NOMENCLATURE AND CLASSIFICATION OF THE GRADES IN FREEMASONRY

SYMBOLIC GRADES

Conferred only in regular Lodges of Master Masons, duly constituted by Grand Lodges

1° Entered Apprentice   2° Fellowcraft
3° Master Mason

INEFFABLE GRADES

4° Secret Master
5° Perfect Master
6° Intimate Secretary
7° Provost and Judge
8° Intendant of the building
9° Master Elect of Nine
10° Master Elect of Fifteen
11° Sublime Master Elected
12° Grand Master Architect
13° Master of the Ninth Arch
14° Grand Elect Mason

Conferred in a Lodge of Perfection, 14°, duly constituted under authority of the Supreme Council of the 33°

ANCIENT HISTORICAL AND TRADITIONAL GRADES

15° Knight of the East or Sword   16° Prince of Jerusalem

Conferred in a Council, Princes of Jerusalem, 16°.

APOCALYPTIC AND CHRISTIAN GRADES

17° Knight of the East and West
18° Knight of Rose Croix de H∴R-D-M
Conferred in a Chapter of Rose Croix
de H-R-D-M, 18°

MODERN HISTORICAL, CHIVALRIC, AND PHILOSOPHICAL GRADES

19° Grand Pontiff
20° Master ad Vitam
21° Patriarch Noachite
22° Prince of Libanus
23° Chief of the Tabernacle
24° Prince of the Tabernacle
25° Knight of the Brazen Serpent
26° Prince of Mercy
27° Commander of the Temple
28° Knight of the Sun
29° Knight of St. Andrew
30° Grand Elect Kadosh or Knight of the White and Black Eagle
31° Grand Inspector Inquistor Commander
32°Sublime Prince of the Royal Secret

Conferred in a Consistory, Sublime Princes of the Royal Secret, 32°.

OFFICIAL GRADES

33° Sovereign Grand Inspector General

Conferred only by the SUPREME COUNCIL, 33°, and upon those who may be elected to receive it by that high body which assembles yearly.

DUNCAN'S
Masonic Ritual and Monitor

OR

GUIDE TO THE THREE SYMBOLIC DEGREES

BY

MALCOLM C. DUNCAN

EXPLAINED AND INTERPRETED BY COPIOUS
NOTES AND NUMEROUS ENGRAVINGS

———

REVISED EDITION

———

PREFACE

THE objects which Freemasonry was founded to subserve are honorable and 'audable; nor is it intended in the following pages to disparage the institution or to undervalue its usefulness. It has, at various times and in several countries, incurred the ill-will of political parties and of religious bodies, in consequence of a belief, on their part, that the organization was not so purely benevolent and philanthropic as its members proclaimed it to be. In the State of New York, many years ago, it was supposed, but we think unjustly, to wield a powerful political influence, and to employ it unscrupulously for sinister ends. The war between Masonry and Anti-Masonry which convulsed the State at that period is still fresh in the remembrance of many a party veteran. The Order, however, has long since recovered from the obloquy then heaped upon it, and is now in a flourishing condition in most parts of the civilized world.

The purpose of this work is not so much to gratify the curiosity of the uninitiated as to furnish a guide for the neophytes of the Order, by means of which their progress from grade to grade may be facilitated. Every statement in the book is authentic, as every proficient Mason will admit to himself, if not to be public, as he turns over its pages. The non-Masonic reader, as he peruses them, will perhaps be puzzled to imagine why matters of so little real importance to society at large should have been so industriously concealed for centuries, and still more surprised that society should have been so extremely inquisitive about them. "But such," as Old Stapleton says, in 'Jacob Faithful,' "is human nature." The object of the Order in making a profound mystery of its proceedings is obvious enough. Sea-birds are not more invariably attracted toward a lighted beacon on a dark night, than men to whatever savors of mystery. Curiosity has had a much greater influence in swelling the ranks of Masonry than philanthropy and brotherly love. The institution, however, is now sufficiently popular to stand upon its own merits, without the aid of clap-trap, so "via the mantle that shadowed Borgia."

It will be observed by the initiated, that the following exposition gives no information through which any person not a Mason could obtain admission to a Lodge. It is due to the Order that its meetings should not be disturbed by the intrusion of persons who do not contribute to its support, or to the furtherance of its humane design, and whose motives in seeking admission to its halls would be impertinent and ungentlemanly. The clew to the *Sanctum Sanctorum* is, therefore, purposely withheld.

In its spirit and intention Masonry is certainly not a humbug, and in its enlightened age so excellent an institution should not incur the liability of being classed with the devices of charlatanry by affecting to wear a mystic veil which has long been lifted, and of which we are free to say, that, unlike that of the false prophet of Kohrassan, it has no repulsive features behind it.

The author of the following work does not conceive that it contains a single line which can in any way injure the Masonic cause; while he believes, on the other hand, that it will prove a valuable *vade mecum* to members of the Order, for whose use and guidance it is especially designed.

It will be seen that the "work" quoted in this treatise differs from that of Morgan, Richardson, and Alleyn; but as this discrepancy is fully explained at the close of the remarks on the Third Degree, it is not deemed necessary to make further allusion to it here.

THE AUTHORITIES REFERRED TO IN THIS WORK ARE AS FOLLOWS:

"THE HISTORICAL LANDMARKS." By the Rev. G. Oliver, D. D. In two volumes. London: R. Spencer. 1845.

"THE THEOCRATIC PHILOSOPHY OF FREEMASONRY." By the same author and publisher. 1840.

"ORIGIN OF THE ENGLISH ROYAL ARCH." By the same, &c., &c., &c.

"A LEXICON OF FREEMASONRY." By Albert G. Mackey, M. D. Charleston: Burges & James. 1845.

"THE FREEMASON'S TREASURY." By the Rev. George Oliver, D. D. London: R. Spencer. 1863.

"THE INSIGNIA OF THE ROYAL ARCH." By the same author. London: R. Spencer. 1847.

"EXPOSITION OF THE MYSTERIES." An Inquiry into the Origin, History, and Purport of Freemasonry. By John Fellows, A. M. New York. 1835.

"BOOK OF THE CHAPTER." By Albert G. Mackey, M. D. New York: Macoy & Sickles. 1864.

"ALLYN'S RITUAL." New York: John Gowan.

"WEBB'S MONITOR." New York: Macoy & Sickles.

"TENT LIFE IN THE HOLY LAND." By Rev. Irenæus Prime, D. D. New York: Harper & Bros.

"MONITOR OF FREEMASONRY." By Jabez Richardson. Philadelphia, Pa.

Publisher's Announcement

Ezra A. Cook, who founded this publishing business in 1867, was unalterably opposed to secret orders. While many of our publications reflect his spirit, our books have been extensively adopted as text books in conferring the secret work of all standard orders, and the publishers, in continuing their sale, believe they are filling a much felt want.

In further justification, we submit the following from the pen of a noted Masonic authority. This quotation will naturally apply to treatises upon other secret orders:—

"The objection to treatises and disquisitions on Masonic subjects, that there is danger through them of giving too much light to the world without, has not the slightest support from experience. In England, in France, and in Germany, scarcely any restriction has been observed by Masonic writers, except as to what is emphatically esoteric; and yet we do not believe that the profane world is wiser in those countries than in our own in respect to the secrets of Freemasonry In the face of these publications, the world without has remained as ignorant of the aporrheta of our art, as if no work had ever been written on the subject, while the world within—the Craft themselves—have been enlightened and instructed, and their views of Masonry (not as a social or charitable society, but as a philosophy, a science, a religion), have been elevated and enlarged.

The truth is that men who are not Masons never read authentic Masonic works. They have no interest in the topics discussed, and could not understand them, from a want of the preparatory education which the Lodge alone can supply Therefore, were a writer even to trench a little on what may be considered as being really the 'arcana' of Masonry, there is no danger of his thus making an improper revelation to improper persons."—Mackey, Ency. of Freemasonry, 1887 ed., p. 617.

DUNCAN'S
RITUAL AND MONITOR

or

FREEMASONRY

ENTERED APPRENTICE, OR FIRST DEGREE.

Seven Freemasons, viz , six Entered Apprentices and one Master Mason, acting under a charter or dispensation from some Grand Lodge, is the requisite number to constitute a Lodge of Masons, and to initiate a candidate to the First Degree of Masonry.

They assemble in a room well guarded from all cowans and eaves-droppers, in the second or third story (as the case may be) of some building suitably prepared and furnished for Lodge purposes, which is, by Masons, termed "the Ground Floor of King Solomon's Temple."

The officers take their seats, as represented in the Plate on page 8. Lodge-meetings are arranged as follows, viz.: a "regular" is held but once a month (i. e. every month on, or preceding, the full of the moon in each month); special meetings are held as often as the exigency of the case may seem to demand, if every night in the week, Sunday excepted. If Tuesday should be Lodge night, by Masons it would be termed, "Tuesday evening on or before the full of the moon, a regular night."

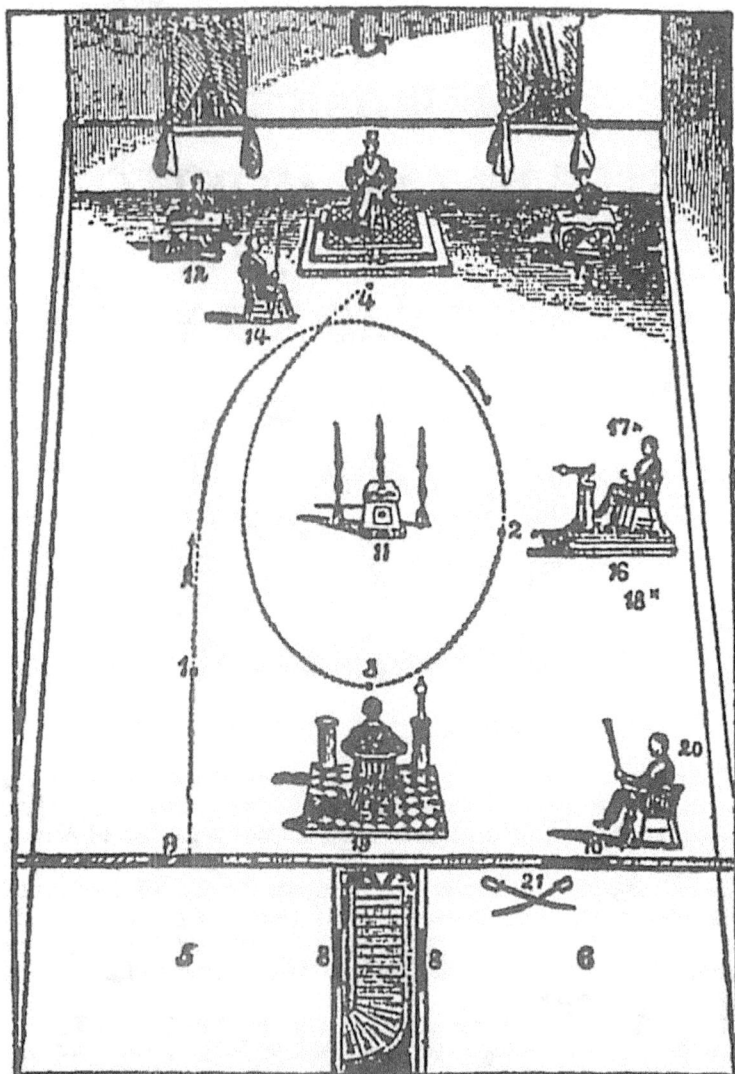

LODGE OF ENTERED APPRENTICES, FELLOW CRAFTS, OR MASTER MASONS.

1. Candidate prays.   2. First stop.   3. Second stop.   4. Third stop.   5. Room where candidates are prepared.   6. Ante-room where members enter the lodge. 7. Hall.   8. Doors.   9. Door through which candidates are admitted into the lodge.   10. Door through which members enter.   11. Altar.   12. Treasurer. 13. Secretary.   14. Senior Deacon.   15. Worshipful Master.   16. Junior Warden. 17 and 18. Stewards.   19. Senior Warden.   20. Junior Deacon.   21. Tylar.

All business relative to Masonry is done at a "regular," and in the Third, or Master Mason Degree. None but Master Masons are allowed to be present at such meetings; balloting for candidates is generally done on a "regular," also receiving petitions, committee reports, &c., &c.

A petition for the degrees of Masonry is generally received at a "regular" (though, as a common thing, Grand Lodges of each State make such arrangements as they may deem best for the regulation of their several subordinate Lodges).

At the time of receiving a petition for the degrees of Masonry, the Master appoints a committee of three, whose duty it is to make inquiry after the character of the applicant, and report good or bad, as the case may be, at the next regular meeting, when it is acted upon by the Lodge.

Upon reception of the committee's report, a ballot is had: if no black balls appear, the candidate is declared duly elected; but if one black ball or more appear, he is declared rejected.

No business is done in a Lodge of Entered Apprentices, except to initiate a candidate to the First Degree in Masonry, nor is any business done in a Fellow Crafts' Lodge, except to pass a Fellow Craft from the first to the second degree. To explain more thoroughly: when a candidate is initiated to the First Degree, he is styled as "entered"; when he has taken the Second Degree, "passed"; and when he has taken the Third, "raised" to the sublime Degree of a Master Mason. No one is allowed to be present, in any degree of Masonry, except he be one of that same degree or higher. The Master always wears his hat when presiding as such, but no other officer, in a "Blue Lodge" (a "*Blue Lodge*" is a Lodge of Master Masons, where only three degrees are conferred, viz.: Entered Apprentice, 1st; Fellow Craft, 2d; Master Mason, 3d. Country Lodges are mostly all "*Blue Lodges*").

A Lodge of Fellow Craft Masons consists of five, viz.: Worshipful Master, Senior and Junior Wardens, Senior and Junior Deacons; yet seven besides the Tyler generally assist, and take their seats as in the Entered Apprentice's Degree. The Fellow Craft Lodge is styled by Masons "the Middle Chamber of King Solomon's Temple."

Three Master Masons is the requisite number to constitute a Masters' Lodge, which is called by Masons "the *Sanctum Sanctorum*, or, Holy of Holies of *King Solomon's Temple*." Although three are all that is required by "Masonic Law" to open a Third Degree Lodge, there are generally seven besides the Tyler, as in the other degrees.

All the Lodges meet in one room, alike furnished, for the conferring of the different degrees (E. A., F. C., and M. M.); but they are masonically styled by the Craft as the Ground Floor, Middle Chamber, and *Sanctum Sanctorum*.

MOST WORSHIPFUL MASTER IN THE EAST

A person being in the room, while open on the First Degree, would not see any difference in the appearance of the room from a Master Masons' Lodge. It is the duty of the Tyler to inform all the brethren on what degree the Lodge is at work, especially those that arrive too late (i. e., after the Lodge has been opened), so that none will be liable to give the wrong sign to the Worshipful Master when he enters. If the Lodge is opened on the First Degree, there might be present those who had taken only one degree, and, if the brother arriving late should be ignorant of this fact, and make a Third Degree sign, they would see it; consequently, caution on this point should always be given to such brethren by the Tyler, before entering the Lodge.

Usual way: Brethren that arrive too late come up to the anteroom, which they find occupied by the Tyler, sword in hand; after inquiring of the Tyler on what degree the Lodge is at work (opened), they put on an apron, and request the Tyler to let them in; the Tyler steps to the door, gives one rap (●), *i.e.* if opened on the First Degree; two raps (● ●), if Second Degree; three raps (● ● ●), if the Third Degree; which being heard by the Junior Deacon, on the inside, he reports to the Master the alarm, as follows, viz.:

J. D.—Worshipful Master, there is an alarm at the inner door of our Lodge.

W. M.—Attend to the alarm, Brother Junior, and ascertain the cause.

Junior Deacon opens the door and inquires of the Tyler the cause of the alarm; when the Tyler will report the brethren's names (which we will suppose to be Jones, Brown, and Smith).

J. D. (to the Master)—Brothers. Jones, Brown, and Smith are without, and wish admission.

If they are known to the Master, he will say, "Admit them."

Deacon opens the door, and says, in an under tone of voice, "Come in." These brothers advance to the centre of the Lodge, at the altar make the duegard, and sign of the degree on which the Lodge is opened, which is responded to by the Master, and then take their seats among the brethren. No brother is allowed to take his seat until he has saluted the Worshipful Master on entering a Lodge; and if one omits his duty in this respect, he is immediately reminded of it by either the Master or some one of the brethren present. The Tyler generally cautions the brethren, before entering the Lodge, about giving the sign, before passing them through the door; the Junior Deacon the same, as soon as they are in. This officer's station is at the inner door, and it is his duty to attend to all alarms from the outside, to report the same to the Master, and get his permission before admitting any one.

The author remembers seeing the duegard and sign of a Master Mason given, while yet an Entered Apprentice Mason: he was sitting one evening in the Lodge, when a brother of the Third Degree came in, and very carelessly saluted the Master with the Master's duegard and sign, undoubtedly supposing the Lodge open on that degree—a very common error among Masons.

In large cities there are often more than one Lodge. Some cities have ten or twenty, and even more; in the cities of New York and Brooklyn there are one hundred and thirty-five Lodges, besides Chapters, Councils, Commanderies, &c., &c. Consequently, there are Lodge-meetings of some sort every night in the week, excepting Sunday, and of course much visiting is going on between the different Lodges. The visitors are not all known to the Masters personally; but the brethren are, generally, acquainted with each other, and of course have often to be vouched for in some of the Lodges, or pass an examination; and for the purpose of giving the reader an idea of the manner in which they are admitted, the author will suppose a case, in order to illustrate it. Jones, Smith, and Brown, belonging to Amity Lodge, No. 323, in Broadway, New York, wish to visit Hiram Lodge, No. 449, of Twenty-fifth Street, and for that purpose go on Lodge night to the hall of Hiram Lodge, No. 449, and ask the Tyler for admission. The Tyler, perhaps, will say—Brothers, are you acquainted with our Master, or any of the brethren in the Lodge? Smith, Jones, and Brown will say, perhaps, Yes; or, We can't tell, but pass our names in, and if there are any acquainted with us, they will vouch for our masonic standing. The Tyler does so, in the manner already described; and, if they are vouched for by either Master or any brother, they are admitted, the Tyler telling them on what degree the Lodge is opened, besides furnishing them with aprons.

On the evening of a Lodge-meeting, brethren generally get together at an early hour at the Lodge-room, which has been opened and cleaned out by the Tyler. On arrival of the Master, and the hour of meeting, the Master repairs to his seat in the east, puts on his *hat*,[1] sash, yoke, and apron, with gavel in hand, and says: "Brethren will be properly clothed and in order; officers repair to their stations for the purpose of opening."

At this announcement the brethren put on their aprons, and seat themselves around the Lodge-room, while the officers invest themselves with their yokes and aprons, and take their stations as represented in Plate on page 8, viz.: Senior Warden in the west; Junior Warden in the south; Senior Deacon in front of the Worshipful Master in the east, and a little to his right hand, with a long rod in hand; Junior Deacon at the right hand of the Senior Warden in the west, guarding the inner door of the Lodge, with rod in hand; Secretary at the left of the Worshipful Master, and Treasurer at the right; and, generally, two Stewards on the right and left of the Junior Warden in the south, with rods in hand. After all are thus seated, the Worshipful Master says: "Is the Tyler present? If so, let him approach the east."

At this command, the Tyler, who is all this time near the outer door of the Lodge, approaches the Worshipful Master's seat in the east, with yoke and apron on.

W. M.—Brother Tyler, your place in the Lodge?

Tyler—Without the inner door.

W. M.—Your duty there?

Tyler—To keep off all cowans and eavesdroppers, and not to pass or repass any but such as are duly qualified and have the Worshipful Master's permission.

W. M.—You will receive the implement of your office (handing him the sword). Repair to your post, and be in the active discharge of your duty. (See Note A, Appendix.)

The Tyler retires to the inside of the outer door of the anteroom, and all Lodge-doors are closed after him.

W. M. (gives one rap with his gavel, Junior Deacon rises up)

---

[1] In most foreign Lodges the Master wears his hat, while the rest of the brethren remain uncovered. This practice was followed by Mac-Kenzie Beverly Esq., when he held the office of D. P. G. M. for the East Riding of York.—*Historical Landmarks,* vol. I. p. 189.

—Brother Junior Deacon, the first and constant care of Masons when convened?

Junior Deacon—To see that the Lodge is duly tyled.

W. M.—You will attend to that part of your duty, and inform the Tyler that we are about to open a Lodge of Entered Apprentice Masons (Fellow Crafts, or Master Masons, as the case may be), and direct him to tyle accordingly.

The Deacon opens the door, and says to the Tyler—Brother Tyler, it is the orders of the Worshipful Master that you tyle this Lodge as an Entered Apprentice (Fellow Crafts, or Master Mason, as the case may be); then closes the door, gives one rap (two, if a Fellow Crafts', or three, if a Masters' Lodge), which is responded to by the Tyler.

J. D.—Worshipful Master, the Lodge is tyled.

W. M.—How tyled?

J. D.—By a brother of this degree, without the inner door, invested with the proper implement of his office (the sword).

W. M.—His duty there?

J. D.—To keep off all cowans[1] and eavesdroppers; suffer none to pass or repass, except such as are duly qualified, and have the Worshipful Master's permission. (Sits down.)

W. M. (one rap, Warden rises to his feet). — Brother Senior Warden, are you sure that all present are Entered Apprentice Masons (Fellow Crafts, or Master Masons? as the case may be).

S. W. — I am sure, Worshipful Master, that all present are Entered Apprentice Masons (or as the case may be).

W. M.—Are you an Entered Apprentice Mason?

S. W.—I am so taken and accepted among all brothers and fellows.

W. M.—Where were you first prepared to be made an Entered Apprentice Mason?

S. W.—In my heart.

W. M.—Where secondly?

S. W.—In a room adjacent to a legally constituted Lodge of such, duly assembled in a place representing the Ground Floor of King Solomon's Temple.

W. M.—What makes you an Entered Apprentice Mason?

---

[1] From the affair of Jephthah, an Ephraimite was termed a cowan. In Egypt, cohen was the title of a priest or prince, and a term of honor. Bryant, speaking of the harpies, says, they were priests of the sun; and, as cohen was the name of a dog is well as a priest, they are termed by Apollonius "the dogs of Jove." Now, St. John cautions the Christian brethren, that "without are dogs" (κυνες), cowans or listeners (Rev. xxii. 15), and St. Paul exhorts the Christians to "beware of dogs," because they are evil workers" (Phil. iii. 2). Now, κυων, a dog, or evil worker, is the masonic cowan.—Historical Landmarks, vol. l. p. 349.

S. W.—My obligation.

W. M.—How many constitute a Lodge of Entered Apprentice Masons?

S. W.—Seven or more, consisting of the Worshipful Master; Senior and Junior Wardens, Senior and Junior Deacons, Secretary, and Treasurer.

W. M.—The Junior Deacon's place?

S. W.—At the right hand of the Senior Warden in the west.

W. M. (two raps with his gavel, when all the officers of the Lodge rise to their feet).—Your duty there, brother Junior Deacon?

J. D. (makes the sign of an Entered Apprentice Mason, see Fig. 2, page 17).—To carry orders from the Senior Warden in the west to the Junior Warden in the south, and elsewhere around the Lodge, as he may direct, and see that the Lodge is tyled.

W. M.—The Senior Deacon's place in the Lodge?

J. D.—At the right hand of the Worshipful Master in the east.

W. M.—Your duty there, brother Senior?

S. D.—To carry orders from the Worshipful Master in the east to the Senior Warden in the west, and elsewhere around the Lodge, as he may direct; to introduce and clothe all visiting brethren; to receive and conduct candidates.

W. M.—The Secretary's place in the Lodge?

S. D.—At the left hand of the Worshipful Master in the east.

M. W.—Your duty, brother Secretary?

Sec.—To observe the Worshipful Master's will and pleasure, record the proceedings of the Lodge, transmit a copy of the same to the Grand Lodge, if required, receive all moneys paid into the Lodge by the hands of the brethren, pass the same over to the Treasurer, and take his receipt for the same.

W. M.—The Treasurer's place in the Lodge?

Sec.—At the right hand of the Worshipful Master in the east.

W. M.—Your duty there, brother Treasurer?

Treas.—To receive all moneys paid into the Lodge from the hands of the Secretary, keep a regular and just account of the same, and pay it out by the order of the Worshipful Master and the consent of the Lodge.

W. M.—The Junior Warden's station in the Lodge?

Treas.—In the south, Worshipful.

W. M.—Your duty there, brother Junior Warden?

J. W.—As the sun in the south, at high meridian, is the beauty and glory of the day, so stands the Junior Warden in the south, the better to observe the time, call the craft from labor to refreshment, superintend them during the hours thereof, and see that the means of refreshment be not converted into intemperance or excess; and call them on to labor again, that they may have pleasure and profit thereby.

W. M.—The Senior Warden's station in the Lodge!

J. W.—In the west, Worshipful.

W. M. — Why in the west, brother Senior, and your duty there!

S. W.—To assist the Worshipful Master in opening and closing his Lodge, pay the craft their wages, if any be due, and see that none go away dissatisfied, if in my power to prevent, harmony being the strength of all institutions, more especially of this of ours.

W. M.—The Worshipful Master's station in the Lodge!

S. W.—In the east, Worshipful.

W. M.—Why in the east, and his duty there!

S. W.—As the sun rises in the east, to open and govern the day, so rises the Worshipful Master in the east (here he gives three raps with his gavel, when all the brethren of the Lodge rise, and, himself), to open and govern his Lodge, set the craft to work, and give them proper instructions.

W. M.—Brother Senior Warden, it is my orders that this Lodge be opened on the First Degree of Masonry (or Second, or Third Degree, as the case may be). For the dispatch of business during which time, all private committees, and other improper, unmasonic conduct,* tending to destroy the peace of the same while engaged in the lawful pursuits of Masonry, are strictly forbidden, under no less penalty than a majority of the brethren present, acting under the by-laws of this Lodge, may see fit to inflict: this you will communicate to the Junior Warden in the south, and he to the brethren around the Lodge, that they, having due and timely notice, may govern themselves accordingly.

S. W. (turning to the Junior Warden in the south.)—Brother Junior Warden, you have heard the orders of the Worshipful Master, as communicated to me from the Worshipful Master in the east. You will take notice, and govern yourself accordingly.[1]

---

[1] The ceremony of OPENING THE LODGE is solemn and impressive. Every brother is reminded of his duties and obligations. The necessary precautions are employed to avoid the intrusion of the profane, and every member, being compelled to assume a share of the necessary forms, is thus admonished that Masonry is a whole of which each Mason forms a part.—*Lexicon.*

The first business which occupies the brethren at their stated meetings is what is technically called opening the Lodge. It is a solemn and imposing rite, and strongly fixes the attention of every serious Mason. Every *officer is made acquainted with his duty, and seriously impressed with the importance attached to his situation.*—*Theo. Phil.,* p. 37 &72.

J. W. (to the Lodge).—Brethren, you have heard the orders of the Worshipful Master, as communicated to me through the Senior Warden in the west. You will please take notice, and govern yourselves accordingly.

W. M.—Brethren, together on the signs. (The signs of the three degrees are given, if opening on the Third Degree; but if only on the First Degree, Entered Apprentice, the Master would say, Together on the sign, and not signs. The Master always leads off in giving the sign or signs. The Master first makes the "duegard" of the First Degree, representing the position of the hands when taking the oath of an Entered Apprentice Mason, which is called the "duegard" of an Entered Apprentice, viz.: "My left hand supporting the Bible, and my right hand resting thereon."

FIG. 1

After which the Master makes the sign of an Entered Apprentice Mason, which alludes to the penalty of the Entered Apprentice's obligation, which is imitated by all the brethren present.

[Explanation of Fig. 2.—Draw the right hand rapidly across the neck, as represented in the cut, and drop the arm to the side.—Remember that the duegards and signs are all made with right angles, horizontals, and perpendiculars, with very slight, but marked pauses between each motion or part of the sign.]

The Master then makes the duegard of a Fellow Craft, which alludes to the position of the hands when taking the oath of a Fellow Craft Mason.

[Explanation of Fig. 3.—The left arm, as far as the elbow, should be held in a horizontal position, and the rest of the arm in a vertical position, forming a square. The right hand detached from the stomach, fingers extending outward.]

After which he gives the sign of a Fellow Craft, which alludes to the penalty of the Fellow Craft obligation.

[Explanation of Fig. 4.—In making the duegard and sign of the Fellow Craft, or Second Degree, care must be taken to drop the left arm suddenly and with spirit, as soon as the two motions are accomplished.]

DUEGARD OF AN ENTERED
APPRENTICE

Next is the duegard of a Master Mason, which alludes to the position of the hands when taking the oath of a Master Mason, both hands resting on the Holy Bible, square, and compasses.

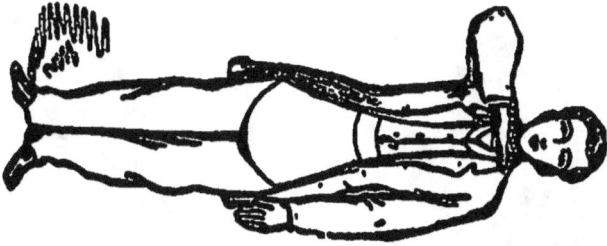

SIGN OF AN ENTERED APPRENTICE

Fig. 2

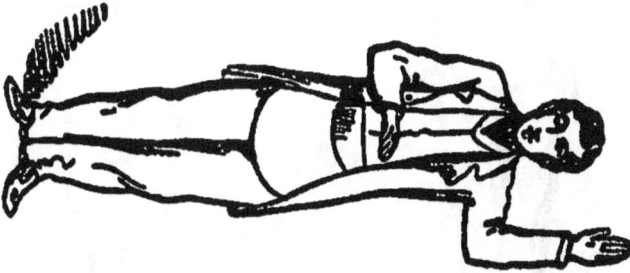

DUEGARD OF A FELLOW CRAFT MASON

Fig. 3

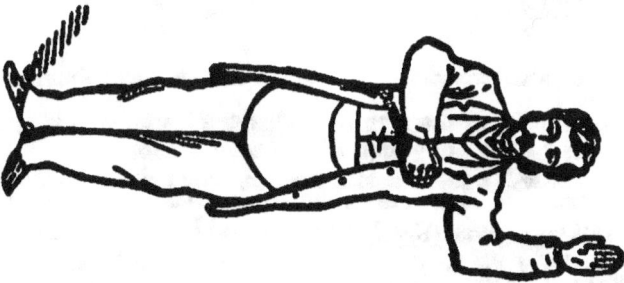

SIGN OF A FELLOW CRAFT MASON

Fig. 4

DUEGARD OF A MASTER MASON

Fig. 5

FIG. 6   FIG. 7

SIGN OF A MASTER MASON   GRAND HAILING SIGN OF DISTRESS

And then (Fig. 6) the sign of a Master Mason, which alludes to the penalty of the obligation of a Master Mason.

[*Explanation of Fig. 6.*—In making this sign, draw the right hand (thumb in) across the stomach as low down as the vest, then drop the hand suddenly.]

The last sign given (Fig. 7) is the "grand hailing sign of distress."

[*Explanation of Fig. 7.*—Raise the hands as represented in the cut, and drop them with spirit. Repeat this three times.]

The words accompanying this sign in the night, or dark, when the sign cannot be seen, are, viz.: "O Lord my God! is there no help for the widow's son?" This sign is given by the Master, at the grave of our "Grand Master Hiram Abiff."[1] (See Note B, Appendix.)

Master gives one rap with his gavel; Senior Warden, one;

---

[1] When a Mason enters a Lodge after it is opened and at work, he proceeds to the centre of the Lodge, at the altar, and, facing the Worshipful Master in the east, gives the duegard and sign of the degree in which the Lodge is working. The duegard is never omitted when the Master is addressed.

Junior Warden, one. Master one the second time, which is responded to by the wardens a second time, in the west and south, when the master makes the third gavel sound, which is responded to by the Wardens. These three raps are made, when opening the Lodge on the Third Degree; if opening on the Second, two raps only are used; First Degree, one rap each, first given by the Master, then Senior Warden, lastly Junior Warden. After which the Master takes off his hat, and repeats the following passage of Scripture:—

"Behold, how good and how pleasant it is for brethren to dwell together in unity! It is like the precious ointment upon the head, that ran down upon the beard, even Aaron's beard; that went down to the skirts of his garments; as the dew of Hermon, and as the dew that descended upon the mountains of Zion: for there the Lord commanded the blessing, even life forever more." Amen!

Responded to by all the brethren present: "Amen! So mote it be!"

W. M.—I now declare this Lodge opened on the First (or, as the case may be) Degree of Masonry. Brother Junior Deacon, you will inform the Tyler. (Deacon opens the Lodge-door, and delivers his message to the Tyler.)

W. M.—Brother Senior Deacon, you will attend at the altar. (Here the Senior Deacon steps to the altar, places the square above the compasses, if opened on the First Degree, viz.:)

W. M. (gives one sound of the gavel).—All are seated and ready for business.

If the Lodge is opened on the Third Degree, and at a regular meeting of the Lodge, the following would be the order of business; but as the reader may be a little anxious, besides curious, about the way and manner of raising the Lodge from the First to the Third Degree, the author will suppose the Lodge open on the First Degree, and, it being a regular Lodge-night, and business to transact, the Lodge must be raised to the Third or Masters' Degree, as no business except that of initiation can be done on the First

COMPASSES, PLACED IN A LODGE OF ENTERED APPRENTICES, "BOTH POINTS COVERED BY THE SQUARE." (See Note C, Appendix.)

Degree. The following manner is generally adopted among Masons at the present day, though there are two or three ways.

W. M (gives one rap with his gavel).—Brother Senior Warden, are you sure that all present are Master Masons? (or Fellow Crafts, as the case may be.)

S. W.—I am not sure that all present are Master Masons, but will ascertain through my proper officers, and report.

S. W.—Deacons will approach the west (Deacons, both Junior and Senior, repair to the Warden's station in the west); first the Senior Deacon whispers the password of a Master Mason in the ear of the Junior Deacon (Tubal Cain), and the Senior Deacon whispers the same in the Senior Warden's ear, when one Deacon passes up one side of the Lodge, and the other the other side, and, as they go, stop at each brother present for the pass-word, which each brother rises up and whispers in the ear of the Deacon (Tubal Cain); if there are any present that cannot give it, the Deacons pass them by, especially if they are lower degree members (Entered Apprentices or Fellow Crafts), and after the Deacons have gone through the entire Lodge, they meet before the Worshipful Master in the east; the Senior Deacon gets the pass again from the Junior Deacon, and passes it up to the Master, and then they return to the Senior Warden in the west, and pass the same up to him in the same way, and take their seats again, as in Plate on page 8. The Warden then rises and says—All present are not Master Masons, Worshipful.

M. W.—All below the degree of Master Mason will please retire while we raise the Lodge. The Junior Deacon says to those below Master Mason, "Brothers, please retire," and he sees that they do so. After they are out, and the door is closed by the Junior Deacon, the Senior Warden says: "All present are Master Masons, Worshipful, and makes the sign of a Master Mason."

W. M.—If you are satisfied that all present are Master Masons, you will have them come to order as such, reserving yourself for the last.

S. W. (gives three raps with his gavel, when all in the Lodge rise to their feet).—Brethren, you will come to order as Master Masons.

Brethren all place their hands in the form of a duegard of a Master Mason. (See Fig. 5, page 17.)

S. W.—In order, Worshipful.

W. M.—Together on the sign, brethren; and makes the sign of a Master Mason (see Fig. 6, page 18), which is imitated by the officers and brethren, and lastly the Senior Warden. The Master gives one rap, Senior Warden one, Junior Warden one, and then the Master again one rap, followed up by the Wardens, until they have rapped three times each.

W. M.—I now declare this Lodge open on the Third Degree of Masonry. Brother Junior Deacon, inform the Tyler. Brother Senior Deacon attend to the altar. (Raps once, and the officers and brethren take their seats.) (See Note D, Appendix.)

Order of business as follows, viz.:—

W. M.—Brother Secretary, you will please read the minutes of our last regular communication.

The Secretary reads as follows, viz.:—

MASONIC HALL, NEW YORK, *December* 8, A. L. 5860.

A regular communication of St. John's Lodge, No. 222, of Free and Accepted Masons, was holden at New York, Wednesday, the 10th of November, A. L. 5860.

Present	*Members*
Brother A. B., Worshipful Master.	Brother Luke Cozzans.
" B. C., Senior Warden.	" John Hart.
" C. D., Junior Warden.	" Peter Lewis.
" D. E., Treasurer.	" George Fox.
" E. F., Secretary.	" Robert Onion.
" F. G., Senior Deacon.	" Frank Luckey.
" G. H., Junior Deacon.	" Samuel Slick.
" H. I., } Stewards.	" Solomon Wise.
" I. J., }	" Henry Wisdom.
" K. L., Tyler.	" Truman Swift.

VISITING BROTHERS

Brother James B. Young, of Union Lodge, No. 16, Broadway, New York.

Brother George J. Jones, Rochester Lodge, No. 28, Rochester, New York.

Brother Benjamin Scribble, of Hiram Lodge, No. 37, New Orleans, Louisiana.

Brother Stephen Swift, of Cleveland Lodge, No. 99, Cleveland, Ohio.

Brother Robert Morris, of Lexington Lodge, No. 7, Lexington, Kentucky.

Lodge was opened in due form on the Third Degree of Masonry.

The minutes of the last communication of St. John's Lodge were read and confirmed.

The committee on the petition of John B. Crockerberry, a candidate for initiation, reported favorably, whereupon he was balloted for, and duly elected.

The committee on the application of D. C. Woolevert, a candidate for initiation, reported favorably; whereupon he was balloted for, and the box appearing foul, he was declared rejected.

The committee on the application of William S. Anderson, a candidate for initiation, having reported unfavorably, he was declared rejected, without a ballot.

A petition for initiation from Robert Chase, of Jersey City, accompanied by the usual fee of ten dollars ($10), and recommended by Brothers Hart, Lewis, and Onion, was referred to a committee of investigation, consisting of Brothers Slick, Wise, and Swift.

Brother Samuel Brevoort, an Entered Apprentice, having applied for advancement, was duly elected to the Second Degree; and Brother Thomas Jansen, a Fellow Craft, was, on his application for advancement, duly elected to the Third Degree in Masonry.

Lodge of Master Masons was then closed, and a Lodge of Entered Apprentices opened in due form.

Mr. Charles Fronde, a candidate for initiation, being in waiting, was duly prepared, brought forward, and initiated as an Entered Apprentice Mason in due and ancient form, he paying the further sum of five dollars ($5).

Lodge of Entered Apprentices closed, and a Lodge of Fellow Crafts opened in due form.

Brother Stephen Currie, an Entered Apprentice, being in waiting, was duly prepared, brought forward, and passed to the degree of a Fellow Craft, he paying the further sum of five dollars ($5).

Lodge of Fellow Crafts closed, and a Lodge of Master Masons opened in due form.

Brother John Smith, a Fellow Craft, being in waiting, was duly prepared, brought forward, and raised to the sublime degree of a Master Mason, he paying the further sum of five dollars ($5).

Amount received this evening, as follows:—

Petition of Robert Chase	$10.00
Fellow Craft Charles Fronde	5.00
Fellow Craft Stephen Currie	5.00
Master Mason John Smith	5.00
	$25.00

All of which was paid over to the Treasurer.

There being no further business, the Lodge was closed in due form and harmony.

SAMUEL SLICK, Secretary.

Approved:
    SOLOMON NORTHUS, W. M.

Such is the form which has been adopted as the most convenient mode of recording the transactions of a Lodge at the present day.

The minutes of a Lodge should be read at the close of each meeting, that the brethren may suggest any necessary alterations or additions, and then at the beginning of the next regular meeting, that they may be confirmed.

W. M.—Brother Senior Warden, have you any alterations to propose?

S. W. (makes the sign of a Master Mason, see Fig. 6, page 18.) —I have none, Worshipful.

W. M.—Have you any, Brother Junior Warden?

J. W. (sign, Fig. 6.)—None, Worshipful.

W. M.—Has any ·brother around the Lodge any alterations to propose? (None offering.) W. M.—Then, brethren, the motion is on the confirmation of the minutes of our last communication; all that are in favor of their confirmation will make it known by the usual sign of a Mason (see Fig 6, page 18—raise the right hand); those opposed, by the same sign, which is called the usual sign of a Mason. The question of confirmation is simply a question whether the secretary has faithfully and correctly recorded the transactions of the Lodge.

If it can be satisfactorily shown by any brother that there are any omissions or misentries, this is the time to correct them.

SECOND ORDER OF BUSINESS

W. M. (reading and referring petitions).—If the secretary has any petitions on his table, he will report to the Lodge, as follows: Worshipful Master, there are two petitions for membership, which are as follows, viz.:—

FORM OF PETITION

To the Worshipful Master, Wardens, and Brethren of St. John's Lodge, No. 222, of Free and Accepted Masons:

The petition of the subscriber respectfully showeth, that, entertaining a favorable opinion of your ancient institution, he is desirous of being admitted a member thereof, if found worthy. His place of residence is New York City, his age thirty-eight years, his occupation a bookseller.   (Signed)   ABNER CRUFF.

Recommended by Brothers Jones, Carson, and Fox.
NEW YORK, *December* 1, 1860.

Sec.—The next petition is from Peter Locke, recommended by Brothers Derby and Jackson. Both these petitions are accompanied by the usual fee of ten dollars each.

W. M.—Brethren, what is your pleasure respecting these petitions of Cruff and Locke?

Brother Hand—I would move that they be received, and a committee of investigation be appointed.

Brother Fast—I second that motion, Worshipful.

W. M.—Brethren, you have heard the motion. All those in favor of the motion, make it known by the usual sign; all to the contrary, the same.

W. M.—The petitions are received, and I would appoint, on the application of Mr. Cruff, Brothers Brevoort, Gore, and Ackerman; and, on the petition of Mr. Locke, Brothers Derby, Hart, and Barnes.

THIRD ORDER OF BUSINESS

W. M. (receiving reports of committees).—Brother Secretary, are there any committee reports due on your desk?

Sec.—There are two reports, Worshipful. One on the application of Mr. Robert Granger, and one on the application of Mr. Brady.

W. M.—Are the chairmen of those committees present?

Brother Pepper—Worshipful, as chairman of the committee to whom was referred the application of Mr. Robert Granger, I would say to the Lodge that I have examined into his character and find it good, and, consequently, report on it favorably. I think he will make a good Mason. In his younger days, he was rather wild; but now he is considered very steady, and a good member of society. (Here, sometimes, great and lengthy discussion arises. Some very conscientious and discreet brother thinks more thorough inquiry should have been made respecting Mr. Robert Granger's early history, the result of which is that he is not balloted for until the next regular meeting. This is no common thing, though.)

W. M.—Is the chairman of the committee to whom was referred the application of Peter Locke present?

Brother Melville—Worshipful, I am chairman of that committee, and report favorably. He is recommended as one of the best of men.

W. M.—Brethren, what's your pleasure with the petition of Mr. Locke?

Brother Jones—I move, Worshipful, that the report be received, committee discharged, and the candidate balloted for.

Brother Jackson—I second that motion.

W. M.—Brethren, you have heard the motion. All in favor of it, make it known by the usual sign; the contrary, the same.

FOURTH ORDER OF BUSINESS

W. M. (balloting for candidates, or admission).—Brother Secretary, are there any candidates to be balloted for?

Sec.—There are, Worshipful, two, viz.: Joseph Locker and Reuben Bruce.

W. M.—Brethren, we are about to ballot for two applicants for the First Degree in Masonry. The first is the petition of Mr. Joseph Locker. Any thing for or against this gentleman is now in order. (Here, if any brother has any thing against or for Mr. Locker, he is privileged to speak on the subject.) If nothing is offered, the Master says:

W. M.—If there is nothing to offer, we will proceed to ballot. Brother Senior Deacon, you will prepare the ballot-box.

Senior Deacon takes the ballot-box (which is a small box, five or six inches square, with two drawers in it, and a small hopper in the top, a hole from which passes down into the first drawer, which is empty and shoved in, while the lower one is drawn out and nearly full of both black and white balls), places the box on the altar in the middle of the Lodge, and takes his seat again.

W. M.—Brethren, you will proceed to ballot.

The balloting is done as follows, viz.: Master first; Secretary calls the names, commencing with the Senior Warden down to the Tyler, and, as their names are called, each Mason steps up to the box at the altar, makes the sign of Master Mason to the Master, and then takes from the lower drawer of the ballot-box a ball (white or black, as he sees fit), deposits it in the hopper above, and retires to his seat. So all vote.

W. M.—Have all voted? If so, Brother Senior Deacon, you will close the ballot.

Senior Deacon closes the drawer, and carries the box to the Junior Warden in the south. He pulls out the top drawer, looks to see if the drawer is "clear" or not, and then closes it and hands it to .the Deacon, who carries it to the Senior Warden in the west for his examination. As the Deacon leaves the Junior Warden's station, the Master says to him:

W. M.—Brother Junior Warden, how stands the ballot in the south?

J. W. (makes the sign of a Master Mason, see Fig. 6, page 18). —Clear in the south, Worshipful. (If not clear, and there should be a black ball or two, he would say—Not clear in the south, Worshipful.)

By this time the Senior Warden has examined, and the Master inquires of him:

W. M.—Brother Senior Warden, how stands the ballot in the west?

S. W.—Clear (or not) in the west, Worshipful. (Making the sign.)

By this time the Deacon has arrived at the Worshipful Master's station in the east. He looks in the box, and says:

W. M.—And clear (or not clear) in the east. Brethren, you have elected (or not) Mr. Joseph Locker to the First Degree in Masonry.

The other candidate is balloted for in the same manner.

FIFTH ORDER OF BUSINESS

W. M. (conferring Degrees).—Brother Junior Deacon, you will ascertain whether there are any candidates in waiting, and for what Degree, and report at once.

The Junior Deacon inquires of the Tyler and brethren generally, and reports. Some one will name a candidate who has been previously balloted for, who will probably be waiting in the ante-room.

J. D.—There is one, or two (as the case may be) now in waiting for the First Degree, Mr. Peter Gabe and Mr. John Milke.

W. M.—Brethren, there seems to be a good deal of business on hand this evening; but my business engagements are such as to render it impossible for me to be present very late, consequently we will confer the Degree upon Mr. Gabe only, and will call a special communication next week to attend to Mr. Milke's wants. You will, inform Mr. Milke, Brother Junior Deacon, of our decision, and not keep him any longer in waiting. You will also say to Mr. Gabe, that as soon as we finish the regular business of the Lodge, he can have the First Degree conferred on him.

Junior Deacon does his duty.

SIXTH ORDER OF BUSINESS

W. M. (considering unfinished business). — No unfinished business.

SEVENTH ORDER OF BUSINESS

W. M. (disposing of such other business as may lawfully come before the Lodge).—Brethren, if there is no further business before this Lodge of Master Masons, we will proceed to close the same, and open an Entered Apprentices' Lodge, for the purpose of initiation.

Here Lodges differ, in the mode of lowering from a Masters' to an Entered Apprentices' Lodge. Some close entirely, and open on the First; but we will adopt a short way, that Lodges have at the present day.

W. M.—Brother Senior Warden, are you sure all present are Entered Apprentice Masons?

S. W.—I am sure, Worshipful, all present are Entered Apprentice Masons.

W. M.—If you are sure all present are Entered Apprentice Masons, you will have them come to order as such, reserving yourself for the last.

S. W. (gives three raps with his gavel, all rise to their feet).— Brethren, you will come to order as Entered Apprentice Masons.

The members place their hands in the position of a duegard of an Entered Apprentice. (See Plate 1, page 10.) When the Master makes the sign, by drawing his hand across his throat, all follow suit; Worshipful then makes one rap with the gavel, Senior Warden one, and the Junior Warden one.

W. M.—I now declare this Lodge of Master Masons closed, and an Entered Apprentice in its stead. Brother Junior Deacon, inform the Tyler; Brother Senior Deacon, attend at the altar (which is placing both points of the compasses under the square). (Worshipful Master gives one rap, which seats the whole Lodge.) Brother Junior Deacon, you will take with you the necessary assistants (the two Stewards), repair to the ante-room, where there is a candidate in waiting (Mr. Gabe, for the First Degree in Masonry), and, when duly prepared, you will make it known by the usual sign (one rap).

The Junior Deacon and his assistants retire to the ante-room, but before they leave the Lodge-room they step to the altar, and make the sign of the First Degree to the Master. It is the duty of the Secretary to go out into the ante-room with them, and before the candidate is required to strip, the Secretary gets his assent to the following interrogations, viz. (*Monitorial*):—

Do you seriously declare, upon your honor, that, unbiassed by friends, and uninfluenced by mercenary motives, you freely and voluntarily offer yourself a candidate for the mysteries of Masonry?

Yes (or, I do).

Do you seriously declare, upon your honor, that you are prompted to solicit the privileges of Masonry by a favorable opinion of the institution, a desire for knowledge, and a sincere wish of being serviceable to your fellow-creatures?

Yes.

Do you seriously declare, upon your honor, that you will conform to all the ancient established usages of the Order?

Yes.

The Secretary returns to the Lodge, and reports that the candidate has given his assent to the interrogations.

The candidate is now requested to strip.

J. D.—Mr. Gabe, you will take off your coat, shoes, and stockings, also your vest and cravat; and now your pantaloons; here is a pair of drawers for you. You will now slip your left arm out of your shirt-sleeve, and put it through the bosom of your shirt, that your arm and breast may be naked. The Deacon now ties a handkerchief or hoodwink over his eyes, places a slipper on his right foot, and afterwards puts a rope, called a cable-tow, once round his neck, letting it drag behind.[1]

The figure is a representation of the candidate duly and truly prepared for the First Degree in Masonry.

The Junior Deacon now takes the candidate by the arm and leads him forward to the door of the Lodge, and gives three distinct knocks, when the Senior Deacon, on the inside, rises to his feet makes the sign of an Entered Apprentice to the Master, and says:

S. D.—Worshipful Master, there is an alarm at the inner door of our Lodge.

---

[1] Every initiated person, whether prince, peer, or peasant, is bound, at least once during his Masonic career, to pass through this emblematical feature of

W. M.—You will attend to the alarm, and ascertain the cause. (The Deacon repairs to the door, gives three distinct knocks, and then opens it.)

S. D.—Who comes here?

J D. (who always responds for the candidate) —Mr Peter Gabe, who has long been in darkness, and now seeks to be brought to light, and to receive a part in the rights and benefits of this worshipful Lodge, erected to God, and dedicated to the holy Sts. John, as all brothers and fellows have done before.

S. D.—Mr. Gabe, is it of your own free-will and accord?

Mr. G.—I is.

S. D.—Brother Junior Deacon, is he worthy, and well qualified?

J. D.—He is.

S. D.—Duly and truly prepared?

J. D.—He is.

S. D.—Of lawful age, and properly vouched for?

J. D.—He is.

S. D.—By what further right or benefit does he expect to gain admission?

J. D.—By being a man, free born, of good repute, and well recommended.

S. D.—Is he such?

J. D.—He is.

S. D.—Since he is in possession of all these necessary qualifications, you will wait with patience until the Worshipful Master is informed of his request, and his answer returned.

Deacon closes the door and repairs to the altar before the Worshipful Master, raps once on the floor with his rod, which is

his profession, as an unmistakable pledge of fidelity. He may not like it. He may object to it. He may think it degrading. But he has no option. He cannot avoid it. If he seriously intends to be a Mason, he must endure it with patience, as an indispensable condition of his tenure. And accordingly no instance is on record where the privilege of initiation has been abandoned from a rejection of this preliminary ceremony. Nor has any one, when the rite has been completed, ever found reason to question its propriety. Such a proceeding is, indeed, utterly improbable, for it bears such a beautiful analogy to the customs of all primitive nations, that its origin may be reasonably ascribed to some unfathomable antiquity, which might probably extend—although we have no evidence of the fact—to a period before the universal deluge.

"The reverence indicated by putting off the covering of the feet," says Dr. Kitto, "is still prevalent in the East. The Orientals throw off their slippers on all those occasions when we should take off our hats. They never uncover their heads, any more than we do our feet. It would everywhere, whether among Christians, Moslems, or pagans, be considered in the highest degree irreverent for a person to enter a church, a temple, or a mosque, with his feet covered. In like manner our Mosaic pavement is accounted pure and immaculate; and therefore no pollution can be tolerated on that sacred floor." — *The Freemason's Treasury*, p. 177.

responded to by the Master with his gavel, when the same thing is passed through with as at the door, and the Master says:

W. M.—Let him enter, and be received in due form.

The Senior Deacon takes the compasses from off the altar, repairs to the door, opens it, and says:

S. D.— Let him enter, and be received in due form.

Senior Deacon steps back, while the Junior Deacon, with candidate, enters the Lodge, followed by the two Stewards. As they advance they are stopped by the Senior Deacon, who presents one point of the compasses to the candidate's naked left breast, and says:

S. D.—Mr. Gabe, on entering this Lodge for the first time, I receive you on the point of a sharp instrument pressing your naked left breast, which is to teach you, as it is a torture to your flesh, so should the recollection of it ever be to your mind and conscience, should you attempt to reveal the secrets of Masonry unlawfully.

The Junior Deacon now leaves the candidate in the hands of the Senior Deacon, and takes his seat at the right hand of the Senior Warden in the west; while the Senior Deacon, followed by the two Stewards, proceeds to travel once regularly around the Lodge-room, as follows, viz.: Senior Deacon takes the candidate by the right arm, advances a step or two, when the Master gives one rap with his gavel. (Deacon and candidate stop.)

W. M.—Let no one enter on so important a duty without first invoking the blessing of the Deity. Brother Senior Deacon, you will conduct the candidate to the centre of the Lodge, and cause him to kneel for the benefit of prayer.

S. D.—Mr. Gabe, you will kneel. (Candidate kneels.)

Worshipful Master now leaves his seat in the east, approaches candidate, kneels by his side, and repeats the following prayer, viz..—

W. M.—Vouchsafe Thine aid, Almighty Father of the Universe, to this our present convention; and grant that this candidate for Masonry may dedicate and devote his life to Thy service, and become a true and faithful brother among us! Endue him with a competency of Thy divine wisdom, that, by the secrets of our art, he may be better enabled to display the beauties of brotherly love, relief, and truth, to the honor of Thy Holy Name. Amen.

Responded to by all, "So mote it be."

W. M. (rising to his feet, taking candidate by the right hand, placing his left on his head).—Mr. "Gabe" (sometimes Masters say, "Stranger!"), in whom do you put your trust?

Candidate (prompted).—In God.[1]

W. M.—Since in God you put your trust, your faith is well

_____

[1] This is the first admission of a candidate before initiation. He avows his belief and trust in God; and it is on that avowal alone that his admis-

founded. Arise (assists candidate to rise), follow your conductor and fear no danger.

The Master retires to his seat in the east, and while the conductor (S. D.) is attending the candidate once around the Lodge-room, he repeats the following passage:—

"Behold, how good and how pleasant it is for brethren to dwell together in unity!" &c., &c. (See opening, or Monitor's.) The reading is so timed as to be concluded when they have passed once around the Lodge-room to the Junior Warden's station in the south; as they pass each officer's station, east, south, and west, they give one sound with their gavels, viz.: first the Master, one (.); J. W., one (.); S. W., one (.); which has a good effect on the candidate, the sounds being near his ears as he passes by this conductor generally passing close up). Having passed once around the Lodge, they halt at the Junior Warden's station in the south.

J. W. (gives one rap; conductor one).—Who comes here?

Conductor (S. D.) — Mr. Peter Gabe, who has long been in darkness, and now seeks to be brought to light, and to receive a part in the rights and benefits of this Worshipful Lodge, erected to God, and dedicated to the holy St. John, as all brothers and fellows have done before.

J. W.—Mr. Gabe, is it of your own free will and accord?

Mr. Gabe—It is.

J. W.—Brother Senior Deacon, is he worthy and well qualified?

S. D.—He is.

J. W.—Duly and truly prepared?

S. D. CONDUCTING CANDIDATE ONCE AROUND THE LODGE—FIRST DEGREE (ENTERED APPRENTICE).[1]

sion among us is based. If he refused to acknowledge the being of a God, he would be at once rejected; but on the receipt of a solemn declaration that he puts his trust in God, the chief officer of the Lodge expresses his satisfaction, and tells him that where the name of God is invoked no danger can possibly ensue.—*Historical Landmarks*, vol. 1. p. 46.

[1] NOTE.—If more than one candidate is being initiated at once, they are required

S. D.—He is.

J. W.—Of lawful age, and properly vouched for?

S. D.—He is.

J. W.—By what further right or benefit does he expect to gain admission?

S. D.—By being a man, free born, of good repute, and well recommended.

J. W.—Since he is in possession of all these necessary qualifications, I will suffer him to pass on to the Senior Warden's station in the west.

Senior Warden, disposing of him in the same manner as the Junior Warden, suffers him to pass on to the Worshipful Master in the east, who makes the same inquiries as did the Wardens in the south and west, after which the Master says:

W. M.—From whence come you, and whither are you travelling?

S. D.—From the west, and travelling toward the east.

W. M.—Why leave you the west and travel toward the east?

S. D.—In search of light.

W. M.—Since light is the object of your search, you will re-conduct the candidate, and place him in charge of the Senior Warden in the west, with my orders that he teach this candidate to approach the east, the place of light, by advancing with one upright, regular step to the first stop, the heel of his right placed in the hollow of his left foot, his body erect at the altar (see Fig. 14), before the Worshipful Master in the east.

Senior Deacon conducts candidate back to the Senior Warden in the west, and says:

S. D.—Brother Senior Warden, it is the orders of the Worshipful Master, that you teach this candidate to approach the east, the place of light, by advancing on one regular upright step to the first stop; the heel of his right foot in the hollow of his left (see Fig. 14, p. 93), his body erect at the altar before the Worshipful Master in the east.

Senior Warden leaves his seat, comes down to the candidate, faces him towards the Worshipful Master, and requests him to step off with his left foot, bringing the heel of his right in the hollow of his left (see step 1, Fig. 14, page 93—before the candidate is requested to do this, he is led by the Warden within one pace of the altar). Senior Warden reports to the Worshipful Master.

S. W.—The candidate is in order, and awaits your further will and pleasure.

to take hold of each other's arms. Five are about as many as can be initiated at once; the same number "passed" to Second Degree; but only one at a time can be raised to the Master's Degree. Small Lodges cannot manage but one at a time conveniently.

The Master now leaves his seat in the east, and, approaching (in front of the altar) the candidate, says:

W. M.—Mr. Gabe, before you can be permitted to advance any farther in Masonry, it becomes my duty to inform you, that you must take upon yourself a solemn oath or obligation, appertaining to this degree, which I, as Master of this Lodge, assure you will not materially interfere with the duty that you owe to your God, yourself, family, country, or neighbor. Are you willing to take such an oath?

Candidate—I am.

W. M.—Brother Senior Warden, you will place the candidate in due·form, which is by kneeling on his naked left knee, his right forming the angle of a square, his left hand supporting the Holy Bible, square, and compasses, his right hand resting thereon.

The Warden now places, or causes the candidate to be placed, in the position commanded by the Worshipful Master, as shown in Figure 8.

W. M.—Mr. Gabe, you are now in position for taking upon

Fig. 8

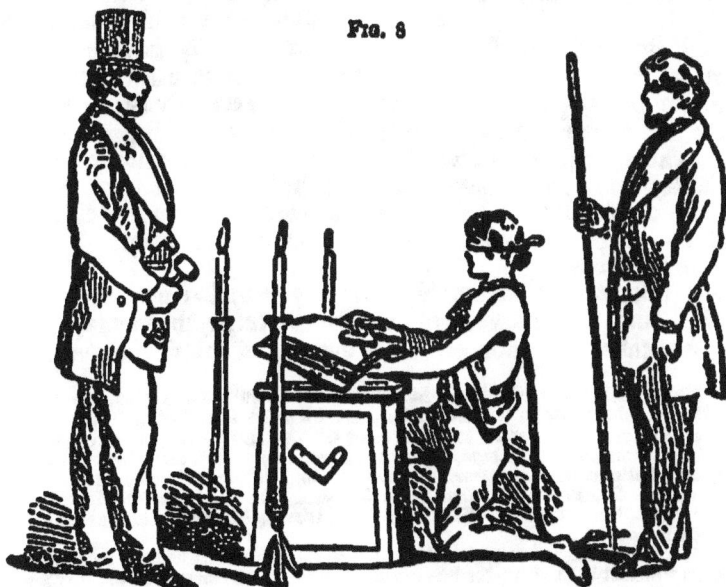

| Master | Altar | Candidate | Conductor |

CANDIDATE TAKING THE OATH OF AN ENTERED APPRENTICE

"Kneeling on my naked left knee, my right forming a square; my left hand supporting the Holy Bible, square, and compasses, my right resting thereon."

yourself the solemn oath of an Entered Apprentice Mason, and, if you have no objections still, you will say I, and repeat your name after me.

Master gives one rap with his gavel which is the signal for all present to assemble around the altar.

OBLIGATION

I, Peter Gabe, of my own free will and accord, in the presence of Almighty God, and this Worshipful Lodge, erected to him, and dedicated to the holy *Sts. John,*[1] do hereby and hereon (Master presses his gavel on candidate's knuckles) most solemnly and sincerely promise and swear, that I will always *hail,*[2] ever conceal, and never reveal, any of the arts, parts, or points of the hidden mysteries of Ancient Free Masonry, which may have been, or hereafter shall be, at this time, or any future period, communicated to me, as such, to any person or persons whomsoever, except it be to a true and lawful brother Mason, or in a regularly constituted Lodge of Masons; nor unto him or them until, by strict trial, due examination, or lawful information, I shall have found him, or them, as lawfully entitled to the same as I am myself. I furthermore promise and swear that I will not print, paint, stamp, stain, cut, carve, mark, or engrave them, or cause the same to be done, on any thing movable or immovable, capable of receiving the least impression of a word, syllable, letter, or character, whereby the same may become legible or intelligible to any person under the canopy of heaven, and the secrets of Masonry thereby unlawfully obtained through my unworthiness.

All this I most solemnly, sincerely promise and swear, with a firm and steadfast resolution to perform the same, without any mental reservation or secret evasion of mind whatever, bind-

---

[1] Neither Adam, nor Nimrod, nor Moses, nor Joshua, nor David, nor Solomon, nor Hiram, nor St. John the Evangelist, nor St. John the Baptist belonged to the Masonic Order. It is unwise to assert more than we can prove, and to argue against probability. There is no record, sacred or profane, to induce us to believe that these holy and distinguished men were Freemasons, and our traditions do not go back to their days.—*Dr. Dalcho, G. M. of South Carolina. Historical Landmarks,* vol. i. p. 89.

[2] "HAIL," or "HALE."—This word is used among Masons with two very different significations:

(1) When addressed as an inquiry to a visiting brother, it has the same import as that in which it is used, under like circumstances, by mariners. Thus, "Whence do you hail?" that is, of what Lodge are you a member?" Used in this sense, it comes from the Saxon term of salutation "*Hael,*" and should be spelled "*hail.*"

(2) Its second use is confined to what Masons understand by the "tye," and in this sense signifies to *conceal,* being derived from the Saxon word "*helan,*" to hide.—*Lexicon.*

ing myself under no less penalty than that of having my throat
cut across,[1] my tongue torn out by its roots, and *my body buried
in the rough sands of the sea,* at low-water mark,[2] where the
tide ebbs and flows twice in twenty-four hours, should I ever
knowingly violate this my Entered Apprentice obligation. So
help me God, and keep me steadfast in the due performance of
the same.

W. M.—In token of your sincerity, you will now detach your
hands, and kiss the book on which your hands rest, which is the
Holy Bible.

After the candidate has kissed the Bible, he is asked by the
Master:

W. M.—In your present condition, what do you most desire?
Candidate (prompted).—*Light.*[3]

W. M.—Brethren, you will stretch forth your hands, and assist
me in bringing our newly made brother to light.

Here the brethren surrounding the altar place their hands in
form of duegard of an Entered Apprenticed Mason (see Fig. 1,
p. 16).

W. M.—"In the beginning God created the heavens and the
earth. And the earth was without form, and void; and darkness
was upon the face of the waters. And God said, Let there be
light, and there was light." (In some Lodges, at the last word,
"light," the brethren stamp their feet and clap their hands once;
but this is nearly done away with now-a-days. Too much "Morganry" about it, as it is styled by Masons.)

Worshipful Master now gives one rap which is the signal for
all to be seated but himself, he remaining at the altar.

I should remark here, that at the word "light," the conductor

---

[1] In some Lodges, at the words *"throat cut across,"* one of the members, or the
conductor, draws his hand across candidate's throat: sometimes they draw the
sword.

[2] A terrible instance of the consequences which attended a violation of this principle has been handed down to us in the story of Hipparchus, a Pythagorean, who,
having out of spleen and resentment violated and broke through the several engagements of the society, was held in the utmost detestation, expelled from the
school as a most infamous and abandoned person; and, as he was esteemed dead to
the principles of virtue and philosophy, they had a tomb erected for him, according
to their custom, as though he had been naturally dead. The shame and disgrace that
justly attended so great a breach of truth and fidelity, drove the unhappy wretch to
such despair that he proved his own executioner; and so abhorred was even his
memory, that he was denied the rites and ceremonies of burial used to the dead in
those times: instead of which, *his body was suffered to lie upon the sands of the
seashore* in the Isle of Samos, to be devoured by rapacious animals.—*Theo. Phil.,*
vol. i. p. 246/47.

[3] Light is the first demand of a candidate at his initiation; and the material
light is succeeded by an intellectual illumination.—*Historical Landmarks,* vol. i.
p. 135.

strips off the hoodwink from the candidate's eyes, but keeps him yet kneeling at the altar.

W. M.—Brother Senior Deacon, I will now thank you to remove the cable-tow. (Rope is taken off candidate's neck.)

Some Masters say—As we now hold the brother by a stronger tie.

W. M.—My brother, on being brought to light in this degree, you discover both points of the compasses hid by the square, which is to signify that you are yet in darkness as respects Masonry, you having only received the degree of an Entered Apprentice. You also discover the three great lights of Masonry, by the help of the three lesser. The three great lights in Masonry are the Holy Bible, square, and compasses, which are thus explained: the Holy Bible is the rule and guide of our faith and practice; the square, to square our actions; the compasses, to circumscribe and keep us within bounds with all mankind, but more especially with a brother Mason. The three lesser lights are the three burning tapers which you see placed in a triangular form about this altar. They represent the sun, moon, and Master of the Lodge; and as the sun rules the day, and the moon governs the night, so ought the Worshipful Master to endeavor to rule and govern his Lodge, with equal regularity.

W. M. (taking a step back from the altar).—You next discover me as the Master of this Lodge, approaching you from the east, under the duegard, sign, and step of an Entered Apprentice Mason (Master making the duegard, sign, and step, as represented and explained in Figs. 1, 2, and 14, pp. 16, 17), and, in token of my brotherly love and favor, present you my right hand (takes the candidate by the right hand, who is yet kneeling at the altar), and with it the grip and word of an Entered Apprentice. (W. M. to candidate.) Grip me, brother, as I grip you. As you are yet uninformed, your conductor will answer for you. (Senior Deacon.)

FIG. 9

THE GRIP OF AN ENTERED APPRENTICE

W. M. (looking the Deacon in the eye, while holding candidate by the right hand).—I hail.

S. D.—I conceal.

W. M.—What do you conceal?

S. D.—All the secrets of Masons, in Masons, to which this (here presses his thumb-nail on the joint) token alludes.

W. M.—What is that?
S. D.—A grip.
W. M.—Of what?
S. D.—Of an Entered Apprentice Mason.
W. M.—Has it a name?
S. D.—It has.
W. M.—Will you give it me?
S. D.—I did not so receive it, neither will I so impart it.
W. M.—How will you dispose of it?
S. D.—I will letter and halve it with you.
W. M.—Letter and begin.
S. D.—No, you begin.
W. M.—You must begin.
S. D.—A.
W. M.—Z.
S. D.—Az.
W. M.—B.
S. D.—O.
W. M.—Bo.
S. D.—Boaz.
S. D. (pronouncing)—Boaz. (The old way of spelling this word, as represented by Morgan, Craft, Allyn, Richardson, and Barnard, was by syllabling it. See those books.)

W. M. (helping candidate to rise from the altar, by the right hand).—Rise, my brother, and salute the Junior and Senior Wardens as an obligated Entered Apprentice.

Here Lodges differ; some only pass candidate once around the room, and, as he passes the officers' stations, he gives the duegard and sign of an Entered Apprentice; while other Lodges require him to halt at the Wardens' stations, and pass through with the following ceremony, viz.: The Deacon takes candidate by the right arm, and passes around the altar to the Junior Warden's station in the south, stops, gives one rap with his rod on the floor, which is responded to by the Junior Warden with his gavel, once.

J. W.—Who comes here?
S. D.—An obligated Entered Apprentice.
J. W.—How shall I know him to be such?
S. D.—By signs and tokens.
J. W.—What are signs?
S. D.—Right angles, horizontals, and perpendiculars (⌐, ═, ‖).
J. W.—What are tokens?
S. D.—Certain friendly or brotherly grips, by which one Mason may know another, in the dark as well as in the light.
J. W.—Give me a sign.

Senior Deacon gives the duegard, and directs the candidate to do likewise. (See duegard, Fig. 1, p. 16.)

J. W.—What is that?

S. D.—A duegard.

J. W.—Has it an allusion?

S. D.—It has; it alludes to the manner in which my hands were placed when I took upon myself the obligation of an Entered Apprentice Mason.

J. W.—Have you any further sign?

S. D.—I have. (Makes the sign of an Entered Apprentice. See Fig. 2, p. 17.)

J. W.—What is that?

S. D.—Sign of an Entered Apprentice Mason.

J. W.—Has it an allusion?

S. D.—It has, to the penalty of my obligation.[1]

J. W.—Have you any further sign?

S. D.—I have not; but I have a token.

J. W.—Advance your token.

Senior Deacon makes candidate take the Junior Warden by the right hand.

J. W.—I hail.

S. D.—I conceal.

J. W.—What do you conceal?

S. D.—All the secrets of Masons, in Masons, to which this (here presses his thumb-nail on the joint) token alludes.

J. W.—What is that?

S. D.—A grip.

J. W.—Of what?

S. D.—Of an Entered Apprentice Mason.

J. W.—Has it a name?

S. D.—It has.

J. W.—Will you give it me?

S. D.—I did not so receive it, neither will I so impart it.

J. W.—How will you dispose of it?

S. D.—I will letter it, or halve it.

J. W.—Letter it, and begin.

S. D.—No, you begin.

J. W.—Begin you.

---

[1] The palate and throat being the chief seat of irregular appetites, we are instructed by the first sign to avoid temptation by a proper restraint on our passions; that we may be temperate in all our indulgences, and never exceed the boundary-line of decency and decorum, under the penalty of disobedience, or the violation of those engagements which, as Masons, we have voluntarily assumed.— Theo. Phil., p. 289.

S. D.—A.
J. W.—Z.
S. D.—Az.
J. W.—B.
S. D.—O.
J. W.—Bo.

S. D. (pronounces) — Boaz. In spelling this word — Boaz — always begin with the letter "A." This is one way that Masons detect impostors, *i. e.,* Morgan or book Masons.—(See Note E, Appendix.)

J. W.—I am satisfied, and will suffer you to pass on to the Senior Warden in the west for his examination.

The conductor and candidate pass on to the Senior Warden's station, where the same ceremony is gone through with, and suffers them to pass on to the Worshipful Master in the east. As they leave the west, and are nearly to the Master's station in the east, he gives one rap with his gavel, when they halt. The Master takes a white linen apron (sometimes a lambskin, which is kept for such purposes), approaches the candidate, hands it to him rolled up, and says:

W. M.—Brother, I now present you with a lambskin or white apron, which is an emblem of innocence and the badge of a Mason, more ancient than the Golden Fleece or Roman Eagle, and, when worthily worn, more honorable than the Star and Garter, or any other order that can be conferred on you at this time, or any future period, by kings, princes, and potentates, or any other persons, except it be by Masons. I trust that you will wear it with equal pleasure to yourself and honor to the fraternity. You will carry it to the Senior Warden in the west, who will teach you how to wear it as an Entered Apprentice.

ENTERED APPRENTICE'S APRON

Deacon conducts candidate back to the west, and says:

S. D.—Brother Senior Warden, it is the order of the Worshipful Master, that you teach this new-made brother how to wear his apron as an Entered Apprentice.

The Senior Warden takes the apron and ties it on the candidate, with the flap turned up, remarking to the candidate as he does so: This is the way, Brother Gabe, that Entered Apprentices wore their aprons at the building of King Solomon's Temple, and so you will wear yours until further advanced. Senior Deacon now reconducts the candidate to the Worshipful Master in the east.

W. M.—Brother Gabe, agreeably to an ancient custom, adopted among Masons, it is necessary that you should be requested to deposit something of a metallic kind or nature, not for its intrinsic valuation, but that it may be laid up among the relics in the archives of this Lodge, as a memento that you were herein made a Mason. Anything, brother, that you may have about you, of a metallic nature, will be thankfully received—a button, pin, five or ten cent piece—anything, my brother.

Candidate feels for something—becomes quite confused. On examination, or reflection, finds himself very destitute, not being able to contribute one pin, his conductor having been careful to take every thing from him, in the ante-room, before he entered the Lodge;—finally stammers out that he has nothing of the kind with him, but if permitted to pass out into the ante-room, where his clothes are, he will contribute. This the Master refuses to do, of course, which only helps confuse the candidate more and more. After the Master has kept the candidate in this suspense some moments, he says:

W. M.—Brother Gabe, you are indeed an object of charity—almost naked, not one cent, no, not even a button or pin to bestow on this Lodge. Let this ever have, my brother, a lasting effect on your mind and conscience; and remember, should you ever see a friend, but more especially a brother, in a like destitute condition, you will contribute as liberally to his support and relief as his necessities may seem to demand and your ability permit, without any material injury to yourself or family.[1]

W. M.—Brother Senior Deacon, you will now reconduct this candidate to the place from whence he came, and reinvest him with that which he has been divested of, and return him to the Lodge for further instruction.

Senior Deacon takes candidate by the arm, leads him to the centre of the Lodge, at the altar before the Worshipful Master in the east, makes duegard and sign of an Entered Apprentice, and then retires to the ante-room.

After candidate is clothed, the deacon ties on his apron, and, returning to the Lodge, conducts him to the Worshipful Master in the east, who orders the Deacon to place him in the northeast corner of the Lodge, which is at the Master's right.

W. M.—Brother Gabe, you now stand in the northeast corner of this Lodge, as the youngest Entered Apprentice, an upright man and Mason, and I give it to you strictly in charge as such ever to walk and act. (Some Masters preach great sermons to

---

[1] The Master, assisted by the Senior Warden, lays the chief corner-stone of a beautiful fabric.—*Theo. Phil.*, p. 274.

candidate on this occasion.) Brother, as you are clothed as an Entered Apprentice, it is necessary you should have the working-tools of an Entered Apprentice, which are the twenty-four-inch gauge and common gavel.

W. M.—The twenty-four-inch gauge is an instrument made use of by operative masons to measure and lay out their work; but we, as Free and Accepted Masons, are taught to make use of it for the more noble and glorious purpose of dividing our time. It being divided into twenty-four equal parts, is emblematical of the twenty-four hours of the day which we are taught to divide into

three parts, whereby we find a portion for the service of God and the relief of a distressed worthy brother, a portion for our usual avocations, and a portion for refreshment and sleep.

W. M.—The common gavel is an instrument made use of by operative masons to break off the superfluous corners of rough stones, the better to fit them for the builder's use; but we, as Free and Accepted Masons, are taught to make use of it

for the more noble and glorious purpose of divesting our minds and consciences of all the vices and superfluities of life, thereby fitting us, as living stones, for that spiritual building, that house not made with hands, eternal in the heavens.

W. M.—Brother Gabe, there is a lecture to this Degree, consisting of three sections, which you will at your earliest opportunity commit to memory.[1] The first section treats of the manner of your initiation; the second section, the reasons why, &c.; the third section, the form, furniture, lights, &c., &c. This lecture commences as follows:

FIRST SECTION

Q. From whence came you? (Some say, As an Entered Apprentice Mason.)

A. From a Lodge of the Sts. John of Jerusalem.

[1] The labors are conducted on a plan which is intended to produce an exciting spirit of emulation. Every individual is personally and in turn requested by the Worshipful Master to give his opinion on some specific doctrine or ceremony propounded from the Chair. He may, or he may not, be willing or able to comply with the demand. If the former, he enlightens the members by his disquisition; and if he declines the task, a slight sign is a sufficient negative, and the query is transferred to the next in succession, whose absolute freedom of will is acknowledged by leaving him at full liberty to act as he may feel disposed.—*The Freemason's Treasury,* p. 149.

Q. What came you here to do?

A. To learn to subdue my passions and improve myself in Masonry.

Q. Then I presume you are a Mason?

A. I am so taken and accepted among all brothers and fellows. (See Note F, Appendix.)

Q. How do you know yourself to be a Mason?

A. By having been often tried, never denied, and willing to be tried again.

Q. How shall I know you to be a Mason?

A. By certain signs, a token, a word, and the perfect points of my entrance.

Q. What are signs?

A. Right angles, horizontals, and perpendiculars (⌐, =, ‖).

Q. What are tokens?

A. Certain friendly or brotherly grips, by which one Mason may know another in the dark as well as in the light.

Q. Give me a sign.

Here give sign of Entered Apprentice. (See Fig. 2, p. 17.)

Q. Has that an allusion?

A. It has; to the penalty of my obligation.

Q. Give me a token.

Here give sign of Entered Apprentice. (See Fig. 2, p. 17.)

Q. I hail.

A. I conceal.

Q. What do you conceal?

A. All the secrets of Masons, in Masons, to which this (here press with thumb-nail the first joint hard) token alludes.

Q. What is that?

A. A grip.

Q. Of what?

A. Of an Entered Apprentice Mason.

Q. Has it a name?

A. It has.

Q. Will you give it me?

A. I did not so receive it, neither will I so impart it.

Q. How will you dispose of it?

A. I will letter it or halve it.

Q. Letter it, and begin.

A. No, you begin.

Q. Begin you. (Some say, No, you begin.)

A. A.

Q. Z.

A. Az.

Q. B.

A. O.

Q. Bo.

A. Boaz.

Q. Where were you first prepared to be made a Mason?

A. In my heart.

Q. Where were you next prepared?

A. In a room adjacent to a regularly constituted Lodge of Free and Accepted Masons. (See Note G, Appendix.)

Q. How were you prepared?

A. By being divested of all metals, neither naked nor clothed, barefoot nor shod, hoodwinked, with a cable-tow around my neck; in which condition I was conducted to the door of a Lodge by a friend, whom I afterward found to be a brother.[1]

Q. How did you know it to be a door, being hoodwinked?

A. By first meeting with resistance, afterward gaining admission.

Q. How gained you admission?

A. By three distinct knocks.

Q. What were said to you from within?

A. Who comes here?

Q. Your answer?

A. Mr.——, who has long been in darkness, and now seeks to be brought to light, and to receive a part in the rights and benefits of this worshipful Lodge, erected to God, and dedicated to the holy Sts. John, as all brothers and fellows have done before.

Q. What were you then asked?

A. If it was of my own free will and accord; if I was worthy and well qualified; duly and truly prepared; of lawful age and properly vouched for. All of which being answered in the affirmative, I was asked by what further right or benefit I expected to gain admission.

Q. Your answer?

A. By being a man, free born, of good repute, and well recommended.

Q. What followed?

A. I was directed to wait with patience until the Worshipful Master should be informed of my request, and his answer returned.

Q. What answer did he return?

[1] The Tracing Board combines all the Landmarks of the Degree, and includes the essence of its lectures and illustrations. It opens with mortality in its feeblest state; poor and penniless, and blind and naked; and conducts the pious inquirer to a glorious immortality.—*Historical Landmarks*, vol. I. p. 134.

A. Let him enter, and be received in due form.

Q. How were you received?

A. On the point of a sharp instrument pressing my naked left breast.

Q. How were you then disposed of?

A. I was conducted to the centre of the Lodge, caused to kneel, and attend at prayer.

Q. After attending at prayer, what were you then asked?

A. In whom I put my trust.

Q. Your answer?

A. In God.

Q. What followed?

A. My trust being in God, I was taken by the right hand, and informed that my faith was well founded; ordered to arise, follow my conductor, and fear no danger.

Q. Where did you follow your conductor?

A. Once around the Lodge, to the Junior Warden's station in the south, where the same questions and like answers were asked and returned as at the door. (See Note H, Appendix.)

Q. How did the Junior Warden dispose of you?

A. He bid me be conducted to the Senior Warden in the west, and he to the Worshipful Master in the east, where the same questions were asked and like answers returned as before.

Q. How did the Worshipful Master dispose of you?

A. He ordered me to be reconducted to the Senior Warden in the west, who taught me to approach the east by one upright, regular step, my feet forming an angle of an oblong square, my body erect, at the altar before the Worshipful Master in the east.[1]

Q. What did the Worshipful Master then do with you?

A. He made me a Mason in due form.

Q. What was that due form?

A. Kneeling on my naked left knee, my right forming a square, my left hand supporting the Holy Bible, square, and compasses, my right resting thereon, in which due form I took the solemn oath of an Entered Apprentice, which is as follows, viz.; (some Lodges require the obligation repeated, but not as a general thing).

Q. After the obligation, what were you then asked?

A. What I most desired.

---

[1] The candidate is obligated in the east and invested in the west; advances from west to east by right lines and angles, to typify the necessity of an upright life and well-squared actions; and he is subsequently placed in the northeast to receive instruction, as a corner-stone, from which a superstructure is expected to rise, perfect in its parts and honorable to the builder.—*The Freemason's Treasury*, p. 24.

Q. Your answer?

A. Light.

Q. Did you receive light?

A. I did, by the order of the Worshipful Master and the assistance of the brethren.

Q. On being brought to light, what did you first discover?

A. The three great lights in Masonry, by the help of the three lesser.

Q. What are the three great lights in Masonry?

A. The Holy Bible, square, and compasses.

Q. What are their Masonic use?

A. The Holy Bible is the rule and guide to our faith and practice; the square, to square our actions; and the compasses, to circumscribe and keep us within bounds with all mankind, but more especially with a brother Mason.

Q. What are the three lesser lights?

A. Three burning tapers, in a triangular position.

Q. What do they represent?

A. The sun, moon, and Master of the Lodge.

Q. Why so?

A. Because, as the sun rules the day, and the moon governs the night, so ought the Worshipful Master to endeavor to rule and govern his Lodge, with equal regularity.

Q. What did you then discover?

A. The Worshipful Master approaching me from the east, under the duegard and sign of an Entered Apprentice; who, in token of his brotherly love and favor, presented me with his right hand, and with it the grip and word of an Entered Apprentice and ordered me to arise and salute the Junior and Senior Wardens as an Entered Apprentice.

Q. After saluting the Wardens, what did you then discover?

A. The Worshipful Master approaching me from the east a second time, who presented me with a lambskin or white linen apron which he informed me was an emblem of innocence and the badge of a Mason; that it had been worn by kings, princes, and potentates of the earth; that it was more ancient than the Golden Fleece or Roman Eagle; more honorable than the Star or Garter, or any other order that could be conferred on me at that or any time thereafter by king, prince, potentate, or any other person, except he be a Mason; and hoped that I would wear it with equal praise to myself and honor to the fraternity; and ordered me to carry it to the Senior Warden in the west, who taught me how to wear it as an Entered Apprentice.

Q. How should an Entered Apprentice wear his apron?

A. With the flap turned up.

Q. After being taught to wear your apron as an Entered Apprentice, what were you then informed?

A. That, agreeably to an ancient custom, adopted in every regulated and well-governed Lodge it was necessary that I should be requested to deposit something of a metallic kind, not from its intrinsic valuation, but that it might be laid up, among the relics in the archives of the Lodge, as a memorial that I was therein made a Mason; but, on strict examination, I found myself entirely destitute.

Q. How were you then disposed of?

A. I was ordered to be returned to the place from whence I came, and reinvested of what I had been divested of, and returned to the Lodge for further instructions.

Q. On your return to the Lodge, where were you placed, as the youngest Entered Apprentice?

A. In the northeast corner, my feet forming a right angle, my body erect, at the right hand of the Worshipful Master in the east, an upright man and Mason, and it was given me strictly in charge ever to walk and act as such.

Q. What did the Worshipful Master then present you with?

A. The working-tools of an Entered Apprentice Mason, which are the twenty-four-inch gauge and common gavel.

Q. What is their use?

A. The twenty-four-inch gauge is an instrument made use of by operative masons, to measure and lay out their work; but we, as Free and Accepted Masons, are taught to make use of it for the more noble and glorious purpose of dividing our time. It being divided into twenty-four equal parts is emblematical of the twenty-four hours of the day, which we are taught to divide into three parts, whereby we find a portion for the service of God and the relief of a distressed worthy brother, a portion for our usual avocations, and a portion for refreshment and sleep.

The common gavel is an instrument made use of by operative masons, to break off the superfluous corners of rough stones, the better to fit them for the builder's use; but we, as Free and Accepted Masons, are taught to make use of it for the more noble and glorious purpose of divesting our minds and consciences of all the vices and superfluities of life, thereby fitting us, as living stones of that spiritual building, that house not made with hands, eternal in the heavens.

This generally ends the first section of the lecture as given in Lodges at the present day; but as some Lodges persist still in keeping up the old lecture as revealed by William Morgan, in 1826,

and by Bernard, Allyn, Richardson, and others, the author will give
it, that it may go to the world a complete Masonic lecture.

Q. What were you next presented with?

A. A new name.

Q. What was that?

A. Caution.

Q. What does it teach?

A. It teaches me, as I was barely instructed in the rudiments
of Masonry, that I should be cautious over all my words and
actions, especially when before its enemies.

Q. What were you next presented with?

A. Three precious jewels.

Q. What were they?

A. A listening ear, a silent tongue, and a faithful heart.

Q. What do they teach?

A. A listening ear teaches me to listen to the instructions of
the Worshipful Master, but more especially to the cries of a
worthy distressed brother. A silent tongue teaches me to be
silent in the Lodge, that the peace and harmony thereof may
not be disturbed, but more especially before the enemies of Masonry. A faithful heart, that I should be faithful and keep and
conceal the secrets of Masonry and *those of a brother when delivered to me in charge as such, that they may remain as secure
and inviolable in my breast as in his own, before being communicated to me.*

Q. What were you next presented with?

A. The Grand Master's check-word.

Q. What was that?

A. Truth.

Q. How explained?

A. Truth is a divine attribute, and the foundation of every
virtue. To be good and true are the first lessons we are taught
in Masonry. On this theme we contemplate, and by its dictates
endeavor to regulate our conduct; hence while influenced by this
principle, hypocrisy and deceit are unknown among us, sincerity
and plain-dealing distinguish us, and the heart and tongue join
in promoting each other's welfare, and rejoicing in each other's
prosperity.

With a few other interrogations and answers the old lecture
ends. These interrogations and answers are embodied in the new-
fangled lecture as already given; they relate only to the demand
for something of a metallic kind, reinvestment of candidate's
clothing, northeast corner of the Lodge, &c., &c.

SECOND SECTION

Q. Why were you divested of all metals when made a Mason?

A. For the reason, first, that I should carry nothing offensive or defensive into the Lodge; second, at the building of King Solomon's Temple, there was not heard the sound of an axe, hammer, or any tool of iron.

Q. How could a building of that stupendous magnitude be erected without the aid of some iron tool?

A. Because the stones were hewed, squared, and numbered at the quarries where they were raised; the trees felled and prepared in the forests of Lebanon, carried by sea in floats to Joppa, and from thence by land to Jerusalem, where they were set up with wooden mauls, prepared for that purpose; and, when the building was completed, its several parts fitted with such exact nicety, that it had more the resemblance of the handy workmanship of the Supreme Architect of the universe than of that of human hands.

Q. Why were you neither naked nor clothed?

A. Because Masonry regards no one for his worldly wealth or honors; it is the internal, and not the external qualifications of a man that should recommend him to be made a Mason.

Q. Why were you neither barefoot nor shod?

A. It was in conformity to an ancient Israelitish custom: we read in the book of Ruth, that it was their manner of changing and redeeming; and to confirm all things, a Mason plucked off his shoe and gave it to his neighbor, and that was testimony in Israel. This then we do in confirmation of a token, and as a pledge of our fidelity; thereby signifying that we will renounce our own will in all things, and become obedient to the laws of our ancient institution.[1]

Q. Why were you hoodwinked, and a cable-tow put about your neck?

A. For the reason, first, as I was then in darkness,[2] so I should keep the whole world in darkness so far as it related to the secrets of Free-Masonry. Secondly: in case I had not sub-

---

[1] Among the ancient Israelites, the SHOE was made use of in several significant ways. To *put off the shoe* imported reverence, and was done in the presence of God, or on entering the dwelling of a superior. To *unloose one's shoe, and give it to another*, was the way of confirming a contract.—*Lexicon.*

[2] DARKNESS among Freemasons is emblematical of Ignorance; for as our science has technically been called "Lux," or light, the absence of light must be the absence of knowledge. Hence the rule, that *the eye should not see until the heart has conceived* the true nature of those beauties which constitute the mysteries of our Order. Freemasonry has restored Darkness to its proper place, as *a state of preparation.*—*Lexicon.*

mitted to the manner and mode of my initiation, that I might
have been led out of the Lodge, without seeing the form and
beauty thereof.

Q. Why were you caused to give three distinct knocks?

A. To alarm the Lodge, and inform the Worshipful Master
that I was prepared for Masonry, and, in accordance to our ancient custom, that I should ask. "Ask, and ye shall receive; seek,
and ye shall find; knock, and it shall be opened unto you."

Q. How did you apply this to your then situation in Masonry?

A. I asked the recommendation of a friend to become a Mason;
through his recommendation I sought admission; I knocked at
the door of the Lodge and it was opened unto me.

Q. Why were you received on the point of a sharp instrument
pressing your naked left breast?

A. As that was an instrument of torture to my flesh, so might
the recollection of it be to my conscience, should I ever presume
to reveal the secrets of Free-Masonry.

Q. Why were you caused to kneel and attend at prayer?

A. Because no man should ever enter upon a great and important undertaking without first imploring the blessings of Deity.

Q. Why were you asked in whom you put your trust?

A. Because, agreeably to our most ancient institution, no
Atheist could be made a Mason; it was therefore necessary that
I should put my trust in Deity, or no oath would have been con-
sidered binding among Masons.

Q. Why were you taken by the right hand, ordered to arise,
follow your conductor, and fear no danger?

A. It was to assure me, as I could not foresee nor avoid
danger, that I was in the hands of a true and trusty friend, in
whose fidelity I might with safety confide.

Q. Why were you conducted *once around the Lodge?*

A. That the brethren might see that I was duly and truly
prepared.

Q. Why were you caused to meet with the several obstructions on your passage?

A. Because there were guards placed at the south, west, and
east gates of the courts of King Solomon's Temple, to see that
none passed or repassed but such as were duly and truly prepared and had permission; it was therefore necessary that I
should meet with these several obstructions, that I might be duly
examined before I could be made a Mason.

Q. Why were you caused to kneel on your naked left knee?

A. Because the left side is considered to be the weakest part
of man; it was therefore to show that it was the weaker part of

Masonry I was then entering upon, being that or an Entered Apprentice.

Q. Why were you caused to rest your right hand on the Holy Bible, square, and compasses?

A. Because the right hand was supposed by our ancient brethren to be the seat of fidelity, and so they worshipped Deity under the name of *Fides,* which was supposed to be represented by the right hands joined, and by two human figures holding each other by the right hand; the right hand, therefore, we masonically use to signify in the strongest manner possible the sincerity of our intentions in the business in which we are engaged.

Q. Why were you presented with a lambskin or white linen apron, which is the badge of a Mason?

A. Because the lamb, in all ages, has been deemed an emblem of innocence; he, therefore, who wears the lambskin as a badge of a Mason is thereby continually reminded of that purity of life and conduct which is essentially necessary to his gaining admission into that celestial Lodge above, where the Supreme Architect of the universe presides.

Q. Why were you requested to deposit something of a metallic kind?

A. To remind me of my extremely poor and penniless state, and that, should I ever meet with a friend, more especially with a brother, in like destitute circumstances, I should contribute as liberally to his relief as his circumstances demanded, without any material injury to myself.

Q. Why were you conducted to the northeast corner of the Lodge, as the youngest Entered Apprentice, and there caused to stand upright like a man, your feet forming a square—receiving at the same time a solemn charge ever to walk and act uprightly before God and man?[1]

A. Because the first stone of a building is usually laid in the northeast corner. I was therefore placed there to receive my first instructions where to build my future Masonic and moral edifice.

THIRD SECTION

Q. What is a Lodge?

A. A certain number of Masons duly assembled, with the Holy Bible, square, and compasses, and charter, or warrant empowering them to work.

[1] It was asserted by Aristotle, that "he who bears the shocks of fortune valiantly and demeans himself uprightly, is truly good, and of a SQUARE POSTURE, without reproof."—*Historical Landmarks,* vol. I. p. 189.

Q. Where did our ancient brethren usually meet?
A. On a high hill or in a low valley. (See Note 1, Appendix.)

Q. Why so?
A. The better to observe the approach of cowans, or eaves-droppers, ascending or descending.

Q. What is the form and covering of a Lodge?
A. An oblong square, extending from east to west, between the north and south, from the earth to the heavens, and from the surface to the centre.

Q. Why of such vast dimension?
A. To signify the universality of Masonry, and that a Mason's charity should be equally extensive.

Q. What supports this vast fabric?
A. Three great pillars, constituting Wisdom, Strength, and Beauty.

Q. Why are they so called?
A. Because it is necessary there should be wisdom to contrive, strength to support, and beauty to adorn all great and important undertakings.

Q. By whom are they represented?
A. By the Worshipful Master, and the Senior and Junior Wardens

Q. Why are they said to represent them?
A. The Worshipful Master represents the pillar of Wisdom, because he should have wisdom to open his Lodge, set the craft at work, and give them proper instructions. The Senior Warden represents the pillar of Strength, it being his duty to assist the Worshipful Master in opening and closing his Lodge, to pay the craft their wages, if any be due, and see that none go away dis-satisfied, harmony being the strength of all institutions, more especially of ours. The Junior Warden represents the pillar of Beauty, it being his duty at all times to observe the sun at high meridian, which is the glory and beauty of the day.

Q. What covering has a Lodge?
A. A clouded canopy, or starry-decked heavens, where all good Masons hope to arrive, &c., &c. (See *Masonic Monitor*.)

Q. What furniture has a Lodge?
A. The Holy Bible, square, and compasses.

Q. To whom are they dedicated?
A. The Bible is dedicated to God, the square to the Master, and the compasses to the craft.

Q. Why are they thus dedicated?
A. The Bible is dedicated to God, because it is the inestimable gift of God to man, &c., &c. (See *Monitor*.)

Q. What are the ornaments of a Lodge?

A. The mosaic pavement, the indented tessel, and the blazing star.

Q. What are they?

A. The mosaic pavement is a representation of the Ground Floor of King Solomon's Temple, with a blazing star in the centre; the indented tessel, that beautiful tessellated border which surrounds it.

Q. Of what are they emblematical?

A. The mosaic pavement represents this world, which, though checkered over with good and evil, yet brethren may walk together thereon, and not stumble. (See *Monitor*.)

Q. How many lights has a Lodge?

A. Three.

Q. How are they situated?

A. East, west, and south.

Q. None in the north?

A. No.

Q. Why none in the north?

A. Because this and every other Lodge is, or ought to be, a true representation of King Solomon's Temple, which was situated north of the ecliptic; the sun and moon, therefore, darting their rays from the south, no light was to be expected from the north. We therefore, masonically, term the north a place of darkness.

Q. How many jewels has a Lodge?

A. Six: three movable, and three immovable.[1]

Q. What are the movable jewels?

A. The rough ashler, the perfect ashler, and the trestle-board.

Q. What are they?

A. Rough ashler is a stone in its rough and natural state; the perfect ashler is also a stone, made ready by the working-tools of the fellow craft, to be adjusted in the building; and the trestle-board is for the master workman to draw his plans and designs upon.

Q. Of what do they remind us?

A. By the rough ashler we are reminded of our rude and imperfect state by nature; by the perfect ashler of that state of perfection at which we hope to arrive by a virtuous education, our

---

[1] Every Lodge is furnished with six JEWELS, three of which are movable and three immovable. The movable jewels, so called because they are not confined to any particular part of the Lodge, are the rough ashler, the perfect ashler, and the trestleboard. The immovable jewels are the square, the level, and the plumb. They are termed immovable, because they are appropriated to particular parts of the Lodge, where alone they should be found, namely, the square in the east, the level to the west, and the plumb to the south.—*Lexicon*.

own endeavors, and the blessing of God; and by the trestle-board we are also reminded that, as the operative workman erects his temporal buildir g agreeably to the rules and designs laid down by the Master on his tiestle-board, so should we, both operative and speculative, endeavor to erect our spiritual building agreeably to the rules and designs laid down by the Supreme Architect of the universe, in the great book of Revelation, which is our spiritual, moral, and Masonic trestle-board.

Q. What are the three immovable jewels?

A. The square, level, and plumb.

Q. What do they masonically teach us?

A. The square teaches morality; the level, equality; and the plumb teaches rectitude of life.

Q. How should a Lodge be situated?

A. Due east and west.

Q. Why so?

A. Because, after Moses had safely conducted the children of Israel through the Red Sea, by Divine command he erected a tabernacle to God, and placed it due east and west, which was to commemorate to the latest posterity that miraculous east wind that wrought their mighty deliverance—this was an exact model of Solomon's Temple; since which time every well regulated and governed Lodge is, or ought to be, so situated.

Q. To whom were Lodges dedicated in ancient times?

A. To King Solomon.

Q. Why so?

A. Because it was said he was our most ancient Grand Master, or the founder of our present system.

Q. To whom in modern times?

A. To St. John the Baptist and St. John the Evangelist, who were two eminent Christian patrons of Masonry; and since their time there is, or ought to be, represented in every regular and well-governed Lodge a certain "point within a circle," the point representing an individual brother, the circle the boundary-line of his conduct beyond which he is never to suffer his prejudices or passions to betray him. This circle is embodied by two perpendicular parallel lines, representing St. John the Baptist and St. John the Evangelist; and upon the top rest the Holy Scriptures. In going round this circle, we necessarily touch upon these two lines, as well as upon the Holy Scriptures; and while a Mason keeps himself circumscribed within their precepts it is impossible that he should materially err.

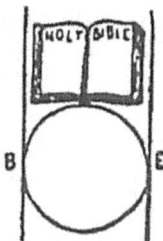

This ends the lecture[1] on the Entered Apprentices' Degree. But very few Masons are sufficiently posted in these lectures to answer every inquiry respecting them. Not one in a hundred ever gets them perfect, none but a few aspiring members seeking after office take the trouble to commit them to memory, and some of these do so very imperfectly. Most Masters, at the present day, qualify themselves for the office of Master by purchasing Richardson's or Avery Allyn's Masonic exposures. These works have, of course, to be amended. On perusing the present work the reader will be greatly surprised at the striking resemblance it bears to the works just mentioned, especially in the lectures; but let him mark the alterations, principally at the commencement of each lecture.

In some Lodges the following lecture is used, especially in the Northwestern States:

Q. What are the points of your profession?

A. Brotherly love, relief, and truth.

Q. Why so? (See *Masonic Monitors*, on "Brotherly Love, Relief, and Truth.")

Q Brother, you informed me that I should know you by certain signs, and tokens, and words, and the points of your entrance. You have already satisfied me as to the signs and words. I now require you to explain to me the points of your entrance: how many, and what are they?

A. They are four: the Guttural, the Pectoral, the Manual, and the Pedestal, which allude to the four cardinal virtues, viz.: Temperance, Fortitude, Prudence, and Justice.

Temperance is that due restraint upon our affections and passions which renders the body tame and governable and frees the mind from the allurements of vice. This virtue should be the constant practice of every Mason, as he is thereby taught to avoid excess, or contracting any licentious or vicious habit, the indulgence of which might lead him to disclose some of those valuable secrets which he has promised to conceal and never reveal, and which would consequently subject him to the contempt and detestation of all good Masons. See "*Guttural,*" (p. 248.)

---

[1] Each Degree of Masonry contains a course of instruction, in which the ceremonies, traditions, and moral instruction appertaining to the Degree are set forth. This arrangement is called a LECTURE. In the Entered Apprentices' Degree, the first section describes the proper mode of initiation, and supplies the means of qualifying us for our privileges, and of testing the claims of others. The second section rationally accounts for all the ceremonies peculiar to this Degree. The third section explains the nature and principles of our institution, and instructs us in the form and construction of the Lodge, furnishing, in conclusion, some important lessons on the various virtues which should distinguish a Freemason.— *Lexicon.*

This virtue alludes to the Mason's obligation, which is the Guttural.

Fortitude is that noble and steady purpose of the mind, whereby we are enabled to undergo any pain, peril, or danger, when prudentially deemed expedient. This virtue is equally distant from rashness and cowardice; and, like the former, should be deeply impressed upon the mind of every Mason, as a safeguard or security against any illegal attack that may be made, by force or otherwise, to extort from him any of those secrets with which he has been so solemnly intrusted; and which virtue was emblematically represented upon his first admission into the Lodge, on the point of a sharp instrument pressing his naked left breast. This alludes to the Pectoral.[1]

Prudence teaches us to regulate our lives and actions agreeably to the dictates of our reason, and is that habit by which we wisely judge, and prudentially determine, on all things relative to our present, as well as to our future happiness. This virtue should it be the invariable practice of every Mason never to for the government of his conduct while in the Lodge, but also when abroad in the world. It should be particularly attended to in all strange and mixed companies, never to let fall the least sign, token, or word, whereby the secrets of Masonry might be unlawfully obtained. Especially, brother in Masonry, you should always remember your oath as an Entered Apprentice, while kneeling at the altar, on your naked left knee, your left hand supporting the Holy Bible, square, and compasses, your right resting thereon, which alludes to the Manual.

Justice is that standard or boundary of right which enables us to render to every man without distinction his just due. This virtue is not only consistent with Divine and human laws, but is the very cement and support of civil society; and as justice in a great measure constitutes the real good man, so should it be the invariable practice of every Mason never to deviate from the minutest principles thereof.

The charge you received while standing in the northeast corner of the Lodge, your feet forming a right angle, was an allusion to the Pedestal.

Q. How did Entered Apprentices serve their Master in ancient times, and how should they in modern?

A. With freedom, fervency, and zeal.

Q. How were they represented?

---

[1] Pectoral a breastplate; especially, a sacerdotal habit or vestment worn by the Jewish High Priest.—*Webster.*

A. By Chalk, Charcoal, and Clay. (See *Webb's Monitor.*)

Q. Why were they said to represent them?

A. Because it was said there was nothing more free than chalk, which, under the slightest touch, leaves a trace behind; nothing more fervent than charcoal to melt—when well lit, the most obdurate metals will yield; nothing more zealous than clay, or our mother earth, to bring forth.

CHARGE AT INITIATION INTO THE FIRST DEGREE

BROTHER: As you are now introduced into the first principles of Masonry, I congratulate you on being accepted into this ancient and honorable order; ancient, as having existed from time immemorial; and honorable, as tending in every particular so to render all men who will conform to its precepts. No human institution was ever raised on a better principle, or more solid foundation; nor were ever more excellent rules and useful maxims laid down than are inculcated in the several Masonic lectures. The greatest and best of men in all ages have been encouragers and promoters of the art, and have never deemed it derogatory to their dignity to level themselves with the fraternity, extend their privileges, and patronize their assemblies.

There are *three great duties*, which, as a Mason, you are strictly to observe and inculcate—to God, your neighbor, and yourself. To God, in never mentioning His name but with that reverential awe which is due from a creature to his Creator; to implore His aid in all your laudable undertakings, and to esteem Him as your chief good. To your neighbor, in acting upon the square, and doing unto him as you would he should do unto you: and to yourself, in avoiding all irregularity and intemperance, which may impair your faculties or debase the dignity of your profession. A zealous attachment to these duties will insure public and private esteem.

In the State you are to be a quiet and peaceable citizen, true to your government, and just to your country; you are not to countenance disloyalty or rebellion, but patiently submit to legal authority, and conform with cheerfulness to the government of the country in which you live.

In your outward demeanor be particularly careful to avoid censure or reproach. Let not interest, favor, or prejudice bias your integrity, or influence you to be guilty of a dishonorable action. And although your frequent appearance at our regular meetings is earnestly solicited, yet it is not meant that Masonry should interfere with your necessary avocations, for these are on no account to be neglected; neither are you to suffer your zeal for the institution to lead you into arguments with those who, through ignorance, may ridicule it. But, at your leisure hours, that you may improve in Masonic knowledge, you are to converse with well informed brethren, who will be always as ready to give as you will be ready to receive instruction.

Finally, keep sacred and inviolable the mysteries of the Order, as these are to distinguish you from the rest of the community, and mark your consequence among Masons. If, in the circle of your acquaintance, you find a person desirous of being initiated into Masonry, be particularly careful not to recommend him, unless you are convinced he will conform to our rules; that the honor, glory, and reputation of the institution may be firmly established, and the world at large convinced of its good effects.

[*If the candidate be a clergyman, add the following.*]

You, brother, are a preacher of that religion, of which the distinguishing characteristics are universal benevolence and unbounded charity. You cannot, therefore, but be fond of the Order, and zealous for the interests of Freemasonry, which, in the strongest manner, inculcates the same charity and benevolence, and which, like that religion, encourages every moral and social virtue; which introduces peace and good-will among mankind, and is the centre of union to those who otherwise might have remained at a perpetual distance. So that whoever is warmed with the spirit of Christianity, must esteem, must love Freemasonry. Such is the nature of our institution, that, in all our Lodges, union is cemented by sincere attachment, hypocrisy and deceit are unknown, and pleasure is reciprocally communicated by the cheerful observance of every obliging office. Virtue, the grand object in view, luminous as the meridian sun, shines refulgent on the mind, enlivens the heart, and converts cool approbation into warm sympathy and cordial affection.

Though every man, who carefully listens to the dictates of reason, may arrive at a clear persuasion of the beauty and necessity of virtue, both public and private, yet it is a full recommendation of a society to have these pursuits continually in view, as the sole objects of their association; and these are the laudable bonds which unite *us* in one indissoluble fraternity.

For the ceremony of closing a Lodge, see the end of the Third, or Master Masons' Degree, page 142.

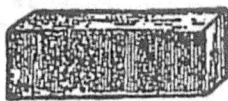

PERFECT ASHLER   ROUGH ASHLER

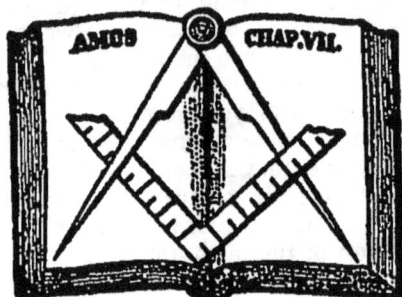

FELLOW CRAFT, OR SECOND DEGREE

I SHALL omit the ceremonies incident to opening a Lodge of Fellow Crafts, as they are very similar to those employed in opening the First Degree, and will be explained hereafter more clearly to the reader. Five are required by Masonic law to make a legal Lodge of Fellow Crafts, viz.: Worshipful Master, Senior and Junior Wardens, Senior and Junior Deacons; yet seven, besides the Tyler, generally officiate, and take their seats as in the Entered Apprentice Degree. (See Plate, page 8.)

COMPASSES PLACED IN A LODGE OF FEL-
LOW CRAFT MASONS, "ONE POINT
ELEVATED ABOVE THE SQUARE."
(See Note B.)

When the Lodge is opened on the Fellow Craft Degree, the altar is arranged as represented in the accompanying engraving.

We will suppose the Lodge to be opened on the Fellow Craft Degree, and Mr. Gabe, who has previously taken the degree of Entered Apprentice, and been elected to that of Fellow Craft, is in the ante-room in waiting. The Master, being aware of this fact, will say:

W. M.—Brother Junior Deacon, you will take with you the necessary assistance and repair to the ante-room, where there is a candidate in waiting for the second degree in Masonry; and when you have him prepared, make it known by the usual sign.

The Junior Deacon, with the two Stewards accompanying him, steps to the centre of the Lodge, makes the duegard and sign of a Fellow Craft, and passes out of the Lodge into the ante-room. (For duegard and sign see Figs. 3 and 4, page 17.)

J. D.—Well, Brother Gabe, you will have to be prepared for this Degree as all have been before you. You, of course, can have no serious objection?

Brother Gabe.—I have not.

J. D.—Then you will take off your boots, coat, pants, vest, necktie, and collar; and here is a pair of drawers, unless you have a pair of your own. Now you will slip your right arm out of your shirtsleeve, and put it through the bosom of your shirt, that your right arm and breast may be naked.

The Deacon here ties a hoodwink, or hand-kerchief, over both eyes. (In the time of Morgan, it was the usage to cover only one eye.) The Junior Deacon then ties a rope, by Masons called a cable-tow, twice around his arm. (Formerly, the rope was put twice round the candidate's neck.) Some Lodges follow the old custom now, but this is rather a rare thing. The reader will, however, do well to recollect these hints, as they are particular points.

The right foot and knee of the candidate are made bare by rolling up the drawers, and a slipper should be put on his left foot. This being accomplished, the candidate is duly and truly prepared. (See engraving.)

The Deacon now takes the candidate by the arm, and leads him forward to the door of the Lodge; and upon arriving there he gives three raps, when the Senior Deacon, who has taken his station on the inside door of the Lodge, reports to the Master as follows:

S. D.—Worshipful Master (making the sign of a Fellow Craft), there is an alarm at the inner door of our Lodge.

W. M.— You will attend to the alarm, and ascertain the cause.

The Deacon gives three raps, which are responded to by the

Junior Deacon, and answered to by one rap from the Senior Deacon inside, who opens the door, and says:

S. D.—Who comes here?

J. D. (conductor).—Brother Gabe, who has been regularly initiated as Entered Apprentice, and now wishes to receive more light in Masonry by being passed to the degree of Fellow Craft.

S. D. (turning to candidate).—Brother Gabe, is it of your own free-will and accord?

Candidate—It is.

S. D.—Brother Junior Deacon, is he duly and truly prepared, worthy and well qualified?

J. D.—He is.

S. D.—Has he made suitable proficiency in the preceding degree?

J. D.—He has.

S. D.—And properly vouched for?

J. D.—He is.

S. D.—Who vouches for him?

J. D.—A brother.

S. D.—By what further right, or benefit, does he expect to gain admission?

J. D.—By the benefit of a pass.

S. D.—Has he that pass?

J. D.—He has it not, but I have it for him.

S. D.—Advance, and give me the pass. (Some say, advance the pass.)

Junior Deacon whispers in the Senior Deacon's ear the password, "Shibboleth."

S. D.—The pass is right. You will wait with patience until the Worshipful Master is informed of your request, and his answer returned.

The Senior Deacon then closes the door, and repairs to the centre of the Lodge, before the Worshipful Master in the east, and sounds his rod twice on the floor, which is responded to by the Master with his gavel, when the same interrogations and answers are repeated by the Master and Deacon as at the door. The Master then says:

W. M.—Let him enter, in the name of the Lord, and be received in due form.

The Senior Deacon then takes the square from the altar, and, repairing to the door, he opens it, and says:

S. D.—Let him enter in the name of the Lord, and be received in due form.

The Junior Deacon advances through the door, followed by the two Stewards, when the Senior Deacon stops them by placing the angle of the square against the candidate's right breast.

S. D. (pressing square against candidate's breast).—Brother Gabe, on entering this Lodge the first time you were received on the points of the compass: I now receive you on the angle of the square, which is to teach you that the square of virtue should be the rule and guide of your conscience in all future transactions with mankind.

The Senior Deacon now takes the candidate by the right arm, followed by the Stewards, and conducts him twice around the Lodge, counting from the Junior Warden's station in the south, during which time the Master reads the following passage of Scripture:

"Thus he showed me: and behold, the Lord stood upon a wall made by a plumb-line, with a plumb-line in his hand. And the Lord said unto me, Amos, what seest thou? And I said, A plumb-line. Then said the Lord, Behold, I will set a plumb-line in the midst of my people Israel; I will not again pass by them any more."—*Amos* VII. 7, 8.

While going around the Lodge, as the conductor and candidate pass the officers' stations in the south, west, and east, they (the officers) sound the gavel as follows: the first time going round, one rap each; the second time, two raps each. By the time the Master has finished reading the above passage of Scripture, the candidate and conductor have passed around the room twice, and arrived at the Junior Warden's station in the south.

J. W. (giving two raps, which are responded to by the deacon). —Who comes here?

S. D. (conductor).—Brother Gabe, who has been regularly initiated Apprentice, and now wishes to receive more light in Masonry, by being passed to the Degree of Fellow Craft.

J. W. (turning to candidate).—Brother Gabe, is it of your own free-will and accord?

Candidate—It is.

J. W.—Brother Senior Deacon, is he duly and truly prepared, worthy, and well qualified?

S. D.—He is.

J. W.—Has he made suitable proficiency in the preceding Degree?

S. D.—He has.

J. W.—And properly vouched for?

S. D.—He is.

J. W.—Who vouches for him?

S. D.—A brother.

J. W.—By what further right, or benefit does he expect to gain admission?

S. D.—By the benefit of the pass.

J. W.—Has he that pass?

S. D.—He has it not, but I have it for him.

J. W.—Advance, and give me the pass.

Senior Deacon advances, and whispers in the Junior Warden's ear, "Shibboleth."

J. W.—The pass is right; I will suffer you to pass on to the Senior Warden's station in the west.

S. W.—Who comes here?

S. D.—Brother Gabe, who has been regularly initiated Apprentice, and now wishes to receive more light in Masonry, by being passed to the Degree of Fellow Craft.

S. W. (turning to candidate).—Brother Gabe, is it of your own free will and accord?

Candidate—It is, &c., &c.

Precisely the same questions and answers transpire as at the Junior Warden's station and at the door, and the candidate and conductor are permitted by the Warden to pass to the Worshipful Master's station in the east.

W. M.—Who comes here?

S. D. (for candidate).—Brother Gabe, who has been regularly initiated Apprentice, and now wishes to receive more light in Masonry, by being passed to the Degree of Fellow Craft.

W. M.—(turning to candidate).—Brother Gabe, is it of your own free-will and accord?

Brother Gabe.—It is.

W. M.—Brother Senior Deacon (the Master speaking in a very deep tone of voice), is he duly and truly prepared, worthy, and well qualified?

S. D.—He is.

W. M.—Has he made suitable proficiency in the preceding Degree?

S. D.—He has.

W. M.—And properly vouched for?

S. D.—He is.

W. M.—Who vouches for him?

S. D.—A brother.

W. M.—By what further right or benefit does he expect to gain admission?

S. D.—By the benefit of the pass.

W. M.—Has he that pass?

S. D.—He has it not, but I have it for him.

W. M.—Advance and give me the pass.

Senior Deacon advances, and whispers in the Master's ear, "Shibboleth."

W. M.—The pass is right; from whence came you, and whither are you travelling?

S. D.—From the west, travelling toward the east.

W. M.—Why leave you the west, and travel toward the east?

S. D.—In search of more light.

W. M.—Since that appears to be the object of the candidate's search, it is my orders that he be reconducted to the Senior Warden in the west, who will teach him how to approach the east, by two upright regular steps, his feet forming an angle of a square, his body erect at the altar before the Worshipful Master in the east.

Senior Deacon conducts the candidate back to the Senior Warden in the west, and says:

S. D.—Brother Senior Warden, it is the orders of the Worshipful Master, that you teach this candidate to approach the east, by two upright regular steps, his feet forming an angle of a square, his body erect at the altar before the Worshipful Master in the east.

Senior Warden leaves his seat, and, approaching the candidate, he leads him toward the altar, and within two steps of it, and says:

Brother, you will first step off one full step with your left foot, bringing the heel of your right in the hollow of your left foot, now you will step off with your right foot, bringing the heel of your left in the hollow of your right. (Steps 1 and 2, Fig. 14, p. 93.)

The candidate is now within kneeling distance of the altar, and the Senior Warden makes the following report to the Master:—

Worshipful Master, the candidate is now in order, and awaits your further will and pleasure.

W. M.—Brother Senior Warden, you will place him in due form for taking upon himself the solemn oath or obligation of a Fellow Craft.

The Senior Warden, with the assistance of the Senior Deacon, now causes the candidate to kneel on his naked right knee, before the altar, making his left knee form a square. His left arm, as far as the elbow, should be held in a horizontal position, and the rest of the arm in a vertical position, forming another square —his arm supported by the square, held under his elbow, and his right hand resting on the open Bible. (See Fig. 10.)

W. M.—Brother Gabe, you are kneeling for the second time

at the sacred altar of Masonry, to take upon yourself the solemn oath or obligation of a Fellow Craft; and I take pleasure, as Master of this Lodge, to say to you (as on a former occasion), there is nothing in this oath that will interfere with the duty that you owe to your God, your family, country, neighbor, or self. Are you willing to take it?

FIG. 10

Master   Altar and Lights   Candidate   Conductor

CANDIDATE TAKING THE OATH OF A FELLOW CRAFT

"Kneeling on my naked right knee, my left forming a square; my right hand on the Holy Bible, square, and compasses, my left arm forming an angle, supported by the square, and my hand in a vertical position."

Candidate—I am.

W. M.—Then, if you have no objections, you will say, I, and repeat your name after me (here the Master gives two raps with his gavel (● ●), which is the signal for all the brethren to assemble around the altar).

OATH

I, Peter Gabe, of my own free-will and accord, in the presence of Almighty God, and this worshipful Lodge, erected to Him, and dedicated to the holy STS. JOHN,[1] do hereby and hereon (Master presses candidate's hand with the gavel), most solemnly and sincerely promise and swear that I will always hail, and ever conceal, and never reveal any of the secret arts, parts, or points of the Fellow Craft Degree to any person whomsoever, except it be to a true and lawful brother of this degree, or in a regularly constituted Lodge of Fellow Crafts; nor unto him or them until, by strict trial, due examination, or lawful information, I shall find him, or them, as lawfully entitled to the same as I am myself.

I furthermore promise and swear that I will stand to, and abide by, all the laws, rules, and regulations of the Fellow Craft Degree, as far as the same shall come to my knowledge.

Further, I will acknowledge and obey all due signs and summons sent to me from a Lodge of Fellow Crafts, or given me by a brother of that degree, if within the length of my cable-tow.

Further, that I will aid and assist all poor, distressed, worthy Fellow Crafts, knowing them to be such, as far as their necessities may require, and my ability permit, without any injury to myself.

Further, that I will not cheat, wrong, nor defraud a brother of this degree, knowingly, nor supplant him in any of his laudable· undertakings.

All this I most solemnly promise and swear with a firm and steadfast resolution to perform the same, without any hesitation, mental reservation, or self-evasion of mind whatever, binding myself under no less penalty than of having my breast torn open[2] (see sign of Fellow Craft, Fig. 4, p. 17) my heart[3] plucked out, and placed on the highest pinnacle of the temple (some say, "My heart and vitals taken from thence, and thrown over my left shoulder, and carried into the valley of Jehoshaphat, &c., &c.), there to be devoured by the vultures of the air, should I ever knowingly violate the Fellow Craft obligation. So help me God, and keep me steadfast in the due performance of the same.

[1] We are challenged by our opponents to prove that St. John was a Freemason. The thing is incapable of direct proof. Calmet positively asserts that he was an Essene, which was the secret society of the day, that conveyed moral truths under symbolical figures, and may, therefore, be termed Freemasonry, retaining the same form, but practised under another name.—*Historical Landmarks*, vol. I. p. 167.

[2] Gives candidate a rake across his breast with the hand; this is to draw candidate's attention to the penalty.

[3] The *breast* being the abode of fortitude, we are taught by the second sign to suppress the *risings* of apprehension and discontent; and to endure with patience the attacks of adversity, or distress, pain, or disappointment, rather than induce, by a weak and temporizing compliance with the persuasion of friends, or the denunciations of enemies, the bitter stings of remorse which must inevitably result from *a betrayal of secrets* with which we have been intrusted on the faith of a solemn obligation.—*Theo. Phil.*, p. 389.

W. M.—Brother Gabe, you will detach your hand, and kiss the book on which your hand rests, which is the Holy Bible.

Candidate kisses the book once (some Lodges say twice).

W. M.—In your present condition, what do you most desire?

The candidate, prompted by his conductor, answers—More light in Masonry.

W. M.—Brethren, you will stretch forth your hands, and assist me in bringing our brother to light.

Here all the brethren place their hands in the form of the duegard of a Fellow Craft. (See Fig. 3, p. 17.)

W. M.—Let the brother receive light.

At this point the conductor unties the hoodwink, and lets it fall from the candidate's eyes. The Master then gives one rap on the altar with his gavel, when all the brethren but himself and the conductor (S. D.) take their seats. The Master then says to the candidate:

W. M.—My brother, on being brought to light in this Degree, you behold one point of the compasses elevated above the square (see altar and compasses in this Degree, p. 58), which is to signify that you have received light in Masonry by points.

Then, stepping back a few feet from the altar, the Worshipful Master continues:

W. M.—Brother, you discover me approaching you from the east, under the duegard (here he makes the duegard) and sign (here he makes the sign of a Fellow Craft, see Figs. 3, 4, p. 17); and in token of the continuance of brotherly love and favor, I present you with my right hand (takes candidate by the right hand), and with it the pass, token, token of the pass, grip, and word of a Fellow Craft. As you are yet uninformed, your conductor will answer for you.

The Worshipful Master now takes the candidate by the Entered Apprentice's grip (see Entered Apprentice's grip, Fig. 9, p. 36), and says to his conductor, the S. D., while holding the candidate by this grip:

Fig. 11

PASS GRIP OF A FELLOW CRAFT

W. M. — Here I left you, and here I find you. Will you be off or from?

S. D. (for candidate). From.

W. M. — From what, and to what?

S. D.—From the real grip of an Entered Apprentice to the pass grip of a Fellow Craft.

W. M.—Pass.

Here the candidate is requested to pass his thumb from the first joint to the space between the first and second joints, which is the pass grip of a Fellow Craft. (See Fig. 11.)

W. M.—What is that?

Conductor—The pass grip of a Fellow Craft?

W. M.—Has it a name?

Conductor—It has.

W. M.—Will you give it me?

Conductor—"Shibboleth." (Some letter it, Shib-bo-leth.)

W. M.—Will you be off or from?

Conductor—From.

W. M.—From what, and to what?

Conductor—From the pass grip of a Fellow Craft to the real grip of the same.

W. M. (moving his thumb to the second joint).—Pass.

Fig. 12

REAL GRIP OF A FELLOW CRAFT

W. M.—What is that?

Conductor—The real grip of a Fellow Craft.

W. M.—Has it a name?

Conductor—It has.

W. M.—Will you give it me?

Conductor—I did not so receive it, neither can I so impart it.

W. M.—How will you dispose of it?

Conductor—I will letter it with you.

W. M.—Letter and begin.

Conductor—No, you begin.

W. M.—You must begin.

Conductor—A.

W. M.—J.

Conductor—C.

W. M.—H.

Conductor—I.

W. M.—N.

Conductor—Ja.

W. M.—Chin.

Conductor—Jachin.

W. M.—The pass is right. (At the words, "is right," lifting candidate from his knees at the altar.) You will arise, and salute the Junior and Senior Wardens as a Fellow Craft.

The conductor having previously removed the cable-tow from the candidate's arm, he conducts him to the Junior Warden's station in the south, halts before that officer, and gives two raps on the floor with his rod, or stamps twice on the floor with his foot, which is responded to by the Junior Warden, in like manner, with his gavel.

J. W.—Who comes here?

Conductor—Brother Gabe, an obligated Fellow Craft.

J. W.—How shall I know him to be such?

Conductor—By signs and tokens.

J. W.—Give me a sign.

Conductor gives the duegard of a Fellow Craft (see Fig. 3, p. 17), and makes the candidate·or candidates—if there are more than one—do likewise.

J. W.—What is that?

Conductor—Duegard of a Fellow Craft Mason.

J. W.—Has it an allusion?

Conductor—It has; it alludes to the manner in which my hands were placed when I took upon myself the solemn oath of a Fellow Craft.

J. W.—Have you any other sign?

Conductor—I have. (At the same time he makes the sign of a Fellow Craft, see Fig. 4, p. 17, and the candidate does the same.)

J. W.—What is that?

Conductor—The sign of a Fellow Craft Mason.

J. W.—Has it an allusion?

Conductor—It has; it alludes to the penalty of my obligation.

J. W.—Have you any further signs?

Conductor—I have not; but I have a pass, token, token of the pass, grip, and word.

J. W.—Advance, and give me the pass.

Warden takes hold of candidate by the right hand, and places his thumb on the first joint of candidate's hand (see Entered Apprentice grip, Fig. 9, p. 36), and says to the conductor:

J. W.—Will you be off or from?

Conductor—From.

J. W.—From what, and to what?

Conductor—From the real grip of an Entered Apprentice to the pass grip of a Fellow Craft. (See Fig. 11, p. 66.)

J. W.—Pass. (They move their thumbs, as already described.)

J. W.—What is that?

Conductor—The pass grip of a Fellow Craft.

J. W.—Has it a name?

Conductor—It has.

J. W.—Will you give it me?

Conductor—"Shibboleth."

J. W.—Will you be off or from?

Conductor—From.

J. W.—From what, and to what?

Conductor—From the pass grip of a Fellow Craft, to the real grip of the same.

J. W.—Pass. (They pass the thumbs, as before described. See Fig. 12, p. 67.)

J. W.—What is that?

Conductor—The real grip of a Fellow Craft.

J. W.—Has it a name?

Conductor—It has.

J. W.—Will you give it me?

Conductor—I did not so receive it, neither can I so impart it.

J. W.—How will you dispose of it?

Conductor—I will letter it or halve it.

J. W.—Halve it, and begin.

Conductor—No, you begin.

J. W.—Begin you.

Conductor—Ja.

J. W.—Chin.

Conductor—Jachin.

J. W.—The pass is right, and the word is right. I will suffer you to pass on to the Senior Warden's station in the west.

The conductor and candidate now pass on to the Senior Warden in the west, where they pass precisely the same examination as that just described with the Junior Warden. The Senior Warden then permits them to pass on to the Worshipful Master in the east for his examination. As they (the candidate and conductor) approach the Master's station in the east, and when nearly there, he (the Master) says:

W. M.—Brother Senior Deacon, you will reconduct the candidate to the Senior Warden in the west, with my orders that he teach him how to wear his apron as a Fellow Craft.

It should be here remarked, that when a candidate is prepared in the ante-room for the Fellow Craft's degree, he has an apron tied on him, with the flap up, as worn by an Entered Apprentice, which he wears until he arrives at this part of the ceremony.

The Deacon now conducts the candidate to the Senior Warden's station. This officer leaves his seat, and, approaching candidate, turns the flap of his apron down, at the same time saying— Brother, at the building of King Solomon's Temple, the Fellow Crafts wore their aprons with the flap turned down and the corner turned up, and thus you will wear yours, until further advanced. (Tucks a corner under the string.)

The conductor now reconducts the candidate to the Worshipful Master in the east.

FELLOW CRAFT'S APRON

W. M.—I now present you with the working tools of a Fellow Craft Mason, which are the plumb, square, and level.

The Master here shows the candidate these tools, which are generally made of rosewood or ebony, and kept for these occasions on the Master's desk.

WORKING TOOLS OF A FELLOW CRAFT

W. M.—The plumb is an instrument made use of by operative masons to raise perpendiculars, &c.

This is monitorial, and is generally read to candidates by the Master. The reader will see the Masonic Monitors. After reading this, the Master says:

W. M.—Brother Senior Deacon, it is my orders that you reconduct this candidate to the place from whence he came (ante-room), and invest him of what he has been divested of, preparatory to making an ascent through a porch, by a flight of winding stairs, consisting of three, five, and seven steps, to a place representing the Middle Chamber of King Solomon's Temple, there to receive instructions relative to the wages and jewels of a Fellow Craft.

The conductor then leads the candidate to the centre of the Lodge, before the altar, and makes the duegard and sign of a Fellow Craft, which is responded to by the Master. They then retire from the Lodge to the ante-room. After the candidate is out of the room, the Lodge is arranged for his second reception and the completion of the Degree. Two large pillars, each from six and a half to seven feet high, are placed near the door, about five feet apart, and fifteen pieces of painted board, of a rectangular form, are arranged upon the carpet so as to represent three, five, and seven steps, or stairs. Some Lodges, especially those

FIG. 13

REPRESENTATION OF THE CRAFTSMAN'S ROAD TO THE MIDDLE CHAMBER OF KING
SOLOMON'S TEMPLE.

1. Treasurer.   2. Worshipful Master.   3. Secretary.   4, 4. Conductor.   5, 5. Candidate.   6. Junior Warden.

in the large cities, employ real steps, but in most country Lodges the painted boards are used. For a more definite idea of this arrangement, the reader is referred to Fig. 13.

After the candidate is dressed, the conductor ties upon him a white apron, with the flap turned down, as worn by Fellow Crafts. The conductor then opens the Lodge-door, and, taking the candidate by the left arm, he leads him forward through the door in front of the pillars. For the first position of the parties see Fig. 13, the two stars representing the conductor (i. e. S. D.) and the candidate.

Conductor—Brother Gabe, we are now about to make an ascent through a porch, by a flight of winding stairs, consisting of three, five, and seven steps, to a place representing the Middle Chamber of King Solomon's Temple, there to receive instructions relative to the wages due, and jewels of a Fellow Craft.

Masonry is considered under two denominations—namely, Operative and Speculative. By Operative Masonry, we allude to the proper application of the useful rules of architecture, whence a structure will derive figure, strength, and beauty; and whence will result a due proportion and a just correspondence in all its parts. It furnishes us with dwellings, and convenient shelters from the vicissitudes and inclemencies of the seasons; and while it displays the effects of human wisdom, as well in the choice as in the arrangement of the sundry materials of which an edifice is composed, it demonstrates that a fund of science and industry is implanted in man, for the best, most salutary, and beneficent purposes.

By Speculative Masonry, we learn to subdue the passions, act upon the square, keep a tongue of good report, maintain secrecy, and practise charity. It is so far interwoven with religion as to lay us under obligations to pay that rational homage to the Deity, which at once constitutes our duty and our happiness. It leads the contemplative to view with reverence and admiration the glorious works of creation, and inspires him with the most exalted ideas of the perfections of his Divine Creator.

Our ancient brethren worked at both Operative and Speculative Masonry; they worked at the building of King Solomon's Temple, besides numerous other Masonic edifices. They wrought six days, but did not work on the seventh (7th), for in six days God created the heavens and the earth, and rested on the seventh day; therefore our ancient brethren consecrated this day as a day of rest from their labors; thereby enjoying frequent opportunities to contemplate the glorious works of creation, and to adore their great Creator.

Brother, the first thing that particularly attracts our attention are (here the conductor steps forward) two large brazen pillars (pointing at them with his rod), one on the right and one on the left hand. The name of the one on the left hand is Boaz, and signifies strength; the name of the one on the right is Jachin, and denotes establishment; they, collectively, denote establishment and strength, and allude to a passage in Scripture: "In strength shall this house be established."[1] These are representations of the two pillars erected at the outer porch of King Solomon's Temple. They are said to have been in height thirty-five (35) (Morgan, Richardson, Bernard, and Allyn say only eighteen) cubits, twelve in circumference, and four in diameter; they are said to have been adorned with two large chapiters of five cubits each, making their entire height forty (40) cubits. These chapiters were ornamented with a representation of network, lily-work, and pomegranates, and are said to denote Unity, Peace, and Plenty. The network, from its connection, denotes unity; the lily-work, from its whiteness, and the retired place in which it grows, purity and peace; the pomegranates, from the exuberance of their seed, denote plenty. These chapiters have on the top of each a globe, or ball; these globes are two artificial spherical bodies; on the convex surfaces of which are represented the countries, seas, and various parts of the earth, the face of the heavens, the planetary revolutions; and are said to be thus extensive, to denote the universality of Masonry, and that a Mason's charity ought to be equally extensive. The principal use of these globes, besides serving as maps, to distinguish the outward parts of the earth, and the situation of the fixed stars, is to illustrate and explain the phenomena arising from the annual revolution and the diurnal rotation of the earth around its own axis. They are the noblest instruments for improving the mind, and giving it the most distinct idea of any problem or proposition, as well as enabling it to solve the same.

Contemplating these bodies, we are inspired with a due reverence for the Deity and his works and are induced to encourage the studies of astronomy, geography, navigation, and the arts

[1] One of the rules of the Jewish Cabala is called Transposition, and is used by finding an appropriate meaning to a word formed anagrammatically from any other word. Acting on this rule, Brother Rosenberg, an eminent Jewish Mason, residing in Paris, thus improves the names of these pillars: "In the First Degree, the candidate receives in his preparation the elements of the sciences; it remains for him to instruct or to *fortify* himself by means of the higher sciences; the word *fortify* in Hebrew is ZAON. At the moment when the young neophyte is about to receive the physical light, he should also prepare himself to receive the moral light. The word *prepared* in Hebrew is NIKAJ."—*Historical Landmarks*, vol. 1. p. 450.

dependent on them, by which society has been so much benefited.

The composition of these pillars is molten or cast brass; they were cast whole, on the banks of the river Jordan, in the clay grounds between SUCCOTH and ZAREDATHA, where King Solomon ordered these and all holy vessels to be cast.

They were cast hollow, and were four inches or a hand's breadth thick. They were cast hollow the better to withstand inundation and conflagrations, and are said to have contained the archives of Masonry.

Conductor—Brother, we will pursue our journey. (Stepping to the three steps on the floor or carpet.) The next thing that attracts our attention are the winding stairs which lead to the Middle Chamber of King Solomon's Temple, consisting of three, five, and seven steps.

The first three allude to the three principal stages of human life, namely, youth, manhood, and old age. In youth, as Entered Apprentices, we ought industriously to occupy our minds in the attainment of useful knowledge; in manhood, as Fellow Crafts, we should apply our knowledge to the discharge of our respective duties to God, our neighbors, and ourselves; so that in old age, as Master Masons, we may enjoy the happy reflections consequent on a well-spent life, and die in the hope of a glorious immortality.

They also allude to the three principal supports in Masonry, namely, Wisdom, Strength, and Beauty; for it is necessary that there should be wisdom to contrive, strength to support, and beauty to adorn all great and important undertakings.

They further allude to the three principal officers of the Lodge, viz.: Master, and Senior and Junior Wardens.

Stepping forward to the five steps, he continues:

The five steps allude to the five orders of architecture and the five human senses.

The five orders of architecture are Tuscan, Doric, Ionic, Corinthian, and Composite. (Reads from *Monitor* respecting the orders of architecture.)

The five human senses are hearing, seeing, feeling, smelling, and tasting, the first three of which have ever been highly esteemed among Masons: hearing, to hear the word; seeing, to see the sign; feeling, to feel the grip, whereby one Mason may know another in the dark as well as in the light. (Steps forward to the seven steps.)

The seven steps allude to the seven Sabbatical years, seven years of famine, seven years in building the Temple, seven golden candlesticks, seven wonders of the world, seven wise men of the east, seven planets; but, more especially, the seven liberal arts and sciences, which are grammar, rhetoric, logic, arithmetic, geometry, music, and astronomy. For this and many other reasons the number seven has ever been held in high estimation among Masons. (Reads from *Monitor* respecting grammar, rhetoric, &c., &c.)

By this time the Senior Deacon has passed the entire representation of the flight of stairs, and is now at the Junior Warden's station in the south. Upon arriving here, he (the Senior Deacon) says to the candidate:

Brother, we are now approaching the outer door of King Solomon's Temple, which appears to be tyled or guarded by the Junior Warden. (Some say—our Junior Warden.)

As they approach the Junior Warden's desk, he (the Junior Warden) exclaims:

J W.—Who comes here?

S. D.—A Craftsman, on his way to the Middle Chamber of King Solomon's Temple.

J. W.—How do you expect to gain admission?

S. D.—By the pass, and token of the pass of a Fellow Craft.

J. W.—Give me the pass.

S. D.—Shibboleth.

J. W.—What does that denote?

S. D.—Plenty.

J. W.—How is it represented?

S. D.—By ears of corn hanging near a water-ford.[1]

J. W.—Why originated this word as a pass?

S. D.—In consequence of a quarrel which long existed between Jephthah, judge of Israel, and the Ephraimites: the latter had been a stubborn rebellious people, whom Jephthah had endeavored to subdue by lenient measures, but to no effect. The Ephraimites, being highly incensed for not being called to fight, and share in the rich spoils of the Ammonitish war, assembled a mighty army, and passed over the river Jordan to give Jephthah battle; but he, being apprised of their approach, called together the men of *Gilead*, and gave them battle, and put them to flight; and, to make his victory more complete, he ordered guards to be placed on the different passes on the banks of the river Jordan, and

---

[1] SHIBBOLETH. The word in Hebrew has two significations: 1. An ear of grain, and, 2. A stream of water.—*Lexicon.*
The symbolical interpretation of each floor cloth increases in interest as we gradually advance through *the field of corn by the river-side.*—*Theo. Phil.*, p. 174.

commanded, if the Ephraimites passed that way, Say ye *Shibboleth;*
but they, being of a different tribe, could not frame to pronounce
it aright, and pronounced it *Sibboleth;*[1] which trifling defect
proved them to be spies, and cost them their lives; and there
fell at that time, at the different passes on the banks of the
river Jordan, forty and two thousand. This word was also used
by our ancient brethren to distinguish a friend from a foe,
and has since been adopted as a password, to be given before
entering every regulated and well-governed Lodge of Fellow
Crafts.

J. W.—Give me the token (here give the pass grip of a Fellow
Craft).

J. W.—The pass is right, and the token is right; pass on.

They now pass around the Junior Warden's station, and go to
the Senior Warden's Station in the west, and as they approach
the Senior Warden's station the Senior Deacon remarks:

Brother, we are now coming to the inner door of the Middle
Chamber of King Solomon's Temple, which appears to be guarded
by the Senior Warden in the west.

S. W.—Who comes here?

S. D.—A Craftsman, on his way to the Middle Chamber.

S. W.—How do you expect to gain admission?

S. D.—By the grip and word of a Fellow Craft.

S. W.—Give me the grip (here give the real grip of a Fellow
Craft—Fig. 12, p. 67).

S. W.—What is that?

S. D.—The real grip of a Fellow Craft.

S. W.—Has it a name?

S. D.—It has.

S. W.—Will you give it me?

S. D.—I did not so receive it, neither can I so impart it.

S. W.—How will you dispose of it?

S. D.—I will letter it, or halve it with you.

S. W.—Halve it, and begin.

S. D.—No, you begin.

S. W.—Begin you.

---

[1] Shibboleth signifies *waters.* Thus, when the Ephraimites prayed the men of
Gilead to allow them to pass over, and were asked, in return—To pass over what?
they could not answer Shibboleth, or *the waters,* without betraying themselves to the
enemy. . . . The word chosen by the Gileadites, meaning a stream of waters, being
the object immediately before them, was well calculated to put the Ephraimites off
their guard. . . . We can easily understand the peculiarity of conformation in the
organs of speech which produced this defect. A native of the continent of Europe
experiences great difficulty in articulating the English *th.* In countries adjacent to
Palestine the same defect prevails.—*Historical Landmarks,* vol. i. pp. 508/09.

S. D.—Ja.

S. W.—Chin.

S. D.—Jachin.

S. W.—The word is right, and the grip is right; pass on, brother.

They pass on to the Worshipful Master in the east, and, on their arrival at his desk, the Master rises from his seat, and says:

W. M.—Brother Gabe, you have now arrived at the place representing the Middle Chamber of King Solomon's Temple, where you will be received and recorded as a Fellow Craft. Turning to the Secretary's desk, he continues.

W. M.—Brother Secretary, you will make the record.

Sec.—It is so recorded.

W. M.—The first thing that particularly attracted your attention on your passage here, was a representation of two brazen pillars, one on the left hand and the other on the right, which was explained to you by your conductor; after passing the pillars you passed a flight of winding stairs, consisting of three, five, and seven steps, which was likewise explained to you; after passing the stairs, you arrived at the outer door of the Middle Chamber, which you found closely guarded by the Junior Warden, who demanded of you the pass and token of the pass of a Fellow Craft; you next arrived at the inner door of the Middle Chamber, which you found guarded by the Senior Warden, who demanded of you the grip and word of a Fellow Craft. You have now arrived at the Middle Chamber where you are received and recorded a Fellow Craft. You are now entitled to wages, as such; which are, the *Corn* of nourishment, the *Wine* of refreshment, and the *Oil* of joy, which denote peace, harmony, and strength. You are also entitled to the jewels of a Fellow Craft; which are, an attentive ear, an instructive tongue, and faithful breast. The attentive ear receives the sound from the instructive tongue, and the mysteries of Masonry are safely lodged in the repository of faithful breasts.

W. M.—I shall now direct your attention to the letter "G" (here the Master turns and points to a large gilded letter "G," which is generally placed on the wall back of the Master's seat, and above his head; some Lodges suspend it in front of the Master, by a cord or wire), which is the initial of geometry, the fifth science, it being that on which this Degree was principally founded.

Geometry, the first and noblest of sciences, is the basis upon which the superstructure of Masonry is erected. By geometry, we may curiously trace nature through her various windings to her most concealed recesses. By it we discover the power, the wisdom, and the goodness of the Grand Artificer of the Universe, and view with delight the proportions which connect this vast machine. By it we discover how the planets move in their different orbits, and demonstrate their various revolutions. By it we account for the return of the seasons, and the variety of scenes which each season displays to the discerning eye. Numerous worlds are around us, all formed by the same Divine Artist, and which roll through the vast expanse, and are all conducted by the same unerring law of nature. A survey of nature, and the observation of her beautiful proportions, first determined man to imitate the Divine plan, and study symmetry and order. This gave rise to societies, and birth to every useful art. The architect began to design, and the plans which he laid down, being improved by experience and time, have produced works which are the admiration of every age.

The lapse of time, the ruthless hand of ignorance, and the devastations of war have laid waste and destroyed many valuable monuments of antiquity on which the utmost exertions of human genius have been employed. Even the Temple of Solomon, so spacious and magnificent, and constructed by so many celebrated artists, escaped not the unsparing ravages of barbarous force. Freemasonry, notwithstanding, has still survived. The *attentive ear* receives the sound from the *instructive tongue*, and the mysteries of Masonry are safely lodged in the repository of faithful breasts. Tools and implements of architecture are selected by the fraternity, to imprint on the memory wise and serious truths; and thus, through a succession of ages, are transmitted unimpaired the excellent tenets of our institution.

W. M.—Brother Gabe, this letter has a higher signification; it alludes to the sacred name of Deity (here he gives three raps with his gavel (● ● ●), when all in the Lodge rise to their feet), to whom we should all, from the youngest Entered Apprentice, who stands in the northeast corner, to the Worshipful Master, who presides in the east, with all sincerity humbly bow (here all bow their heads), with reverence most humbly bow. (Master gives one rap, when all the brethren take their seats again.)

W. M.—Brother Gabe, this ends this degree, with the exception of a charge, which I will now give to you.

CHARGE

Brother: Being passed to the second degree of Masonry, we congratulate you on your preferment. The internal, and not the external qualifications of a man, are what Masonry regards,

As you increase in knowledge you will improve in social intercourse.

It is unnecessary to recapitulate the duties which, as a Mason, you are bound to discharge, or to enlarge on the necessity of a strict adherence to them, as your own experience must have established their value.

Our laws and regulations you are strenuously to support, and be always ready to assist in seeing them duly executed. You are not to palliate, or aggravate, the offences of your brethren; but, in the decision of every trespass against our rules, you are to judge with candor, admonish with friendship, and reprehend with justice.

The study of the liberal arts, that valuable branch of education, which tends so effectually to polish and adorn the mind, is earnestly recommended to your consideration—especially the science of geometry, which is established as the basis of our art. Geometry, or Masonry, originally synonymous terms, being of a divine and moral nature, is enriched with the most useful knowledge: while it proves the wonderful properties of nature, it demonstrates the more important truths of morality.

Your past behavior and regular deportment have merited the honor which we have now conferred; and in your new character it is expected that you will conform to the principles of the Order, by steadily persevering in the practice of every commendable virtue.

Such is the nature of your engagements as a Fellow Craft; and to these duties you are bound by the most sacred ties.

LECTURE ON THE FELLOW CRAFT DEGREE

SECTION FIRST

Q. Are you a Fellow Craft?
A. I am. Try me.
Q. How will you be tried?
A. By the square.
Q. Why by the square?
A. Because it is an emblem of morality, and one of the working-tools of my profession.
Q. What is a square?
A. An angle of ninety degrees, or a fourth part of a circle.
Q. Where were you made a Fellow Craft?
A. In a regularly constituted Lodge of Fellow Crafts.
Q. How were you prepared?

A. By being divested of all metals, neither naked nor clothed, barefoot nor shod, hoodwinked, with a cable-tow twice about my right arm, in which condition I was conducted to the door of a Lodge by a brother.

Q. Why had you a cable-tow twice about your right arm?

A. To signify, as a Fellow Craft, that I was under a double tie to the fraternity.

Q. How gained you admission?

A. By three distinct knocks.

Q. To what do they allude?

A. To the three jewels of a Fellow Craft—an attentive ear, an instructive tongue, and a faithful breast.

Q. What was said to you from within?

A. Who comes there.

Q. Your answer?

A. Brother A. B., who has been regularly initiated Entered Apprentice, and now wishes to receive more light in Masonry, by being passed to the degree of Fellow Craft.

Q. What were you then asked?

A. If it was of my own free-will and accord, if I was worthy and well qualified, duly and truly prepared, had made suitable proficiency in the preceding degree, and was properly vouched for; all of which being answered in the affirmative, I was asked by what further right or benefit I expected to gain admission.

Q. Your answer?

A. By the benefit of the pass.

Q. Did you give the pass?

A. I did not; but my conductor gave it for me.

Q. What followed?

A. I was bid to wait with patience until the Worshipful Master should be informed of my request and his answer returned.

Q. What answer did he return?

A. Let him enter, in the name of the Lord, and be received in due form.

Q. How were you received?

A. On the angle of the square presented to my naked right breast, which was to teach me that the square of virtue should be the rule and guide of my conduct, in all my future transactions with mankind.

Q. How were you then disposed of?

A. I was conducted twice around the Lodge to the Junior Warden in the south, where the same questions were asked and like answers returned as at the door.

Q. How did the Junior Warden dispose of you?

A. He directed me to pass on to the Senior Warden in the west, and he to the Worshipful Master in the east, where the same questions were asked and like answers returned as before.

Q. How did the Worshipful Master dispose of you?

A. He ordered me to be returned to the Senior Warden in the west, who taught me to approach the east by two upright regular steps, my feet forming an angle of a square, my body erect at the altar before the Worshipful Master in the east.

Q. What did the Worshipful Master then do with you?

A. He made me a Fellow Craft in due form.

Q. What was that due form?

A. Kneeling on my naked right knee, my left forming a square, my right hand on the Holy Bible, square, and compasses, my left arm forming a right angle supported by the square in which due form I took the oath of a Fellow Craft. (Some repeat the oath.)

Q. After the obligation, what were you then asked?

A. What I most desired.

Q. Your answer?

A. More light in Masonry.

Q. Did you receive light?

A. I did, by the order of the Worshipful Master, and the assistance of the brethren.

Q. On being brought to light, what did you first discover, more than you had heretofore discovered?

A One point of the compasses elevated above the square, which was to signify that I had received light in Masonry by points.

Q. What did you then discover?

A. The Worshipful Master approaching me from the east, under the duegard and sign of a Fellow Craft; who, in token of the continuance of his brotherly love and favor, presented me with his right hand, and with it the pass, token, token of the pass, grip and word of a Fellow Craft, and ordered me to arise and salute the Junior and Senior Warden as such.

Q. After saluting the Wardens, what did you then discover?

A. The Worshipful Master ordered me to the Senior Warden in the west, who taught me to wear my apron as a Fellow Craft.

Q. How should a Fellow Craft wear his apron?

A. With the flap turned down, and the corner turned up.

Q. After being taught to wear your apron as a Fellow Craft, how were you then disposed of?

A. I was conducted to the Worshipful Master in the east, who presented me with the working-tools of a Fellow Craft (the plumb, square, and level), and taught me their use.

Q. What is their use?

A. The plumb is an instrument made use of, by operative masons, to raise perpendiculars; the square, to square their work; and the level, to lay horizontals. But we, as Free and Accepted Masons are taught to make use of them for more noble and glorious purposes: the plumb admonishes us to walk upright, in our several stations, before God and man; squaring our actions by the square of virtue; and remembering that we are travelling, upon the level of time, to "that undiscovered country from whose bourne no traveller returns."

Q. How were you then disposed of?

A. I was ordered to be returned to the place from whence I came, and invested of what I had been divested of, and was informed that, agreeably to an ancient custom in every well-governed Lodge, it therefore became necessary that I should make a regular ascent, by a flight of winding stairs, consisting of three, five, and seven steps, to a place representing the Middle Chamber of King Solomon's Temple, there to receive instructions relative to the wages and jewels of   Fellow Craft.

SECOND SECTION

Q. Have you ever worked as a Fellow Craft?

A. I have, in speculative; but our forefathers wrought in both speculative and operative Masonry.

Q. Where did they work?

A. At the building of King Solomon's Temple, and of many other Masonic edifices.

Q. How long did they work?

A. Six days.

Q. Did they work on the seventh?

A. They did not.

Q. Why so?

A. Because in six days God created the heavens and the earth, and rested on the seventh day; the seventh day, therefore, our ancient brethren consecrated as a day of rest from their labors, thereby enjoying more frequent opportunities to contemplate the glorious works of creation, and adore their great Creator.

Q. Did you ever return to the *sanctum sanctorum*, or holy of holies, or King Solomon's Temple?

A. I did.

Q. By what way?

A. Through a long porch or alley.

Q. Did any thing in particular strike your attention on your return?

A. There did, viz.: two large columns, or pillars, one on the left hand, and the other on the right.

Q. What was the name of the one on the left hand?

A. Boaz, which denotes strength.

Q. What was the name of the one on the right hand?

A. Jachin, denoting establishment.

Q. What do they collectively allude to?

A. A passage in Scripture, wherein God has declared in his word, "In strength shall this house be established."

Q. What were their dimensions?

A. Thirty-five cubits in height, twelve in circumference, and four in diameter.

Q. Were they adorned with any thing?

A. They were; with two large chapiters, one on each.

Q. What was the height of these chapiters?

A. Five cubits.

Q. Were they adorned with any thing?

A. They were; with wreaths of net-work, lily-work, and pomegranates.

Q. What do they denote?

A. Unity, Peace, and Plenty.

Q. Why so?

A. Net-work, from its connection, denotes union; lily-work, from its whiteness and purity, denotes peace; and pomegranates, from the exuberance of their seed, denote plenty.

Q. Were those columns adorned with any thing further?

A. They were, viz.: with two large globes or balls, one on each.

Q. What was the entire height of these pillars?

A. Forty cubits.

Q. Did they contain any thing?

A. They did, viz.: all the maps and charts of the celestial and terrestrial bodies.

Q. Why are they said to be so extensive?

A. To denote the universality of Masonry, and that a Mason's charity ought to be equally extensive.

Q. What was their composition?

A. Molten or cast brass.

Q. Who cast them?

A. Our Grand Master, Hiram Abiff.

Q. Where were they cast?

A. On the banks of the river Jordan, in the clay ground between Succoth and Zaredatha, where King Solomon ordered these and all other holy vessels to be cast.

Q. Were they cast solid or hollow?

A. Hollow.

Q. What was their thickness?

A. Four inches, or a hand's breadth.

Q. Why were they cast hollow?

A. The better to withstand inundations or conflagrations; they were said to contain all the archives of Masonry.

Q. What did you next come to?

A. A long, winding staircase, or flight of winding stairs, consisting of three, five, and seven steps.

Q. To what do the three steps allude?

A. The three principal supports in Masonry, namely: wisdom, strength, and beauty; they also allude to the three stages in human life: youth, manhood, and age; they further allude to the three degrees in Masonry: Entered Apprentice, Fellow Craft, and Master Mason.

Q. What do the five steps allude to?

A. The five orders in architecture, and the five human senses.

Q. What are the five orders in architecture?

A. The Tuscan, Doric, Ionic, Corinthian, and Composite.

Q. What are the five human senses?

A. Hearing, seeing, feeling, smelling, and tasting; the first three of which have ever been deemed highly essential among Masons: hearing, to hear the word; seeing, to see the sign; and feeling, to feel the grip, whereby one Mason may know another in the dark as well as in the light.

Q. What do the seven steps allude to?

A. The seven Sabbatical years, seven years of famine, seven years of war, seven years in building the Temple, seven golden candlesticks, seven wonders of the world, seven planets; but, more especially, the seven liberal arts and sciences, which are grammar, rhetoric, logic, arithmetic, geometry, music, and astronomy. For these and many other reasons the number seven has ever been held in high estimation among Masons.

Q. What did you next come to?

A. The outer door of the Middle Chamber of King Solomon's Temple, which I found partly open, but closely tyled by the Junior Warden in the south.

Q. How did you gain admission?

A. By the pass, and token of the pass of a Fellow Craft.

Q. What was the name of the pass?

A. SHIBBOLETH.

Q. What does it denote?

A. Plenty.

Q. How is it represented?

A. By ears of corn hanging near a water-ford.

Q. Why originated this word as a pass?

A. In consequence of a quarrel which had long existed between Jephthah, Judge of Israel, and the Ephraimites, &c., &c. (for the balance, see page 75).

Q. What did you next discover?

A. The inner door of the Middle Chamber of King Solomon's Temple.

Q. How did you gain admission?

A. By the grip and word of a Fellow Craft—Jachin.

Q. How did the Senior Warden dispose of you?

A. He ordered me to be conducted to the Worshipful Master in the east, who informed me that I had arrived at a place representing the Middle Chamber of King Solomon's Temple, where I would be received and recorded as such; which record was then made by the Secretary (by the orders of the Worshipful Master), and I was presented with the wages of a Fellow Craft, and also the jewels of a Fellow Craft.

Q. What are the wages of a Fellow Craft?

A. The corn of nourishment, the wine of refreshment, and the oil of joy.

Q. What do they denote?

A. Peace, harmony, and strength.

Q. What are the jewels of a Fellow Craft?

A. An attentive ear, an instructive tongue, and a faithful breast.

Q. How explained?

A. The attentive ear receives the sound from the instructive tongue, and the mysteries of Masonry are lodged in the repository of a faithful breast.

Q. What were you next shown?

A. The letter G.

Q. To what does it allude?

A. Geometry, the fifth science; but more particularly to the sacred name of the Deity, to whom we should all, from the youngest Entered Apprentice who stands in the northeast corner, to the Worshipful Master who presides in the east, with reverence most devoutly and humbly bow.

This is the end of the Fellow Craft Degree, or Second Degree in Masonry.[1]

[1] LECTURE. In the Fellow Crafts' Degree, the first section recapitulates the ceremonies of passing a candidate. The second section gives an account of the ancient division of our institution into operative and speculative Masons, and by striking emblems directs the candidate to an attentive study of the liberal arts and sciences. —*Lexicon.*

During the preparation, according to the legends of Freemasonry, the workmen's wages were paid daily, weekly, monthly, and quarterly, in their respective Lodges; and, when the Temple was nearly completed, *they were paid in the Middle Chamber.* This celebrated apartment was accessible by a *winding staircase* of stone; the foot of which was guarded by the Junior Warden, and the summit by the Senior Warden of a Fellow Crafts' Lodge. And how were these wages paid? Without fear or scruple, says the legend, because their employers were entitled to their unlimited confidence. —*Theo. Phil.,* p. 199.

MASTER MASON, OR THIRD DEGREE [1]

THE ceremony of opening and conducting the business of a Lodge of Master Masons is nearly the same as in the Entered Apprentice and Fellow Crafts' Degrees, already explained. All the business of a "Blue Lodge" (a Lodge of three Degrees) is done in the Lodge while opened on this Degree, except that of entering an Apprentice or passing a Fellow Craft, when the Lodge is lowered from the Masters' Degree for that purpose.

The Third Degree is said to be the height of Ancient Freemasonry, and the most sublime of all the Degrees in Masonry (Royal Arch not even excepted); and when it is conferred, the Lodge is generally well filled with the members of the Lodge and visiting brethren.

The traditional account of the death, several burials, and resurrections of one of the craft, Hiram Abiff, the widow's son, as developed in conferring this Degree, is very interesting.

We read in the Bible, that Hiram Abiff was one of the head workmen employed at the building of King Solomon's Temple, and other ancient writings inform us that he was an arbiter between King Solomon and Hiram, king of Tyre; but his tragical death is nowhere recorded, except in the archives of Freemasonry. Not even the Bible, the writings of Josephus, nor any other writings, however ancient, of which we have any knowledge, furnish any information respecting his death. It is very singular, that a man

---

[1] Our present Third Degree is not architectural, but traditionary, historical, and legendary; its traditions being unfortunately hyperbolical; its history apocryphal, and its legends fabulous.— The Freemason's Treasury, p. 222.

so celebrated as Hiram Abiff was, universally acknowledged as the third most distinguished man then living, and, in many respects, the greatest man in the world, should pass from off the stage of action, in the presence of King Solomon, three thousand three hundred grand overseers, and one hundred and fifty thousand workmen, with whom he had spent a number of years, and with King Solomon, his bosom friend, without any of his numerous *confrères* even recording his death, or any thing about it.

COMPASSES, PLACED IN A LODGE OF MASTER MASONS, "BOTH POINTS ELEVATED ABOVE THE SQUARE." (See Note B, Appendix.)

A Master Masons' Lodge is styled by the Craft the "Sanctum Sanctorum, or Holy of Holies, of King Solomon's Temple," and when the Lodge is opened on this Degree, both points of the compasses are elevated above the square. (See engraving.)

A candidate for the sublime Degree of a Master Mason is generally (as in the preceding Degrees), prepared by the Junior Deacon and the two Stewards, or some other brethren acting as such.

PREPARING THE CANDIDATE

The candidate is divested of all wearing apparel, except his shirt and drawers, and if he has not the latter, he is furnished with a pair by the brethren preparing him. The drawers are rolled up just above the candidate's knees, and both arms are taken out of his shirt-sleeves, leaving his legs and breast bare. A rope, technically called, by Masons, a cable-tow, is wound around his body three times, and a bandage, or hoodwink, is tied very closely over his eyes. (See engraving.)

When the candidate is prepared, the Deacon takes him by the left arm, leads him up to the door of the Lodge, and gives three *loud, distinct knocks*.

The Senior Deacon, who has stationed himself at the inner door, at the right of the Senior Warden, on hearing these raps rises to his feet, makes the sign of a Master Mason to the Master (see Fig. 6, p. 18), and says:

Worshipful Master, while engaged in the lawful pursuit of Masonry, there is an alarm at the inner door of our Lodge.

W. M.—You will attend to the alarm, and ascertain the cause.

Senior Deacon gives three loud knocks (● ● ●), which are responded to by one (●) from the parties outside. The Senior Deacon then answers with one rap (●), and opens the door. (See Note J, Appendix.)

S. D.—Who comes here?

J. D. — Brother Gabe, who has been regularly initiated Entered Apprentice, passed to the Degree of Fellow Craft, and now wishes to receive further light in Masonry, by being raised to the sublime Degree of a Master Mason.

S. D.—Brother Gabe, is it of your own free-will and accord?

Candidate—It is.

S. D. — Brother Junior Deacon, is he worthy and well qualified?

J. D.—He is.

S. D.—Duly and truly prepared?

J. D.—He is.

S. D.—Has he made suitable proficiency in the preceding degrees?

J. D.—He has.

S. D.—And properly vouched for?

J. D.—He is.

S. D.—Who vouches for him?

J. D.—A brother.

S. D.—By what further right or benefit does he expect to gain admission?

J. D.—By the benefit of the password.

S. D.—Has he the password?

J. D.—He has it not, but I have it for him.

S. D.—Advance, and give it me.

Junior Deacon here steps forward and whispers in the Senior Deacon's ear, "Tubal Cain."

S. D.—The pass is right; you will wait with patience until the Worshipful Master is informed of your request and his answer returned.

The Deacon then closes the door, repairs to the centre of the Lodge-room before the altar, and sounds his rod on the floor three times (● ● ●), which is responded to by the Master with three raps of the gavel, when the Senior Deacon makes the sign of a Master Mason (see Fig. 6, p. 18), and says:

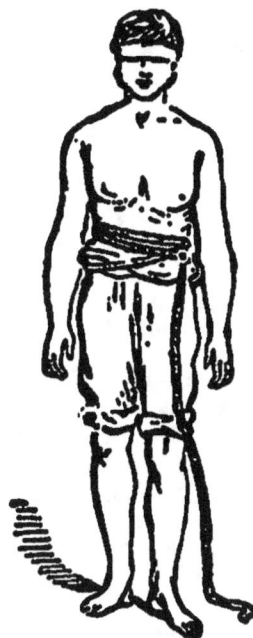

CANDIDATE DULY AND TRULY PREPARED

S. D.—Brother Gabe, who has been regularly initiated Entered Apprentice, passed to the Degree of Fellow Craft, and now wishes to receive further light in Masonry, by being raised to the sublime Degree of a Master Mason

W. M.—Is it of his own free-will and accord?

S. D.—It is.

W. M.—Is he worthy and well qualified, duly and truly prepared?

S. D.—He is.

W. M.—Has he made suitable proficiency in the preceding degree?

S. D.—He has.

W. M.—And properly vouched for?

S. D.—He is.

W. M.—Who vouches for him?

S. D.—A brother.

W. M.—By what further right or benefit does he expect to gain admission?

S. D.—By the benefit of the password.

W. M.—Has he that pass?

S. D.—He has it not, but I have it for him.

W. M.—Advance, and give it me.

The Senior Deacon steps to the Master, and whispers in his ear, "Tubal Cain."

W. M.—The password is right. Let him enter, and be received in due form.

The Senior Deacon steps to the altar, takes the compasses, repairs to the door, opens it, and says:

S. D.—Let him enter, and be received in due form.

The Junior Deacon advances, followed by the Stewards, with rods, when the Senior Deacon stops them, by placing his hand against the candidate, at the same time saying:

S. D.—Brother Gabe, on entering this Lodge the first time, you were received on the point of the compasses, pressing your naked left breast, the moral of which was explained to you. On entering the second time, you were received on the angle of the square, which was also explained to you. I now receive you on both points of the compasses, extending from your naked left to your naked right breast (he here places both points against candidate's breasts), which is to teach you, that as the vital parts of man are contained within the breasts, so the most excellent tenets of our institution are contained between the points of the compasses— which are Friendship, Morality, and Brotherly Love.

The Junior Deacon now passes the candidate over to the Senior

Deacon, and he (Junior Deacon) takes his seat near the door, at the right hand of the Senior Warden in the west, while the Senior Deacon proceeds to conduct the candidate, followed by the two Stewards, three times around the Lodge, during which time the Worshipful Master reads the following passage of Scripture:

"Remember now thy Creator in the days of thy youth, while the evil days come not, nor the years draw nigh when thou shalt say, I have no pleasure in them: while the sun, or the moon, or the stars be not darkened, nor the clouds return after the rain; in the day when the keepers of the house shall tremble, and the strong men shall bow themselves, and the grinders cease, because they are few; and those that look out of the windows be darkened, and the doors shall be shut in the streets, when the sound of the grinding is low, and he shall rise up at the voice of the bird, and all the daughters of music shall be brought low. Also when they shall be afraid of that which is high, and fears shall be in the way, and the almond-tree shall flourish, and the grasshopper shall be a burden, and desire shall fail; because man goeth to his long home, and the mourners go about the streets; or ever the silver cord be loosed, or the golden bowl be broken at the fountain, or the wheel at the cistern. Then shall the dust return to the earth as it was; and the spirit shall return unto God, who gave it."

In some Lodges the following paraphrase of the above is sung; and if the Lodge have an organ, or melodeon, the singers are generally accompanied on the instrument:

"Let us remember in our youth,
  Before the evil days draw nigh,
Our Great Creator, and his Truth,
  Ere memory fail, and pleasures fly;
Or sun, or moon, or planet's light
  Grow dark, or clouds return in gloom;
Ere vital spark no more incite;
  When strength shall bow and years consume."

For balance of this paraphrase, see *Freemason's Monitor, or Illustrations of Masonry,* by Thomas S. Webb, p. 61.

As the Senior Deacon and candidate pass the different stations of the officers, they (the officers) sound their gavels as follows; when they pass the Junior Warden in the south the first time, he gives one rap (●), Senior Warden one rap, and Worshipful Master one rap; the second time, Junior Warden two raps, Senior Warden two raps, and Worshipful Master two raps (●●); the third time round, Junior Warden three raps (●●●); Senior

Warden three raps, and the Worshipful Master three raps. The Master so times his reading of the passage of Scripture, as to finish just as the parties reach the Junior Warden's station in the south, on the third round, when they halt.

J. W.—Who comes here?

Conductor (S. D.)—Brother Gabe, who has been regularly initiated Entered Apprentice, passed to the degree of Fellow Craft, and now wishes to receive further light in Masonry, by being raised to the sublime Degree of a Master Mason.

J. W.—Brother Gabe, is it of your own free-will and accord?

Candidate—It is.

J. W.—Brother Senior Deacon, is he worthy and well qualified, duly and truly prepared?

S. D.—He is.

J. W.—Has he made suitable proficiency in the preceding Degrees?

S. D.—He has.

J. W.—And properly vouched for?

S. D.—He is.

J. W.—Who vouches for him?

S. D.—A brother.

J. W.—By what further right or benefit does he expect to gain admission?

S. D.—By the benefit of the password.

J. W.—Has he the password?

S. D.—He has it not, but I have it for him.

J. W.—Advance and give the password.

Senior Deacon steps forward, and whispers in the Warden's ear, "Tubal Cain."

J. W.—The password is right. I will suffer you to pass on to the Senior Warden's station in the west, for his examination.

Senior Deacon passes on to the west, where the same questions are asked and answered as before, and the Senior Warden suffers them to pass on to the Worshipful Master in the east, where the same questions and answers are repeated.

W. M.—From whence came you, and whither are you travelling?

S. D.—From the west, travelling toward the east.

W. M.—Why leave you the west, and travel toward the east?

S. D.—In search of further light in Masonry.

W. M.—Since that is the object of your search, you will reconduct this candidate to the Senior Warden in the west, with my orders that he be taught to approach the east, the place of further light in Masonry, by three upright, regular steps, his body erect at the altar before the Worshipful Master in the east.

The Senior Deacon then conducts the candidate to the Senior Warden in the west, and reports:

S. D.—Brother Senior Warden, it is the orders of the Worshipful Master that you teach this candidate to approach the east, the place of further light in Masonry, by three upright, regular steps, his body erect at the altar before the Worshipful Master in the east.

The Senior Warden approaches the candidate, faces him toward the east (*i. e.* towards the Master), and says:

Brother, you will step off with your left foot one full step, and bring the heel of your right in the hollow of your left foot; now step off with your right foot, and bring the heel of your left in the hollow of your right foot; now step off with your left foot, and bring both heels together. (See Fig. 14.)

Fig. 14

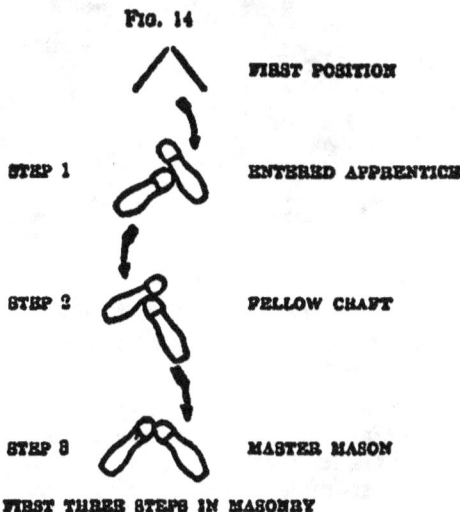

S. W.—The candidate is in order, Worshipful, and awaits your further will and pleasure.

W. M.—You will cause him to kneel on his naked knees, both hands resting on the Holy Bible, square, and compasses.

W. M.—Brother Gabe, you are kneeling, for the third time, at the altar of Masonry, to take upon yourself the solemn oath of a Master Mason; and I, as Master of this Lodge, take pleasure, as on former occasions, in informing you that there is nothing in it which will interfere with the duty you owe to your God, your neighbor, your country, or self. Are you willing to take the oath?

FIG. 15

Worshipful Master   Altar   Candidate   Conductor

CANDIDATE TAKING THE OATH OF A MASTER MASON

"Kneeling on both my naked knees, both hands resting on the Holy Bible, square, and compasses."

Candidate—I am.

W. M.—You will repeat your name, and say after me:

"I, Peter Gabe (Master gives three raps with his gavel, when all present assemble round the altar), of my own free-will and accord, in the presence of Almighty God, and this worshipful Lodge, erected to him and dedicated to the holy Sts. John, do hereby and hereon most solemnly and sincerely promise and swear, that I will always hail, ever conceal, and never reveal any of the secrets, arts, parts, point or points, of the Master Masons' Degree, to any person or persons whomsoever, except it be to a true and lawful brother of this Degree, or in a regularly constituted Lodge of Master Masons, nor unto him, or them, until by strict trial, due examination, or lawful information, I shall have found him, or them, as lawfully entitled to the same as I am myself.

"I furthermore promise and swear, that I will stand to and abide by all laws, rules, and regulations of the Master Masons' Degree, and of the Lodge of which I may hereafter become a member, as far as the same shall come to my knowledge; and that I will ever maintain and support the constitution, laws, and edicts of the Grand Lodge under which the same shall be holden.

"Further, that I will acknowledge and obey all due signs and summonses sent to me from a Master Masons' Lodge, or given me by a brother of that Degree, if within the length of my cable-tow.

"Further, that I will always aid and assist all poor, distressed, worthy Master Masons, their widows and orphans, knowing them to be such, as far as their necessities may require, and my ability permit, without material injury to myself and family.

"Further, that I will keep a worthy brother Master Mason's secrets inviolable, when communicated to and received by me as such, murder and treason excepted.

"Further, that I will not aid, nor be present at, the initiation, passing, or raising of a woman, an old man in his dotage, a young man in his nonage, an atheist, a madman, or fool, knowing them to be such.

"Further, that I will not sit in a Lodge of clandestine-made Masons, nor converse on the subject of Masonry with a clandestine made Mason, nor one who has been expelled or suspended from a Lodge, while under that sentence, knowing him or them to be such.

"Further, I will not cheat, wrong, nor defraud a Master Mason's Lodge, nor a brother of this Degree, knowingly, nor supplant him in any of his laudable undertakings, but will give him due and timely notice, that he may ward off all danger.

"Further, that I will not knowingly strike a brother Master Mason, or otherwise do him personal violence in anger, except in the necessary defence of my family or property.

"Further, that I will not have illegal carnal intercourse with a Master Mason's wife, his mother, sister, or daughter, nor suffer the same to be done by others, if in my power to prevent.

"Further, that I will not give the Grand Masonic word, in any other manner or form than that in which I shall receive it, and then in a low breath.

"Further, that I will not give the Grand Hailing Sign of Distress, except in case of the most imminent danger, in a just and lawful Lodge, or for the benefit of instruction; and if ever I should see it given, or hear the words accompanying it, by a worthy brother in distress, I will fly to his relief, if there is a greater probability of saving his life than losing my own.

"All this I most solemnly, sincerely promise and swear, with a firm and steady resolution to perform the same, without any hesitation, mental reservation, or secret evasion of mind whatever, binding myself, under no less penalty than that of having my body severed in two,[1] my bowels taken from thence and burned to ashes, the ashes scattered before the four winds of heaven, that no more remembrance might be had of so vile and wicked a wretch as I would be, should I ever, knowingly, violate this my Master Mason's obligation. So help me God, and keep me steadfast in the due performance of the same."

M. W.—You will detach your hands and kiss the book. In your present condition, what do you most desire?

Candidate (prompted by conductor). — Further light in Masonry.

W. M.—Let him receive further light.

Conductor here takes off the hoodwink and removes the cabletow, and all around the altar place their hands in the position of the duegard of a Master Mason. (See Fig. 5, p. 17.) The Worshipful Master gives one rap with his gavel, when all the brethren retire to their seats, leaving at the altar the Master, conductor, and candidate.

W. M.—Brother Gabe, on receiving further light, you perceive more than you have heretofore. Both points of the compasses are elevated above the square, which is to teach you never to lose sight of those truly Masonic virtues, which are friendship, morality, and brotherly love.

The Master now steps back about three paces from the altar, and says,

Brother Gabe, you discover me approaching you from the east, under the duegard (some say—step, duegard, and sign) of a Master Mason; and, in token of the further continuance of my brotherly love and favor, I present you with my right hand, and with it the pass and token of the pass of a Master Mason.

Takes the candidate by the "real grip" of a Fellow Craft, and says,

Your conductor will answer for you.

W. M.—Will you be off or from?

Conductor—From.

W. M.—From what and to what?

---

[1] Here the conductor or some brother draws his hand across candidate's naked belly: the sword is often used, especially if the initiation takes place in winter, the sword is left in a cold place—and when it is drawn across candidate's belly, it has a very shocking effect, causing the candidate to jump or tremble.

Conductor—From the "real grip" of a Fellow Craft to the pass grip of a Master Mason.

W. M.—Pass.

FIG. 18

Conductor here instructs candidate to pass his thumb from the second joint to space beyond, which is the second space.

W. M. (looking conductor in the eye).— What is that?

PASS GRIP OF MASTER MASON

Conductor—The pass grip of a Master Mason.

W. M.—Has it a name?

Conductor—It has.

W. M.—Will you give it me?

Conductor—I did not so receive it, neither can I so impart it.

W. M.—How will you dispose of it?

Conductor—I will letter it or halve it.

W. M.—Halve it, and begin.

Conductor—No, you begin.

W. M.—Begin you.

Conductor—Tu.

W. M.—Bal.

Conductor — Cain. (Pronounced by the conductor — Tubal Cain.)[1]

W. M. (lifting the candidate up.)—You will arise, and salute the Junior and Senior Wardens as an obligated Master Mason.

Here Lodges differ in their mode of work; some only pass the candidate around the Lodge once, and as he passes the Junior and Senior Wardens he gives the Master's sign. (See Fig. 6, p. 18.) The Master should instruct the candidate (and he generally does) how to make the signs before he gets up from the altar, after taking the obligation.

The following appears to be the proper way:—After the candidate gets up from the altar, the conductor should lead him from the altar direct to the Junior Warden's station in the south, and

[1] What does it denote? Worldly possession.—*Dr. Hemming.*

That Tubal Cain gave first occasion to the name and worship of Vulcan hath been very probably conceived, both from the very great affinity of the names, and that Tubal Cain is expressly mentioned to be an instructor of every artificer in brass and iron; and as near relation as Apollo had to Vulcan, Jubal had to Tubal Cain, who was the inventor of music, or the father of all such as handle the harp and organ, which the Greeks attribute to Apollo.—*Historical Landmarks,* vol. II. pp. 204/05.

give three raps on the floor with his rod, the Junior Warden responding by three raps with his gavel.

J. W.—Who comes here?

Conductor—Brother Gabe, an obligated Master Mason.

J. W.—How shall I know him to be such?

Conductor—By the pass and token of the pass of a Master Mason.

J. W. (offering his hand to candidate.)—Advance the token. (They take hold of each other's hands by the real grip of a Fellow Craft. See real grip of a Fellow Craft, Fig. 12, p. 67.)

J. W.—Will you be off, or from?

Conductor (for candidate).—From.

J. W.—From what, and to what?

Conductor—From the real grip of a Fellow Craft to the pass grip of a Master Mason.

J. W.—Pass. (They now pass to the pass grip of a Master Mason. (See Fig. 16, p. 97.)

J. W.—What is that?

Conductor—The pass-grip of a Master Mason.

J. W.—Has it a name?

Conductor—It has.

J. W.—Will you give it me?

Conductor—I did not so receive it, neither can I so impart it.

J. W.—How will you dispose of it?

Conductor—I will letter or halve it.

J. W.—Halve it, and begin.

Conductor—No, you begin.

J. W.—Begin you.

Conductor—Tu.

J. W.—Bal.

Conductor—Cain. (Pronounced by conductor—Tubal Cain.)

J. W.—The token is right, and the pass is right. You will pass on to the Senior Warden's station in the west, for his examination.

They then pass on to this officer's station, where the same questions and answers are repeated as at the Junior Warden's station, and he (the Senior Warden) suffers them to pass on to the Worshipful Master's station in the east. As they approach the Worshipful Master's station, he says:

W. M.—Brother Senior Deacon, you will reconduct the candidate to the Senior Warden in the west, with my orders that he teach him how to wear his apron as a Master Mason.

The conductor then turns about to the Senior Warden in the west, and says:

Brother Senior Warden, it is the orders of the Worshipful

Master that you teach this candidate how to wear his apron as a Master Mason.

The Senior Warden approaches the candidate and ties the apron upon him, with the flap and corners turned down, and says:

Master Masons wear their aprons with the flap and corners down, to designate them as Master Masons, or as overseers of the work, and so you will wear yours.

A MASTER MASON'S APRON

The conductor now conducts the candidate back to the Worshipful Master in the east.

W. M. — Brother Gabe, as you are clothed as a Master Mason,[1] it is necessary that you should have the working-tools of a Master Mason. (Master has a small trowel, which he shows the candidate as he commences to read concerning it.)

The working-tools of a Master Mason are all the implements of Masonry appertaining to the first three Degrees indiscriminately, but more especially the trowel.

The trowel is an instrument made use of by operative masons to spread the cement which unites a building into one common mass; but we, as

TROWEL

Free and Accepted Masons are taught to make use of it for the more noble and glorious purpose of spreading the cement of

---

[1] The jewels of a Masters' Lodge are suspended from blue velvet collars, bordered and embroidered with silver. At the point is a blue rosette, in the centre of which is a silver five-pointed star.

The apron is white, lined and bordered with blue. On the flap is delineated an eye, and on the area selections from the Master's carpet. A blue silk scarf, trimmed with silver, having a blue rosette at the shoulder and hip, is worn from left to right.

The following are the jewels:

The Worshipful Master	wears a square.
The Past Master	„ a compass opened on a quarter circle.
The Senior Warden	„ a level.
The Junior Warden	„ a plumb.
The Secretary	„ cross pens.
The Treasurer	„ cross keys.
The Senior Deacon	„ square and compass, with sun.
The Junior Deacon	„ square and compass, with quarter moon.
The Stewards	„ a cornucopia.
The Master of Ceremonies	„ cross swords.
The Tyler	„ a sabre.

brotherly love and affection; that cement which unites us into one sacred band, or society of friends and brothers, among whom no contention should ever exist, but that noble contention, or rather emulation, of who best can work and best agree.

W. M.—Brother Senior Deacon, you will now reconduct this candidate to the place from whence he came, and reinvest him with what he has been divested of, and await my further will and pleasure.

The conductor then leads the candidate to the centre of the Lodge, at the altar, and makes duegard and sign of a Master Mason (see Figs. 5, 6, pp. 17, 18), which is responded to by the Master, after which the conductor and candidate pass out of the Lodge. While they are going out, the Master gives three sounds with his gavel (● ● ●), and says, in a loud tone of voice:

W. M.—Brother Junior Warden, what is the hour?

J. W.—High twelve, Worshipful.

W. M.—If you are satisfied it is high twelve, you will erect your column, and call the craft from labor to refreshment, for the space of thirty minutes (or fifteen minutes, as the case may be), calling them in at the sound of the gavel. On receiving this order, the Junior Warden takes from his desk a small wooden column, about eighteen inches in length, and sets it in an upright position at his right hand, and at the same time he gives three raps (● ● ●) with the gavel, and says:

J. W.—Brethren, you are accordingly at refreshment.

It should be remarked here, that there is a similar column on the Senior Warden's desk, which is always placed in a horizontal position (i. e., turned down on its side) when the Junior Warden's column is up, and *vice versa*. When the Lodge is opened, the Junior Warden's column is turned down, and the Senior Warden's turned up, at his right hand.

The brethren are now allowed a few minutes for recreation, styled by Masons refreshment; during which time the candidate is being prepared in the ante-room, and the Lodge made ready for the remaining portion of the ceremony of initiation.

This latter is accomplished as follows: a canvas, seven feet long and about six feet wide, with five or six strong loops on each side, is produced from a closet or chest in the room; and a buckskin bag, stuffed with hair, about the size of two boxing-gloves, is taken from the same receptacle. These implements are both used as will be described hereafter.

The room is cleared by removing the altar and lights, and the two large pillars used in the Second Degree. By this time the candidate is dressed, his apron is tied on as a Master Mason, with the right-hand corner tucked up, and he wears a yoke with a Senior Warden's jewel attached to it. In some Lodges, the brethren on this occasion attire the candidate with a very rich apron and yoke.

When the candidate is fully dressed, the door is unceremoniously thrown open, and he, in company with others, is permitted to enter the Lodge. His friends now approach him, and congratulate him upon his Masonic appearance, asking him how he likes the degree, and if he is not glad he is through, &c., &c.

The object of this is to mislead the candidate, and to impress upon his mind the idea that there is no more of the ceremony, and that his initiation is completed.

Worshipful Master gives one rap with his gavel (●).

J. W.—Brethren, you are now called from refreshment to labor again. (Gives one rap (●), steps to his desk, and turns the small column down on its side, as already explained.)

At the same time the Senior Warden steps to his stand, and turns up the column on his desk at his right. The brethren then all take their seats, and the candidate with them.

W. M.—Brother Senior Warden, do you know any further business before this Lodge of Master Masons before we proceed to close?

S. W. (rising to his feet and making the sign of a Master Mason.) —Nothing, Worshipful.

W. M.—Have you any thing to offer, Brother Junior Warden?

J. W. (making sign).—Nothing, Worshipful.

W. M.—Have you any thing on your desk, Brother Secretary?

Sec. (makes the sign, see Fig. 8, p. 18).—Nothing, Worshipful.

W. M.—Has any brother present any thing to offer for the benefit of Masonry? (nothing being said, Worshipful Master continues): We will then proceed to close; but, before doing so, I would say to Brother Gabe (the candidate)—Is he present?

Some Brother—He is.

W. M.—Brother Gabe, you will please approach the east.

Conductor (S. D.) leads the candidate up in front of the Master's seat in the east.

(The author would here remark, with regard to the matter of closing the Lodge, and asking the Wardens if they know any thing further before the Lodge, previous to closing, that it is a *ruse* to deceive the candidate, as the Master has no intention of closing until the ceremony of initiation has been concluded.)

After the candidate is conducted to the east, before the Master, the conductor takes his position behind the candidate, with a hoodwink either in his hand or secreted in his pocket.

W. M. (looking candidate seriously in the face).—Brother Gabe, I presume you now consider yourself a Master Mason, and, as such, entitled to all the privileges of a Master Mason, do you not?

Candidate—I do.

W. M.—I presumed that you did from the jewel that you wear, it being the Senior Warden's jewel.

W. M.—Brother Gabe, you are not yet a Master Mason, neither do I know that you ever will be, until I know how well you will withstand the amazing trials and dangers that await you. The Wardens and brethren of this Lodge require a more satisfactory proof of your fidelity to your trust, before they are willing to intrust you with the more valuable secrets of this Degree. You have a rough and rugged road to travel, beset with thieves, robbers, and murderers; and should you lose your life in the attempt, it will not be the first instance of the kind, my brother. You will remember in whom you put your trust, with that divine assurance, that "he who endureth unto the end, the same shall be saved." Heretofore you have had some one to pray for you, but now you have none. You must pray for yourself. You will therefore suffer yourself to be again hoodwinked, and kneel where you are, and pray orally or mentally, as you please. When through, signify by saying Amen, and arise and pursue your journey.

The candidate then kneels, and the conductor ties a hoodwink very closely over both eyes, so that he cannot see.

After the candidate has said Amen, and the Lodge-room has been darkened by turning down the gaslights or lamps, the conductor takes the candidate by the right arm, assists him to arise, and they proceed to travel three times around the room, travelling with the sun. As they start, the conductor commences to relate to the candidate the following:

Conductor—Brother, it was the usual custom of our Grand Master, Hiram Abiff (this is the first he hears about Hiram Abiff), to enter into the unfinished "Sanctum Sanctorum, or Holy of Holies," of King Solomon's Temple, each day at high twelve, while the craft were called from labor to refreshment, for the purpose of drawing out his designs upon the trestle-board, whereby the craft might pursue their labors; after which, it was further his custom to offer up his devotions to the Deity. Then he would retire at the south gate of the outer courts of the Temple; and, in conformity with the custom of our Grand Master, whose memory we all so reverently adore, we will now retire at the south gate of the Temple.

They have now passed around the Lodge three times, and as

they approach the Junior Warden's station in the south, he steps silently out from his seat to the floor, and confronts the blind-folded candidate, clinching him by the collar in a very rough manner, and at the same time exclaiming:

| S. D., or Conductor | Candidate | First Ruffian, Jubela, generally the J. W. in the south |

J. W. (Jubela, First Ruffian).—Grand Master Hiram, I am glad to meet you thus alone. I have long sought this opportunity. You will remember you promised us, that when the Temple was completed, we should receive the secrets of a Master Mason, whereby we might travel in foreign countries, work, and receive Master's wages. Behold! the Temple is now about to be completed, and we have not obtained that which we have so long sought. At first, I did not doubt your veracity; but now I do! (Gives candidate a sudden twitch by the collar.) I therefore now demand of you the secrets of a Master Mason!

Conductor (for candidate).—Brother, this is an unusual way of asking for them. It is neither a proper time nor place; but be true to your engagement, and I will be true to mine. Wait until the Temple is completed, and then, if you are found worthy and well qualified, you will unquestionably receive the secrets of a Master Mason; but, until then, you cannot.

Ruffian—This (shaking candidate) does not satisfy me! Talk not to me of time or place, but give me the secrets of a Master Mason, or I will take your life!

Conductor—I cannot; nor can they be given, except in the presence of Solomon, king of Israel, Hiram, king of Tyre, and myself.

Ruffian—That does not satisfy me. I'll hear no more of your cavilling! (Clinches candidate more fiercely.) Give me the Master's word, or I will take your life in a moment!

Conductor—I shall not!

S. D., or Conductor   Candidate   Second Ruffian, Jubelo, generally the S. W. in the west.

The Ruffian gives the candidate a brush across the throat with his right hand, and at the same time relinquishes his hold with his left, steps quietly to one side, and permits the conductor and candidate to pass on to the Senior Warden's station in the west, which is done by the conductor advancing very rapidly, pulling the candidate along with him. As they approach the west, the Senior Warden steps out as did the Junior Warden, facing the candidate, and, clinching him by the collar more roughly than the Junior Warden, exclaiming as follows:

S. W.:(Second Ruffian).—Give me the secrets of a Master Mason!
Conductor (for candidate).—I cannot.

Ruffian—Give me the secrets of a Master Mason! (Shakes candidate.)

Conductor—I shall not.

Ruffian—Give me the Master's word, or I will take your life in a moment! (Gives candidate a sudden shake.)

Conductor—I will not!

Ruffian (i. e., S. W.) gives candidate a brush with his right hand across the left breast, and at the same time lets him pass, the conductor hurrying him on toward the east end of the Lodge, where the Master is stationed to perform the part of the Third Ruffian, Jubelum, who is generally provided with a buckskin bag stuffed with hair, to represent a setting-maul.

As the candidate is hurried along toward Jubelum (Worshipful Master), the latter seizes him with both hands by the collar of his coat, and swings him round, so as to place his back toward the east, with his heels a few inches from the edge of the canvas before alluded to. This canvas is usually held behind the candidate, in an inclined position, by some of the brethren, and is for the purpose of catching him when he is tripped up by the assumed ruffian, Jubelum. The Master (Third Ruffian) then exclaims:

W. M. (as Third Ruffian).—Give me the secrets of a Master Mason!

Conductor (for candidate).—I cannot!

Ruffian—Give me the secrets of a Master Mason, or I will take your life!

Conductor—I shall not!

Ruffian—You have (here Master seizes the candidate more fiercely, and affects a great earnestness of purpose) escaped "Jubela" and "Jubelo"; me you cannot escape; my name is "Jubelum!" What I purpose, that I perform. I hold in my hand an instrument of death; therefore, give me the Master's word, or I will take your life in a moment!

Conductor—I will not!

Ruffian—Then die!

The Worshipful Master here gives the candidate a blow on his head with a buckskin bag, or setting-maul;[1] at the same time,

---

[1] In the progress of Masonry during the last century the fatal weapons underwent several changes. At the revival in 1717, they were called setting-tool, setting-maul, and setting-beetle; later in the century, it was the twenty-four-inch gauge, square, and gavel; then the setting-tool, square, and rule; and now the plumb-rule, square, and strong or heavy maul.—*The Freemason's Treasury*, p. 808.

pushing him backward, brings the candidate's heels against the edge of the canvas, trips him up, and the candidate falls upon his back, caught in the canvas clear of the floor, unharmed, but, in many instances, badly frightened.

Third Ruffian, Jubelum,   Candidate   Members of the Lodge, in the
generally the W. M.   act of holding the canvas
in the east.   to catch the candidate.

It is the general belief (and it would be readily inferred from most exposures of Masonry) that a candidate is knocked down with a large setting-maul kept for that purpose, but no reasonably sane person would for one moment entertain any such idea of the ceremony of making a Master Mason. The candidate is not intentionally injured in any Degree of Masonry, impressions of a lasting nature being all that are intended by the ceremonies.

As the candidate falls into the canvas the brethren lower it to the floor, when the following dialogue ensues between those who held the canvas and the Master, or the brother acting as the Third Ruffian.

Ruffian—Is he dead?

Answer—He is, his skull is broken in.

Ruffian—What horrid deed is this we have done?

Answer—We have murdered our Grand Master, Hiram Abiff, and have not obtained that which we have sought: this is no time for vain reflection—the question is, what shall we do with the body?

Answer—We will bury it in the rubbish of the Temple, until low twelve, and then we will meet and give it a decent burial.

Answer—Agreed!

They roll the canvas around and over the candidate where he fell, which is in the east or northeast corner of the Lodge, and, for a few moments, retire, when the Lodge becomes still as the hour of midnight; not a sound is permitted to be made; all go—if at all—from place to place on tiptoe. The Master silently steps to the east, near the candidate's head, and strikes the hour of low twelve (which is twelve o'clock at night) on a triangle or bell. As the last sound of twelve dies away, the three ruffians cautiously approach the body, and converse among themselves nearly as follows:

First Ruffian—Is that you, Jubela?

Answer—Yes.

Second Ruffian—Is that you, Jubelum?[1]

Answer—Yes.

Third Ruffian—Is that you, Jubelo?

Answer—Yes.

First Ruffian—Well, we have all met as agreed upon: the question is, what shall we do with the body? It is now past midnight, and if we do not act with decision, daylight will be upon us, and we will be discovered and taken. We will carry the body a westerly course from the Temple to the brow of the hill west of Mount Moriah, where I have dug a grave due east and west, six feet perpendicular.

Answer—Agreed!

A sufficient number of the brethren now take up the body (yet rolled up in the canvas), and, raising it on their shoulders, proceed to carry it around the Lodge, head foremost, three times, in representation of ascending a hill, the last time halting in the west end of the Lodge, nearly in front of the Senior Warden's station, and a little to the right. Upon arriving there they commence to lower it into the grave, as they style it, but in reality only from their shoulders to the floor. After the candidate is lowered, one of the ruffians says:

Let us plant an acacia at the head of the grave, in order to

---

[1] Professor Stuart, of Andover, one of the most skilful linguists and learned men in the United States, has endeavored to show that the legend of the Third Degree is an imposture, "since the names of the criminals are formed from the Latin language, and not from the Hebrew, to which they have no affinity whatever."—*The Freemason's Treasury*, p. 213.

conceal it so that the place may be known should occasion here-after require.

Some Lodges have a small box with a house-plant or dry twig in it, which is set down on the floor near the candidate's head.

One of the ruffians exclaims:

Now let us make our escape out of the country.

And immediately one of the most intelligent brethren stations himself at the door of the ante-room, and when those who have been acting the part of the ruffians approach him, the following colloquy ensues:

First Ruffian—Hallo, friend! Are you a sea-captain?

Captain—I am.

Second Ruffian—Are you going to put to sea soon?

Captain—Immediately.

Third Ruffian—Whither are you bound?

Captain—To Ethiopia.

Ruffian—The very port to which we wish to go. We three should like to take a passage with you.

Captain—Very well, you can have a passage. I suppose you are brothers, workmen from the Temple, and journeying, are you not?

Ruffians—We are.

Captain—I should be glad of your company. You have a pass from King Solomon, I presume?

Ruffians (affecting surprise).—No, we have no pass; we did not know it was necessary. We were sent in haste and on urgent business; there was nothing said about giving us a pass, and we presume it was forgotten, or not deemed necessary.

Captain—What! no pass. What! no pass. If this is the case, you cannot get a passage with me, I assure you. That is strictly forbidden; so you may set your minds at rest.

Ruffians—We will go back and get a pass, if that is the case.

Captain—The sooner the better! Suspicious characters!

The Ruffians now return near to the body, when the following conversation takes place:

First Ruffian—What shall we do in this case?

Second Ruffian—We will go to some other port.

Third Ruffian—But the rules are as strict in other ports as in this.

First Ruffian—If such are the regulations, we shall not get a pass at any port, and what will become of us?

Second Ruffian—We shall be taken and put to death.

Third Ruffian—Let us secrete ourselves until night and steal a small boat and put to sea.

First Ruffian—We cannot make our escape in that way. It is a dangerous coast, and we shall be taken; for before this time our escape is discovered, and the sea-coast will be lined with our pursuers.

Second Ruffian—Then let us flee into the interior parts of the country, and avoid being taken as long as possible.

Third Ruffian—Agreed!

They now retire from the body, in different directions. When all has been again quiet in the Lodge for a few seconds, the brethren jump up, commence laughing, singing, &c., exclaiming:

No work to-day. Craftsmen, we are having good times; I wonder if it will last.

They shuffle about a few moments, when they are called to order by the sound of the gavel from the Master's seat in the east, who inquires in a loud voice as follows:

W. M. (now styled King Solomon).—Brother Junior Grand Warden, what means all this confusion among the workmen? Why are they not at work as usual?

S. W. (now styled J. G. W.)—Most Worshipful King Solomon, there is no work laid out for us, and it is said we can have none. No designs are drawn on the trestle-board, and for this reason many of us are idle.

K. S.—No work laid out—no designs drawn on the trestle-board? What is the meaning of this? Where is our Grand Master, Hiram Abiff?

J. G. W.—We do not know, Most Worshipful King Solomon. He has not been seen since high twelve yesterday.

K. S.—Not been seen since high twelve yesterday! I fear he is indisposed. It is my orders that strict search be made for him through the apartments of the Temple, and due inquiry made. Let him be found, if possible.

The brethren commence, in loud voices to inquire of one another:

Have you seen any thing of our Grand Master Hiram Abiff?

Not since high twelve yesterday, &c., &c.

J. G. W.—Most Worshipful King Solomon, diligent search has been made. He cannot be found. He has not been seen in or about the Temple.

K. S.—I fear that some accident has befallen him. Brother Grand Secretary (turning to the Secretary of the Lodge), you will go out and see to calling the several rolls of the craft, and report to me as soon as possible.

G. Sec.—Assemble, Craftsmen! It is King Solomon's orders that the several rolls be called, and report made as soon as possible.

At this command the Secretary passes out of the Lodge, accompanied by ten or fifteen of the brethren, into the ante-room, leaving the door open, so that the candidate can hear the rolls called. The brethren form around the Secretary like a class at school. The Secretary commences to call off a lot of Bible names, to which each brother responds "Here!" in a loud voice, until he calls that of the First Ruffian, "Jubela! Jubela!! Jubela!!!" After calling a few more names, which are responded to by the brethren, he says: "Jubelo! Jubelo!! Jubelo!!!" and after a few more names, that of the Third Ruffian, "Jubelum! Jubelum!! Jubelum!!!" finishing with a few other names; when he leaves the brethren in the ante-room, closes the door, and reports as follows to King Solomon:

G. Sec.—Most Worshipful King Solomon, the several rolls have been called, and reports made, by which it appears that three Fellow Crafts are missing, namely, Jubela, Jubelo, and Jubelum, who, from the similarity of their names, I presume are brothers, and men from Tyre.

J. G. W.—Most Worshipful King Solomon, there are at the gate twelve Fellow Crafts, who wish to be admitted: they say they come with important tidings.

K. S.—Let them be admitted.

Here the Warden opens the ante-room door, and says: "Come in, you twelve Fellow Crafts;" when all those that were left out by the Secretary come into the Lodge, stamping and scuffling along, especially if only a few of them, to impress upon the candidate's mind the idea that there are more. They advance before the Master in the east, and form across the Lodge, when all make the duegard and sign of a Fellow Craft (Figs. 3 and 4, p. 17), which is responded to by the Master. Then one of the best posted relates the following, in a clear and distinct voice:

"Most Worshipful King Solomon, we come to inform you that fifteen of us Fellow Crafts, seeing the Temple about to be completed, and being desirous of obtaining the secrets of a Master Mason, by which we might travel in foreign countries, and receive Master's wages, entered into a horrid conspiracy to extort them from our Grand Master, Hiram Abiff, or take his life; but, reflecting with horror on the atrocity of the crime, twelve of us recanted; but the other three persisted in their murderous design, and we fear that they have taken the Grand Master's life. We therefore now appear before your Majesty, clothed with white gloves and aprons, in token of our innocence, and, acknowledging our premeditated guilt, we humbly implore your pardon." (They all kneel.)

K. S.—Arise, you twelve Fellow Crafts, divide yourselves into parties and travel—three east, three north, three south, and three west—with others whom I shall appoint, in search of the ruffians.

The brother who has acted the part of sea-captain now takes his station at the door again, when these Fellow Crafts approach him in the west.

First Craftsman—Hallo, friend! have you seen any strangers pass this way?

Capt.—I have, three.

Craftsman—Describe them, if you please.

Capt.—They were three brothers, workmen from the Temple, seeking a passage to Ethiopia, but, not having King Solomon's pass, were not able to obtain one, and returned back into the country.

Second Craftsman—The very fellows of whom we are in pursuit. You say they turned back into the country?

Capt.—Yes.

Craftsman—We will go in pursuit of them; they are the fellows we want. (Moving off, one says:)

Let us report.

And at the same time he steps to the Master's desk, and reports as follows:

"Most Worshipful King Solomon, I, being one of those who pursued a westerly course, coming down near the port of Joppa, met a seafaring man, of whom I inquired if he had seen any strangers pass that way; he informed me that he had—three—who from their appearance were workmen from the Temple, seeking a passage to Ethiopia, but not having King Solomon's pass, were not able to obtain one, and returned back into the country.

K. S.—Divide yourselves and travel, as before, with positive instructions to find the ruffians, and with as positive assurance that, if you do not, the twelve shall be deemed the murderers, and suffer severally, for the crime committed.

They now separate about the Lodge, saying to each other:

"This is very unjust of the King. We are told, if we do not find the ruffians we must be punished—put to death, probably. What have we done? It is very true, we have been associated with these three ruffians, but we have not committed any actual crime."

By this time they have got near the candidate (who is still lying on the floor, rolled up in the canvas), when one of the party sits down near his head, and at the same time says:

"Well, brothers, I am very weary; I must sit down and rest before I can go any farther."

One of his companions exclaims: "I am tired, too!" and sits down near the candidate.

Another says: "What course shall we pursue? we must not go and report ourselves: if we do, the twelve will be put to death. Here are three of the poor fellows with us; we must not go and give them up, to be put to death; rather let us take a northwesterly or a southwesterly course. Which way shall we go?"

One of the brethren then replies: "We will go a southwesterly course, and will come up with our brothers." Attempting to get up, he exclaims, "Hallo! what's this?" at the same time pulling up the evergreen—or acacia, as it is styled—at the head of the grave.[1] "What means this acacia coming up so easily? The ground has been newly broken; this has the appearance of a grave," pointing to the candidate on the floor.

One of the brothers, representing one of the three ruffians, in a corner near by, is now heard to exclaim, in a loud, but deep tone of voice:

"Oh! that my throat had been cut across, my tongue torn out by its roots, and buried in the rough sands of the sea, at low-water mark, where the tide ebbs and flows twice in twenty-four hours, ere I had been accessory to the death of so good a man as our Grand Master, Hiram Abiff."

"Hark! that is the voice of Jubela."

"Oh! that my breast had been torn open, my heart plucked out, and placed upon the highest pinnacle of the Temple, there to be devoured by the vultures of the air, ere I had consented to the death of so good a man as our Grand Master, Hiram Abiff."

"Hark! that is the voice of Jubelo."

"Oh! that my body had been severed in two, my bowels taken from thence and burned to ashes, the ashes scattered to the four winds of heaven, that no more remembrance might be had of so vile and wicked a wretch as I. Ah! Jubela, Jubelo, it was I

---

[1] The system of Freemasonry, as practised in different countries and at different periods, is not uniform on this subject; and I feel so little at liberty to bring forward evidence on such a delicate point, that I am afraid it will be impossible to place it clearly before the brethren. One system says fifteen Fellow Crafts went in search; another, twelve; and asserts that the three (murderers) left the sprig of acacia; others affirm that it was the reanters who placed it there as a mark. Some say, that many days were expended in the search, and that the lost (body) was found near the seaside; others, that it was soon discovered near Jerusalem. The York Masons name the seaside; the Americans say, Mount Moriah; the French, Mount Lebanon. In one account, the brethren disperse widely, east, west, and south; in another, they keep within hail of each other.—Historical Landmarks, vol. II. p. 149.

that struck him harder than you both: it was I that gave him the fatal blow; it was I that killed him."

"That is the voice of Jubelum."

The three craftsmen, having stood by the candidate all this time, listening to the ruffians, whose voices they recognize, say one to another:

"What shall we do? There are three of them, and only three of us."

One says:

"Our cause is just; let us rush in and seize them."

Upon which the three Fellow Crafts rush forward over benches and chairs, and secure the ruffians in no very gentle manner, and lead them to the Worshipful Master's seat in the east, when one of them reports to the Master:

"Most Worshipful King Solomon, I, being one who pursued a westerly course, and, on my return, after several days of fruitless search, being more weary than my companions, sat down on the brow of a hill to rest and refresh myself; and,. on rising, accidentally caught hold of a sprig of acacia,[1] which, easily giving way, excited my suspicions. Having my curiosity aroused, I examined it, and found it to be a grave."

As soon as the craftsman has finished this report, another party arrives with the ruffians, and reports as follows:

"Most Worshipful King Solomon, while sitting down to rest and refresh ourselves, we heard the following horrid exclamations from the clefts of the adjacent rocks. The first was the voice of Jubela exclaiming:[2] 'Oh! that my throat had been cut across, my tongue torn out by its roots, and buried in the rough sands of the

---

[1] CASSIA—sometimes improperly and ignorantly used for acacia. (See ACACIA.) According to the Jewish law, no interments were permitted within the walls of the city, and as it was unlawful for the cohens or priests to pass over a grave, it became necessary to place marks wherever a dead body had been interred, to enable them to avoid it. For this purpose the ACACIA was used.—Lexicon.

[2] Brother Goodacre, of the Witham Lodge, Lincoln, suggests that the various penalties which have been introduced into Freemasonry appear to have reference to a particular kind of covenant which was common among the Hebrews, but which, he adds, "I can find only twice particularly described. Godwyn says: 'Making a covenant was a solemn binding of each other to the performance of a mutual promise, by outward ceremonies of cutting a beast in twain, and passing between the parts thereof' (Jer. xxxiv. 18): as if they would say—Thus let it be done to him, and thus let his body be cut in two, who shall break this covenant. This reference to Jeremiah, where the prophet denounced the curse of the Lord upon the princes and rulers who had broken the covenant which they had made with King Zedekiah, may explain the self-imposed penalty of J—(Jubelum)." But we must look a little closer into the manner of making a covenant, in order to discover the connection of the different penalties as references to one entire ceremony. After an animal had been selected, *his throat was cut across with one single blow, so as to divide the windpipe, arteries,*

sea, at low-water mark, where the tide ebbs and flows twice in twenty-four hours, ere I had been accessory to the death of so good a man as our Grand Master, Hiram Abiff.' The second was that of Jubelo, exclaiming: 'Oh! that my breast had been torn open, my heart plucked out and placed upon the highest pinnacle of the Temple, there to be devoured by the vultures of the air, ere I had consented to the death of so good a man as our Grand Master, Hiram Abiff.' The third was the voice of Jubelum, exclaiming, louder than the rest: 'It was I that gave the fatal blow, it was I that killed him. Oh! that my body had been severed in two, my bowels taken from thence, and burned to ashes, the ashes scattered to the four winds of heaven, that no more remembrance might be had of so vile and wicked a wretch as I. Ah! Jubela! Jubelo! it was I that struck him harder than you both; it was I that gave him the fatal blow; it was I that killed him.' Upon which we rushed in, seized and bound the ruffians, and now have them before your majesty."

K. S.—Jubela, you stand charged as accessory to the death of our Grand Master, Hiram Abiff. What say you, guilty or not guilty?

One answers, in a very penitent manner:

Guilty, my lord.

K. S.—Jubelo, you also stand accessory to the death of our Grand Master, Hiram Abiff. What say you, sir, guilty or not guilty?

Answer—Guilty, my lord.

K. S.—Jubelum, you stand charged as the wilful murderer of our Grand Master, Hiram Abiff. What say you, sir, guilty or not guilty?

Answer—Guilty, my lord.

K. S.—Vile, impious wretches! despicable villains! reflect with horror on the atrocity of your crime, and on the amiable character of your Worshipful Grand Master, whom you have so basely assassinated. Hold up your heads, and hear your sentence. It is my orders that you be taken without the gates of the court, and be executed, according to your several imprecations, in the clefts of the rocks. Brother Junior Grand Warden, you will see my orders duly executed. Begone!

---

and veins, without touching any bone. The next ceremony was to *tear the breast open and pluck out the heart*, and if there were the least imperfection, the body would be considered unclean. The animal was then *divided into two parts*, and placed north and south, that the parties to the covenant may pass between them from east to west, *and the carcase was then left as a prey to voracious animals*. The other example of such a covenant is in Genesis xv.—*Historical Landmarks*, vol. II, p. 178.

They all pass out of the Lodge with a rush, into the ante-room, where they form into a circle. One, acting as the principal mover, raises his right foot from the floor, at the same time his hands, in the manner of slapping them together, makes two false motions, but at the third all bring down their right feet and hands together, producing a very sharp noise. A momentary silence then ensues, during which one of the party groans, as if nearly dying. This is all intended to produce its effect upon the ears of the candidate. It also represents the execution and dying groans of Jubela, the first ruffian, and is repeated twice more to represent the death of the other two ruffians. Some Lodges use a large drum, others roll a large cannon-ball across the ante-room floor, letting it strike on a cushion placed against the wall. This is not, however, practised in city Lodges.

The ruffians being executed, the brethren all return quietly to the Lodge, when one of them reports, in a loud tone of voice:

"Most Worshipful King Solomon, your orders have been duly executed upon the three murderers of Grand Master, Hiram Abiff."[1]

K. S.—You twelve Fellow Crafts will go in search of the body, and, if found, observe whether the Master's word, or a key to it, or any thing that appertains to the Master's Degree, is on or about it.

The brethren representing the twelve repentant conspirators now walk out near the spot where the candidate is lying, and, when close to him, one of the party says:

"Well, brothers, can we find where the acacia was pulled up?"

Approaching the candidate, another replies:

"Yes, this is the place; let us remove the rubbish and dig down here."

A third, lifting up the canvas, says:

"Yes, here is the body of our Grand Master, Hiram Abiff, in a mangled and putrid state. Let us go and report. But what were our orders? We were ordered to observe whether the Master's word, or a key to it, or any thing appertaining to the Master's Degree, was on or about the body; but, brothers, we are only Fellow Crafts, and know nothing about the Master's word, or a key to it, or any thing appertaining to the Master's Degree; we

---

[1] Their real names (if there be any thing real in the whole transaction, which is more than doubtful), as preserved in a subsidiary degree, were GRAVELOT, QUIBO, and AKIROP. In one form of the Degree of Elect of Fifteen, they assume the Protean names of JUBELA-KURMAVIL (another corruption of Cromwell), JUBELO-GRAVELOT, and JUBELUM-AKIROP.—*The Freemason's Treasury*, pp. 305/6.

must, however, make an examination, or we will be put to death."

They then commence to search about the candidate, lifting off the canvas, feeling about his neck, &c., &c.; finally, one of the brethren, taking hold of the jewel which is attached to the yoke about the candidate's neck, exclaims:

"This is the jewel of his office."

Another says:

"Let us go and report that we find nothing on or about the body excepting the jewel of his office."

One of the brothers now takes off the jewel from the candidate's neck, and all repair to the Master's seat in the east, and report:

"Tidings of the body."

K. S.—Where was it found?

Answer—A westerly course, where our weary brother sat down to rest and refresh himself.

K. S.—Was the Master's word, or a key to it, or any thing appertaining to the Master's Degree, on or about it?[1]

Answer—Most Worshipful King Solomon, we are but Fellow Crafts; we therefore know nothing about the Master's word or the Master's Degree. There was nothing found on or about the body excepting the jewel of his office, by which his body was discovered.

They present the jewel to the Master, who, on examination of it, says:

"This is the jewel of our Grand Master, Hiram Abiff; there can be no longer any doubt as to the identity of the body."

K. S.—You twelve Fellow Crafts will now go and assist in raising the body.

Turning in his seat toward the Treasurer's desk, he says to the Treasurer:

"My worthy brother of Tyre, as the Master's word is now lost, the first sign given at the grave, and the first word spoken, after the body is raised, shall be adopted for the regulation of all Masters' Lodges, until future generations shall find out the right."

Treasurer—Agreed.

All now form in a circle around the body, the Master and

---

[1] The occasion of the brethren searching so diligently for their Master was, to receive from him the secret word of Masonry, which should be delivered down as a test to the fraternity of after ages.—*Historical Landmarks*, vol. II. p. 175.

Wardens at the head, when the Master makes the sign of "distress" of a Master Mason, which is done by raising both hands and arms above the head. (See grand hailing sign of distress, Fig. 7, p. 18.) As the Master makes this sign, he says:

"O Lord my God, I fear the Master's word is forever lost!"

I would remark here, that in some Lodges the Master does not make the sign of distress first at the body, but only gives the sign of a Master Mason, which is done by drawing the right hand across the body, with the thumb inward. (See sign of a Master Mason, Fig. 6, p. 18.) After the sign is made, the whole party commence marching around the body with the sun, singing the following dirge; and, if the Lodge has an organ or melodeon, it is played on this occasion, in a very solemn and impressive manner.

Sol-emn strikes the fu-neral chime, Notes of our de-part-ing time; As we jour-ney here be-low, Through a pil-grim-age of woe!

II.

"Mortals, now indulge a tear,
  For Mortality is here:
  See how wide her trophies wave
  O'er the slumbers of the grave!

III.

"Here another guest we bring.
  Seraphs of celestial wing,
  To our funeral altar come:
  Waft this friend and brother home.

IV.

"Lord of all! below—above—
  Fill our hearts with truth and love;
  When dissolves our earthly tie,
  Take us to thy Lodge on High."

Master (as K. S.) makes the "grand hailing sign of distress" (see Fig. 7, p. 18—some Masters make this sign twice), accompanied by the following exclamation, viz.: "O Lord my God, I fear the Master's word is forever lost!" He then turns to the Junior Warden, and says: "You will take the body by the Entered Apprentice grip, and see if it can be raised."

The Junior Warden then takes hold of the candidate's right hand, giving him the Entered Apprentice's grip (see Fig. 9, p. 36), and then lets his hand slip off in a careless manner, and reports:

"Most Worshipful King Solomon, owing to the high state of putrefaction, it having been dead already fifteen days, the skin slips, and the body cannot be raised."

K. S. (making grand hailing sign of distress).—O Lord my God, I fear the Master's word is forever lost!

Turning to the Senior Warden, he continues:

K. S.—My worthy brother of Tyre, I will thank you to endeavor to raise the body by the Fellow Craft's grip.

The Senior Warden then takes the candidate's right hand, giving the real grip of a Fellow Craft (see Fig. 12, p. 67), and letting his hand slip off quickly, he reports as follows:

"Owing to the reason before given, the flesh cleaves from the bone, and the body cannot be so raised."

K. S.—O Lord my God! O Lord my God!! O Lord my God!!! Is there no hope for the widow's son?

At each exclamation he gives the grand hailing sign of distress (see Fig. 7, p. 18), which would be three times, then, turning to the Senior Warden, says:

"My worthy brother of Tyre, what shall we do?"

S. W.—Let us pray.

The brethren now all kneel around the body on one knee. The Master kneels at the head of the candidate, and, taking off his hat, repeats the following prayer, which may be found in all the Masonic Monitors:

PRAYER

Thou, O God! knowest our down-sitting and our uprising, and understandest our thoughts afar off. Shield and defend us from the evil intentions of our enemies, and support us under the trials and afflictions we are destined to endure, while travelling through this vale of tears. Man that is born of a woman is of few days and full of trouble. He cometh forth as a flower, and is cut down: he fleeth also as a shadow, and continueth not. Seeing his days are determined, the number of his months are with thee; thou hast appointed his bounds that he cannot pass, turn from him that he may rest, till he shall accomplish his day. For there is hope of a tree, if it be cut down, that it will sprout again, and that the

BRETHREN KNEELING AT PRAYER AROUND THE GRAVE OF HIRAM ABIFF, THE WIDOW'S SON

tender branch thereof will not cease. But man dieth and wasteth away; yea, man giveth up the ghost, and where is he? As the waters fail from the sea, and the flood decayeth and drieth up, so man lieth down, and riseth not up till the heavens shall be no more. Yet, O Lord! have compassion on the children of thy creation, administer them comfort in time of trouble, and save them with an everlasting salvation. Amen.

Response—So mote it be.

All the brethren now rise to their feet.

K. S. (to the S. W.).—My worthy brother of Tyre, I shall endeavor (with your assistance) to raise the body by the strong grip, or lion's paw, of the tribe of Judah. (See Fig. 17.)

The Master steps to the feet of the candidate, bending over, takes him by the real grip of a Master Mason, places his right

FIG. 17

REAL GRIP OF A MASTER MASON

foot against the candidate's right foot, and his hand to his back, and, with the assistance of the brethren, raises him up perpendicularly in a standing position, and, when fairly on his feet, gives him the grand Masonic word on the five points of fellowship. (See Fig. 18.)

In the mean time, the canvas is slipped out of the Lodge, and as the Master commences to give or whisper the word in the candidate's ear, some one of the brethren slips off the hoodwink, and this is the first time he has seen light, probably, in an hour. The following is the representation of the Master giving candidate the grand Masonic word, or at least this is a substitute, for, according to Masonic tradition, the right one was lost at the death of Hiram Abiff.[1] This word cannot be given in any other way, and by Masons is considered a test of all book Masons.

The Master having given the word, which is MAH-HAH-BONE, in low breath, requests the candidate to repeat it with him, which is in this wise:

Master whispers in candidate's ear—Mah.

Candidate—Hah.

Master—Bone.

---

[1] Respecting the lost word and its substitute, some say that King Solomon advised the change, while others affirm that the three Fellow Crafts adopted the substituted word without consulting him. And Dalcho observes that the interpolated word "is not to be found in any language that ever was used. It is, in fact, not a word, but merely a jumble of letters, forming a sound without meaning."—*The Freemason's Treasury*, p. 801.

Master telling candidate never to give it in any other way than that in which he has received it. The Master, stepping back one pace, now says:

"Brother Gabe, you have now received that grand Masonic word, which you have solemnly sworn never to give in any other way or form than that in which you have received it, which is on the five points of fellowship, and then in low breath. (See p. 247.)

"The five points of fellowship are—foot to foot, knee to knee, breast to breast, hand to back, and cheek to cheek, or mouth to ear.

"1st. Foot to foot—that you will never hesitate to go on foot, and out of your way, to assist and serve a worthy brother.

"2nd. Knee to knee—that you will ever remember a brother's welfare, as well as your own, in all your adorations to Deity.

"3d. Breast to breast—that you will ever keep in your breast a brother's secrets, when communicated to and received by you as such, murder and treason excepted.

"4th. Hand to back—that you will ever be ready to stretch forth your hand to assist and save a fallen brother; and that you will vindicate his character behind his back, as well as before his face.

"5th. Cheek to cheek, or mouth to ear—that you will ever caution and whisper good counsel in the ear of an erring brother, and, in the most friendly manner, remind him of his errors, and aid his reformation, giving him due and timely notice, that he may ward off approaching danger."

All the brethren take their seats but the Master and candidate, when the Master continues:

FIG. 18

MASTER GIVING THE GRAND MASONIC WORD ON THE FIVE POINTS OF FELLOWSHIP

It is done by putting the inside of your right foot to the inside of the right foot of the one to whom you are going to give the word, the inside of your own knee to his, laying your breast close against his, your left hands on each other's back, and each one putting his mouth to the other's right ear.

"Brother Gabe, you will now repair to the east, and receive an historical account of this degree."

Master now takes his seat in the east, and requests candidate to stand before him.

HISTORICAL ACCOUNT

W. M.—Brother Gabe, the second section of this degree exemplifies an instance of virtue, fortitude, and integrity seldom equalled, if ever excelled, in the history of man.

·You have this evening represented one of the greatest men, and perhaps the greatest Mason, the world ever knew, viz., our Grand Master, Hiram Abiff, who was slain just before the completion of King Solomon's Temple. His death was premeditated by fifteen Fellow Crafts, who, seeing the Temple about to be completed, and being desirous of obtaining the secrets of a Master Mason, whereby they might travel in foreign countries and receive Master's wages, entered into a horrid conspiracy to extort them from our Grand Master, Hiram Abiff, or take his life; but, reflecting with horror on the atrocity of the crime, twelve of them recanted; the other three persisted in their murderous designs.

Our Grand Master, Hiram Abiff, was slain at high twelve. It was his usual practice at that hour, while the craft were called from labor to refreshment, to enter into the unfinished "Sanctum Sanctorum, or Holy of Holies," of the Temple, and there offer up his adorations to the Deity, and draw his designs on the trestleboard.

The three Fellow Crafts who persisted in their murderous designs, knowing this to be his usual practice, placed themselves at the south, west, and east gates of the inner courts of the temple, and there awaited his return.

Our Grand Master, Hiram Abiff, having finished his usual exercises, attempted to retire by the south gate, when he was accosted by Jubela, who thrice demanded of him the secrets of a Master Mason, or the Master's word, and, on his being refused, gave him a blow with the twenty-four-inch gauge across his throat, upon which he fled. and attempted to pass out at the west gate, where he was accosted by Jubelo, who, in like manner, demanded of him the secrets of a Master Mason, or the Master's word, and, on his being refused, gave him a blow with the square across his breast, upon which he fled, and attempted to make his escape out at the east gate, where he was accosted by Jubelum, who, in like manner, thrice demanded the secrets of a Master Mason, or the Master's word, and, on his like refusal, gave him a violent blow with the setting-maul on his forehead, which felled him dead on the spot.

The ruffians buried the body in the rubbish of the Temple until low twelve, or twelve at night, when they met by agreement and carried it a westerly course from the Temple, to the brow of a hill west of Mount Moriah, where they buried it in a grave dug due east and west, six feet, perpendicular, at the head of which they planted an acacia, in order to conceal it, and that the place might be known, should occasion ever require, and made their escape.

Our Grand Master, Hiram Abiff, was found to be missing on the following day; his absence was discovered by there being no designs drawn on the trestle-board.

King Solomon, believing him to be indisposed, ordered strict search and due inquiry to be made for him through the several apartments of the Temple, that he might be found, if possible. But nothing could be seen or heard of him.

Then, fearing some accident had befallen him, the king ordered the several rolls of the workmen to be called, and there appeared to be three missing, namely: Jubela, Jubelo, and Jubelum, who, from the similarity of their names, were supposed to be brothers and men from Tyre.

About this time, the twelve Fellow Crafts, who had recanted from their murderous designs, appeared before King Solomon, clothed in white gloves and aprons, in token of their innocence, acknowledging their premeditated guilt, and, kneeling, implored his pardon.

King Solomon then ordered them to divide themselves into parties, and travel three east, three west, three north, and three south; and that they should, with others whom he should appoint, go in search of the ruffians.

The three that pursued a westerly course, coming down near the port of Joppa, met with a seafaring man, of whom they made inquiry, if he had seen any strangers pass that way; he informed them that he had, three, who, from their appearance, were workmen from the Temple, seeking a passage into Ethiopia, but not having King Solomon's pass, were not allowed to obtain one, and had returned back into the country.

They returned and bore this information to King Solomon, who ordered them to disguise themselves and travel as before, with positive instructions to find the ruffians and with as positive assurance that, if they did not, they twelve should be deemed the murderers, and suffer severely for the crime committed.

They travelled as before, and after fifteen days of weary travel and hardships, one of the brethren, being more weary than the rest, sat down on the brow of a hill, west of Mount Moriah, to rest and refresh himself, and, on attempting to rise, caught hold of an acacia, which easily giving way, excited his curiosity: upon examination they found it to be a grave.

About this time a party arrived with the ruffians, and related that while sitting down to rest and refresh themselves, they heard the following horrid exclamations from the clefts of an adjacent rock.

The first was the voice of Jubela, exclaiming:

"Oh! that my throat had been cut across," &c., &c.

The second was the voice of Jubelo, exclaiming:

"Oh! that my body had been cut in two," &c., &c.

The third was the voice of Jubelum, exclaiming:

"Oh! that my body had been cut in two," &c., &c.

Upon which they rushed in, seized, bound, and brought them before King Solomon; who, after a due conviction of their guilt, ordered them to be taken without the gates of the courts of the Temple, and executed according to the several imprecations upon their own heads.

King Solomon then ordered the twelve Fellow Crafts to go in search of the body, and, if found, to observe whether the Master's word, or a key to it, or any thing appertaining to the Master's Degree, was on or about it.

The body of our Grand Master, Hiram Abiff, was found in a westerly course from the Temple, where our weary brothers sat down to rest and refresh themselves.

On removal of the earth, they came to the body of our Grand Master, Hiram Abiff, which they found in a high state of putrefaction, and in a mutilated and mangled condition, it having been buried already fifteen days: the effluvia which arose from it compelled them to place involuntarily their hands thus (Master here places his hands in form of a duegard of a Master Mason, which alludes to the manner in which his hands were placed when he took the oath of a Master Mason), to guard their nostrils—but nothing was found on or about the body excepting the jewel of his office, by which his body was easily discovered.[1]

King Solomon then ordered them to go and assist in raising the body; and it was agreed between him and Hiram, king of Tyre, that as the Master's word was then lost, the first sign given at the grave, and the first word spoken after the body should be raised, should be used for the regulation of all Masters'

[1] Can any living Mason be simple enough to believe that Dr. Anderson, in his "Defence of Masonry," intended to prove a real historical fact when he explained the exhumation of the body of H. A. B.? Why, it is well known that the celebrated artist was living at Tyre many years after the Temple was completed.—*The Freemason's Treasury,* p. 291.

Lodges, until future generations should find out the right one.

They repaired to the grave, when King Solomon ordered one of the Fellow Crafts to take the body by the Entered Apprentice grip, and see if it could be raised; but, on account of its high state of decomposition, it could not be raised—the flesh cleaved from the bone.

King Solomon then ordered them to take it by the Fellow Craft grip; but on trial, for the reason before given, the Fellow Craft's grip failed to benefit any—it could not be raised.

King Solomon then exclaimed:

"O Lord my God, I fear the Master's word is forever lost! My brother of Tyre, what shall we do? Let us pray."

After prayer, King Solomon took the body by the strong grip of a Master Mason, or lion's paw, and raised it on the five points of fellowship, which have been explained to you. The body was then carried to the Temple for a more decent burial, and was interred in due form.

The body of our Grand Master was buried three times: first, in the rubbish of the Temple; secondly, on the brow of a hill west of Mount Moriah; and, thirdly and lastly, as near the "Sanctum Sanctorum, or Holy of Holies," of King Solomon's Temple, as the Jewish law would permit; and Masonic tradition informs us that there was erected to his memory a Masonic monument, consisting of "a beautiful virgin, weeping over a broken column; before her was a book open; in her right hand a sprig of acacia, in her left an urn; behind her stands Time, unfolding and counting the ringlets of her hair."

The beautiful virgin weeping over the broken column denotes the unfinished state of the Temple, likewise the untimely death of our Grand Master, Hiram Abiff; the book open before her, that his virtues lay on perpetual record; the sprig of acacia in her right hand, the divinity of the body; the urn in her left, that his ashes were therein safely deposited, under the "Sanctum Sanctorum, or Holy of Holies," of King Solomon's Temple.

Time, unfolding the ringlets of her hair, denoted that time, patience, and perseverance accomplish all things.

The Master now gives and explains to the candidate the several signs and tokens of this Degree, commencing with the first (see Figs. 5, 6, and 7, pages 17 and 18) and ending with the grips. (See Figs. 16 and 17, pages 97 and 120; also see Note L, Appendix.)

The Master next calls the candidate's attention to the three grand Masonic pillars, usually delineated on Master's carpet (a

Master's carpet is a large map that Lodges generally keep, which is highly embellished with Masonic emblems).

Master, pointing to these pillars, says: "These are called the three grand Masonic columns or pillars, and are designated Wisdom, Strength, and Beauty.

"The pillar of Wisdom represents Solomon, King of Israel, whose wisdom contrived the mighty fabric; the pillar of Strength, Hiram, King of Tyre, who strengthened Solomon in his grand undertaking; the pillar of Beauty, Hiram Abiff, the widow's son, whose cunning craft and curious workmanship beautified and adorned the Temple.

"The construction of this grand edifice was attended with two remarkable circumstances. From Josephus we learn, that although seven years were occupied in building it, yet, during the whole time, it rained not in the daytime, that the workmen might not be obstructed in their labor, and from sacred history it appears that there was neither the sound of hammer, nor axe, nor any tool of iron, heard in the house while it was building. This famous fabric was supported by fourteen hundred and fifty-three columns, and two thousand nine hundred and six pilasters—all hewn from the finest Parian marble.

"There were employed in its building three Grand Masters; three thousand three hundred Masters, or overseers of the work; eighty thousand Fellow Crafts, or hewers on the mountains and in the quarries; and seventy thousand Entered Apprentices, or bearers of burdens. All these were classed and arranged in such a manner, by the wisdom of Solomon, that neither envy, discord, nor confusion was suffered to interrupt that universal peace and tranquillity which pervaded the world at that important period."[1]

---

[1] Among such a vast concourse of people as were assembled together at the construction of this edifice, it is natural to expect every variety of propensities, both good and evil. Accordingly our traditions furnish instances, both among the Apprentices and Craftsmen, of treachery—violation of sacred pledges—and the commission of actual crime. . . . These instances, some of which have been thought worthy of preservation in the ineffable Degrees, were not numerous. . . . From the above causes, however, the connection of the widow's son with the building of the Temple was endeared to the two monarchs; and, to preserve and consecrate his memory, a new arrangement of discipline was adopted; and a legend incorporated into the system, which served to promote a similar object with the fabulous narrative used in the spurious initiations, viz., to inculcate and impress on the candidate's mind the doctrine of a resurrection and a future state.—*Theo. Phil.*, p. 233.

None but he who has visited the Holy of Holies, and travelled the *road of peril*, can have any conception of the mysteries unfolded in this degree. . . . The MASTER MASON represents a man under the doctrine of love, saved from the grave of iniquity, and raised to the faith of salvation. It testifies our faith in the resurrection of the body, and while it inculcates a practical lesson of prudence and unshrinking fidelity,

"Brother Gabe, seven constitute a Lodge of Entered Apprentices —one Master Mason, and six Entered Apprentices. They usually meet on the Ground Floor of King Solomon's Temple.

"Five constitute a Lodge of Fellow Crafts—two Master Masons and three Fellow Crafts. They usually meet in the Middle Chamber of King Solomon's Temple.

"Three constitute a Lodge of Master Masons—three Master Masons. They meet in the Sanctum Sanctorum, or Holy of Holies of King Solomon's Temple."

The Master either reads or repeats the following from a *Monitor*, which by many is committed to memory; but when he has the "work" (*i. e.*, that part which is not monitorial), it is not necessary that he should commit to memory what is called the Master's carpet of emblems, but as it is a part of the initiation of the Third Degree, the author proposes to give it in its regular order of Lodge business.

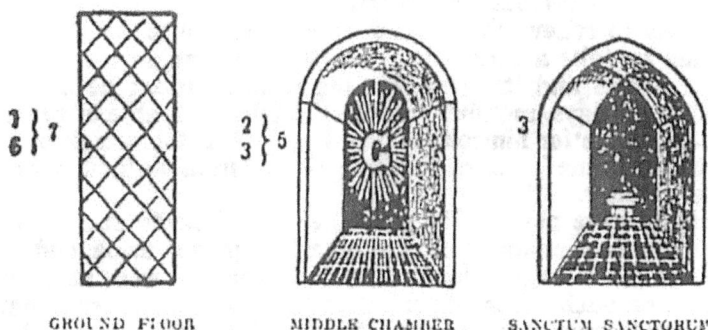

| GROUND FLOOR | MIDDLE CHAMBER | SANCTUM SANCTORUM |

THE THREE STEPS

Usually delineated upon the Master's carpet, are emblematical of the three principal stages of human life, viz.: youth, manhood, and age. In youth, in Entered Apprentices, we ought industriously to occupy our minds in the attainment of useful knowledge; in manhood, as Fellow Crafts, we should apply our knowledge to the discharge of our respective duties to God, our neighbors, and ourselves; so that in age, as Master Masons, we may enjoy the happy reflections consequent on a well-spent life, and die in the hope of a glorious immortality.

It inspires the most cheering hope of that final reward which belongs alone to the "just made perfect."—*Lexicon.*

THE POT OF INCENSE

Is an emblem of a pure heart, which is always an acceptable sacrifice to the Deity; and as this glows with fervent heat, so should our hearts continually glow with gratitude to the great and beneficent Author of our existence, for the manifold blessings and comforts we enjoy.

THE BEEHIVE

Is an emblem of industry, and recommends the practice of that virtue to all created beings, from the highest seraph in heaven to the lowest reptile of the dust. It teaches us that, as we come into the world rational and intelligent beings, so we should ever be industrious ones; never sitting down contented while our fellow-creatures around us are in want, when it is in our power to relieve them without inconvenience to ourselves.

When we take a survey of nature, we view man, in his infancy, more helpless and indigent than the brute creation; he lies languishing for days, months, and years, totally incapable of providing sustenance for himself, of guarding against the attack of the wild beasts of the forest, or sheltering himself from the inclemencies of the weather.

It might have pleased the great Creator of heaven and earth to have made man independent of all other beings; but, as dependence is one of the strongest bonds of society, mankind were made dependent on each other for protection and security, as they thereby enjoy better opportunities of fulfilling the duties of reciprocal love and friendship. Thus was man formed for social and active life, the noblest part of the work of God; and he that will so demean himself as not to be endeavoring to add to the common stock of knowledge and understanding, may be deemed a drone in the hive of nature, a useless member of society, and unworthy of our protection as Masons.

THE BOOK OF CONSTITUTIONS, GUARDED BY THE TYLER'S SWORD,

Reminds us that we should be ever watchful and guarded in our thoughts, words, and actions, particularly when before the enemies of Masonry; ever bearing in remembrance those truly masonic virtues, silence and circumspection.

THE SWORD POINTING TO A NAKED HEART

Demonstrates that justice will sooner or later overtake us; and although our thoughts, words, and actions may be hidden from the eyes of man, yet that

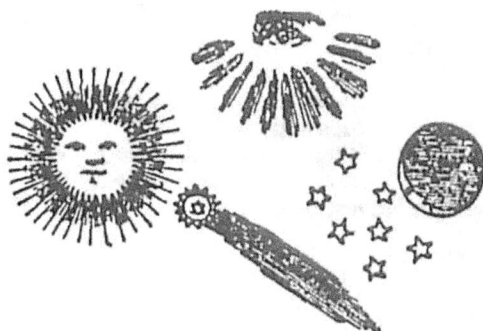

ALL SEEING EYE!

whom the sun, moon, and stars obey, and under whose watchful care even comets perform their stupendous revolutions, beholds the inmost recesses of the human heart, and will reward us according to our works.

THE ANCHOR AND ARK

Are emblems of a well-grounded hope and a well-spent life. They are emblematical of that divine ark which safely bears us over this tempestuous sea of troubles, and that anchor which shall safely moor us in a peaceful harbor, where the wicked cease from troubling, and the weary shall find rest.

THE FORTY-SEVENTH PROBLEM OF EUCLID[1]

This was an invention of our ancient friend and brother, the great Pythagoras, who, in his travels through Asia, Africa, and Europe, was initiated into several orders of priesthood, and raised to the sublime degree of a Master Mason. This wise philosopher enriched his mind abundantly in a general knowledge of things, and more especially in geometry or masonry. On this subject he drew out many problems and theorems, and, among the most distinguished he erected this, which in the joy of his heart he called "Eureka," in the Grecian language signifying, "I have found it;" and upon the discovery of which he is said to have sacrificed a hecatomb. It teaches Masons to be general lovers of the arts and sciences.

[1] THEOREM.—In any right-angled triangle, the square which is described upon

THE HOUR-GLASS

Is an emblem of human life. Behold! how swiftly the sands run, and how rapidly our lives are drawing to a close. We cannot without astonishment behold the little particles which are contained in this machine, how they pass away almost imperceptibly, and yet, to our surprise, in the short space of an hour they are all exhausted. Thus wastes man! To-day he puts forth the tender leaves of hope; to-morrow blossoms, and bears his blushing honors thick upon him; the next day comes a frost, which nips the shoot, and, when he thinks his greatness still aspiring, he falls, like autumn leaves, to enrich our mother earth.

THE SCYTHE

Is an emblem of time, which cuts the brittle thread of life, and launches us into eternity. Behold! what havoc the scythe of time makes among the human race: if by chance we should escape the numerous evils incident to childhood and youth, and with health and vigor arrive at the years of manhood, yet withal we must soon be cut down by the all-devouring scythe of time, and be gathered into the land where our fathers have gone before us.

Brother Gabe, permit me to call your attention to the last emblem on the carpet—the spade, setting-maul, coffin, grave, and sprig of acacia.

The spade, which dug the grave of our Grand Master, may soon dig ours; the setting-maul, which terminated his earthly existence, may be among the casualties which will, sooner or later, terminate ours; the coffin, which received his remains, may soon receive ours; the grave, that abode for the dead, may soon be our grave; the acacia (that evergreen which once marked the temporary resting-place of the illustrious dead), that bloomed and flourished at the head of our Grand Master's grave, and was the cause of its timely discovery, is an emblem of our faith in the immortality of the soul, which never! never—no, never dies.

the side subtending the right angle, is equal to the square described upon the sides which contain the right angle.—*Euclid*, Lib. I. Prop. 47.

SETTING-MAUL   COFFIN, GRAVE, AND ACACIA   SPADE

This, my brother, may soon designate our last resting-place in that everlasting and silent abode, that haven of rest, that peaceful home, "where the wicked cease from troubling, and the weary are at rest."

Brother, be ever mindful of that great change, when we shall be called from labors on earth to that everlasting refreshment in the paradise of God.

Let me admonish you, in the most serious manner, in reference to the close of life, that, when the cold winter of death shall have passed, and the bright summer morn of the resurrection appears, the Sun of Righteousness shall descend and send forth His angels to collect our ransomed dead; then, if we are found worthy, by the benefit of his "pass" we shall gain a ready admission into that celestial Lodge above, where the Supreme Architect of the Universe presides, where we shall see the King in the beauty of holiness, and with him enter into an endless eternity.

Some Masters add the following:

Thus, brother, we close our lecture on the emblems with the solemn thought of death. We are all born to die; we follow our friends to the brink of the grave, and, standing on the shore of a vast ocean, we gaze with exquisite anxiety until the last struggle is over, and we see them sink into the fathomless abyss. We feel our own feet sliding from the precarious brink on which we stand, and a few more suns, and we will be whelmed 'neath death's awful wave, to rest in the stilly shades, and darkness and silence will reign around our melancholy abode. But is this the end of man, and of the aspiring hopes of all faithful Masons? No! blessed be God, we pause not our feet at the first or second step; but, true to our principles, look forward for greater light. As the embers of mortality are faintly glimmering in the sockets of existence, the Bible removes the dark cloud, draws aside the sable curtains of the tomb, bids hope and joy rouse us, and sustains and cheers the departing spirit; it points beyond the silent grave, and bids us turn our eyes with faith and confidence upon the opening scenes of our eternity.

The Worshipful Master gives three raps with his gavel, which brings the whole Lodge to their feet.

CHARGE TO THE LODGE

And now, my brethren, let us see to it, and so regulate our lives by the plumb-line of justice, ever squaring our actions by the square of virtue, that when the Grand Warden of Heaven may call for us, we may be found ready; let us cultivate assiduously the noble tenets of our profession—brotherly love, relief, and truth—and, from the square, learn morality; from the level, equality; from the plumb, rectitude of life. Let us imitate, in all his various perfections, him who, when assailed by the murderous band of rebellious craftsmen, maintained his integrity, even in death, and sealed his pledge with his own blood. Let us emulate his amiable and virtuous conduct, his unfeigned piety to his God, his inflexible integrity to his trust; and as the evergreen that bloomed at the head of the grave betokened the place of his interment, so may virtue's ever-blooming loveliness designate us as free and accepted Masons. With the trowel, spread liberally the cement of brotherly love and affection; and, circumscribed by the compass, let us ponder well our words and actions, and let all the energies of our minds and the affections of our souls be employed in the attainment of our Supreme Grand Warden's approbation. Thus, when dissolution draws nigh, and the cold winds of death come sighing around us, and his chilly dews already glisten on our foreheads, with joy shall we obey the summons of the Grand Warden of Heaven, and go from our labors on earth to everlasting refreshments in the Paradise of God. Then, by the benefit of the pass—a pure and blameless life—with a firm reliance on Divine Providence, shall we gain ready admission into that Celestial Lodge above, where the Supreme Grand Warden forever presides—forever reigns. When, placed at his right hand, he will be pleased to pronounce us just and upright Masons, then shall we be fitted as living stones for that spiritual temple, "that house not made with hands, eternal in the heavens," where no discordant voice shall be heard, but all the soul shall experience shall be perfect bliss, and all it shall express shall be perfect praise, and love divine shall ennoble every heart, and hallelujahs exalted employ every tongue.

The Master gives one rap with his gavel, when all take their seats except the candidate, who remains standing before the Master, by whom he is addressed as follows:

W. M.—Brother Gabe, in closing this Degree. I now give you the following

CHARGE

Brother, your zeal for the institution of Masonry, the progress you have made in the mystery, and your conformity to our regulations, have pointed you out as a proper object for our favor and esteem.

You are now bound by duty, honor, and gratitude, to be faithful to your trust: to support the dignity of your character on every occasion; and to enforce, by precept and example, obedience to the tenets of the Order.

In the character of a Master Mason, you are authorized to correct the errors and irregularities of your uninformed brethren, and to guard them against a breach of fidelity.

To preserve the reputation of the fraternity unsullied must be your constant care; and, for this purpose, it is your province to recommend to your inferiors obedience and submission; to your equals, courtesy and affability; to your superiors, kindness and condescension. Universal benevolence you are always to cultivate; and, by the regularity of your own behavior, afford the best example for the conduct of others less informed. The ancient landmarks of the order, intrusted to your care, you are carefully to preserve; and never suffer them to be infringed, or countenance a deviation from the established usages and customs of the fraternity.

Your virtue, honor, and reputation are concerned in supporting with dignity the character you now bear. Let no motive, therefore, make you swerve from your duty, violate your vows, or betray your trust; but be true and faithful, and imitate the example of that celebrated artist whom you this evening represent. Thus you will render yourself deserving of the honor which we have conferred, and merit the confidence we have reposed.

W M.—Brother Gabe, you will now take your seat in this Lodge as a Master Mason, after stepping to the Secretary's desk, and signing your name to the constitution and by-laws—which will then make you a member of this Lodge.

There is a lecture to this Degree, as well as in the other Degrees, but it is not generally given by the Master to the candidate on the night of his "raising." The candidate generally gets this from some of the brethren who are well posted in the work. This Degree is very lengthy, and to give the lecture at an initiation would take up too much of the night; but if there is time, the Master and Senior Warden usually go through with the first section before closing the Lodge, so that the candidate and brethren may become conversant with it. The lecture is as follows:

FIRST SECTION

Q. Are you a Master Mason?

A. I am.

Q. What induced you to become a Master Mason?

A. In order that I might travel in foreign countries, work and receive Master's wages, being better enabled to support myself and family, and contribute to the relief of worthy distressed Master Masons, their widows and orphans.

Q. What makes you a Master Mason?

A. My obligation.

Q. Where were you made a Master Mason?

A. In a regularly constituted Lodge of Masons.

Q. How were you prepared?

A. By being divested of all metals, neither naked nor clothed, barefoot nor shod, hoodwinked, with a cable-tow three times around my body, in which condition I was conducted to the door of the Lodge by a brother.

Q. Why had you a cable-tow three times around your body?

A. To signify that my duties and obligations become more and more binding as I advance in Masonry.

Q. How gained you admission?

A. By three distinct knocks.

Q. To what do they allude?

A. To the three jewels of a Master Mason, which are friendship, morality, and brotherly love.

Q. What was said to you from within?

A. Who comes here?

Q. Your answer?

A. Brother A. B., who has been regularly initiated Entered Apprentice, passed to the Degree of Fellow Craft, and now wishes further light in Masonry, by being raised to the sublime Degree of a Master Mason.

Q. What were you then asked?

A. If it was of my own free-will and accord, if I was worthy and well qualified, duly and truly prepared, had made suitable proficiency in the preceding Degree, and was properly vouched for; all which being answered in the affirmative, I was asked by what further right or benefit I expected to gain admission.

Q. What followed?

A. I was directed to wait with patience until the Worshipful Master should be informed of my request, and his answer returned.

Q. What answer did he return?

A. Let him enter, and be received in due form.

Q. How were you received?

A. On both points of the compasses, extending from my naked left to my right breast, which was to teach me that, as the most vital parts of man are contained within the breast, so the most excellent tenets of our institution are contained between the points of the compasses, which are, friendship, morality, and brotherly love.

Q. How were you then disposed of?

A. I was conducted three times around the Lodge, to the Junior Warden in the south, where the same questions were asked, and like answers returned as at the door.

Q. How did the Junior Warden dispose of you?

A. He directed me to the Senior Warden in the west, and he to the Worshipful Master in the east, where the same questions were asked, and like answers returned as before.

Q. How did the Worshipful Master dispose of you?

A. He ordered me to be returned to the Senior Warden in the west, who taught me to approach the east by three upright regular steps, my feet forming the angle of a perfect square, my body erect at the altar, before the Worshipful Master in the east.

Q. What did the Worshipful Master do with you?

A. He made me a Master Mason in due form.

Q. What was that due form?

A. Kneeling on both my naked knees, both hands resting on the Holy Bible, square, and compasses; in which due form I took the solemn oath of a Master Mason, which is as follows:

(Here give the obligation; but it is never required—being only a matter of form.)

Q. After the obligation, what were you asked?

A. What I most desired.

Q. Your answer?

A. Further light in Masonry.

Q Did you receive it?

A. I did, by order of the Worshipful Master and the assistance of the brethren.

Q. On being brought to light, what did you discover more than you had heretofore discovered?

A. Both points of the compasses elevated above the square, which was to teach me never to lose sight of those truly Masonic virtues, which are friendship, morality, and brotherly love.

Q. What did you then discover?

A. The Worshipful Master approaching me from the east, under the duegard of a Master Mason, who, in token of further continuance of his brotherly love and favor, presented me with his right hand, and with it the pass and token of the pass of a Master Mason, and ordered me to arise and salute the Junior and Senior Wardens as such.

Q. After saluting the Wardens, what did you first discover?

A. The Worshipful Master, who ordered me to the Senior Warden in the west, who taught me how to wear my apron as a Master Mason.

Q. How should a Master Mason wear his apron?

A. With the flap and corners turned down, which is to distinguish him as a Master Mason, or an overseer of the work.

Q. After being taught to wear your apron as a Master Mason, how were you then disposed of?

A. I was conducted to the Worshipful Master in the east, who presented me with the working-tools of a Master Mason, which are all the implements of Masonry indiscriminately, but more especially the trowel.

Q. What is the use of these tools?

A. The trowel is an instrument made use of by operative masons to spread the cement, which unites a building into one common mass; but we, as free and accepted Masons, are taught to make use of it for the more noble and glorious purpose of spreading the cement of brotherly love and affection, &c., &c (See *Monitor* for the balance of this answer, or page 99 of this work.)

Q. How were you then disposed of?

A. I was ordered to be returned to the place from whence I came, and reinvested of what I had been divested of, and wait the Worshipful Master's will and pleasure.

SECOND SECTION

Q. What does a Master's Lodge represent?

A. The unfinished Sanctum Sanctorum, or Holy of Holies, of King Solomon's Temple.

Q. Did you ever return to the Lodge?

A. I did.

Q. On your return to the Lodge, where were you placed?

A. In the centre, where I was caused to kneel, and implore the blessings of Deity.

Q. After imploring the blessings of Deity, what followed?

A. I arose, and on my passage around the Lodge was accosted by three Fellow Crafts, who thrice demanded of me the secrets of a Master Mason; and, on being refused, the first gave me a blow with the twenty-four-inch gauge, across my throat; the second with a square, across my breast; the third with a setting-maul, on my forehead, which felled me on the spot.

Q. What did you then represent?

A. Our Grand Master, Hiram Abiff, who was slain just before the completion of King Solomon's Temple.

Q. Was his death premeditated?

A. It was, by fifteen Fellow Crafts, who, seeing the Temple about to be completed, and being desirous of obtaining the secrets of a Master Mason, whereby they might travel in foreign countries, work, and receive Master's wages, entered into a horrid conspiracy to extort them from our Grand Master, Hiram Abiff, or take his life; but, reflecting with horror on the atrocity of the crime, twelve of them recanted; the other three persisted in their murderous designs.

Q. At what hour was our Grand Master, Hiram Abiff, slain?

A. At high twelve.[1]

---

[1] We are told that when *the Temple was nearly finished,* it was customary at the hour of H. (high) XII., when the men were called from labor to refreshment, for H. A. B. (Hiram Abiff) to retire to the Most Holy Place, to draw his plans and designs, and offer up his orisons, &c. But how could this be accomplished before the Sanctum Sanctorum was built? And, if finished, he would not have been permitted to enter it; for one living person alone possessed that privilege, viz., the High Priest, and he only once a year. Besides, when a work is nearly completed, the necessity of plans and designs ceases altogether. But we are assured, that not only were the plans drawn and the specifications approved, but every other preparation was made for completing the work *before the foundations were laid;* even the stone and timber were carved, marked, and numbered before they were removed from the quarry and the forest; and hence nothing was required, when the materials were conveyed to Jerusalem, but skilled labor to make it perfect and complete from foundation to cope-stone.

Again, some of the rituals taught that H. A. B. divided the operatives into three classes, viz., Apprentices, Fellow Crafts, and Masters; paying the wages of the

Q. How came he to be assassinated at that hour?

A. It was his usual practice at high twelve, while the Craft were called from labor to refreshment, to enter into the unfinished Sanctum Sanctorum, or Holy of Holies of the Temple, and there to offer up his adorations to Deity, and there to draw his designs on the trestle-board.[1]

Q. Who were the murderers?

A. The three Fellow Crafts who persisted in their murderous designs, knowing this to be his usual practice, placed themselves at the south, west, and east gates of the inner courts of the Temple, and there awaited his return.

Q. What followed?

A. Our Grand Master, Hiram Abiff, having finished his usual exercises, attempted to retire at the South gate, where he was accosted by Jubela, who thrice demanded of him the secrets of a Master Mason, or the Master's word; and, on being refused, gave him a blow with the twenty-four-inch gauge across the throat, upon which he fled, and attempted to pass out at the west gate, where he was accosted by Jubelo, who, in like manner, thrice demanded of him the secrets of a Master Mason, or the Master's word; and, on his being refused, gave him a blow with a square across his breast, upon which he fled, and attempted to make his escape out at the east gate, where he was accosted by Jubelum, who, in like manner, thrice demanded of him the secrets of a Master Mason, or the Master's word: and, on his being refused, gave him a violent blow with a setting-maul, on his forehead, which felled him dead on the spot.[2]

---

former at the pillar of B. *(Boaz)*, the Fellow Crafts at that of J. *(Jachin)*, and the Masters in the Middle Chamber. Now, as in the former case, this arrangement would be impossible before the pillars were erected or the Middle Chamber built: and if it be pretended that any such plan was adopted *after they were finished*, the tragic drama could not be true, because it professes to have been enacted *before* the Temple was completed.

And finally, the veracity of the legend is completely ignored by a reference to the Holy Scriptures, which constitute our authority for affirming that no such event ever happened; for H. A. B. not only lived to finish all the work, in whatever capacity he might have been engaged, but also, according to the testimony of Josephus, who calls him ABDXMON, he returned to Tyre, and died there at a good old age.—*The Freemason's Treasury*, pp. 299—300.

[1] Our traditions further say, that the time when this celebrated man went into the H. of H. *(Holy of Holies)* to offer up his orisons to God, at the hour of H. *(high)* twelve, the Ark of the Covenant had not been removed thither, for that took place at the dedication, after which no one was permitted to enter but the H. P. *(High Priest)*, and he only once a year, on the great day of expiation, at which time he had a string or belt around his waist, which extended into the court of the tabernacle, that he might be drawn forth from the S. S. *(Sanctum Sanctorum)* in case sudden death should occur while he officiated there.—*Historical Landmarks*, vol. II. p. 164.

[2] A similar divergence from uniformity will be found in describing the places

Q. What did they do with the body?

A. They buried it in the rubbish of the Temple until low twelve, or twelve at night, when they met by agreement and carried it a westerly course from the Temple, to the brow of a hill west of Mount Moriah, where they buried it in a grave dug due east and west, six feet perpendicular, at the head of which they planted an acacia, in order to conceal it, and that the place might be known, should occasion ever require; and then made their escape.

Q. When was our Grand Master, Hiram Abiff, found to be missing?

A. On the following day.

Q. How was his absence discovered?

A. By there being no designs drawn on the trestle-board.

Q. What followed?

A. King Solomon, being informed of this, supposed him to be indisposed, and ordered strict search to be made for him through the several apartments of the Temple, and due inquiry made; search and inquiry were accordingly made, but he could not be found.

Q. What followed?

A. King Solomon, fearing some accident had befallen him, ordered the several rolls of the workmen to be called; and, after roll-call, it was found that three Craftsmen were missing, namely, Jubela, Jubelo, and Jubelum, who, from the similarity of their names, were supposed to be brothers, and men from Tyre.

Q. What followed?

A. At this time, the twelve Fellow Crafts, who had recanted from their murderous designs, appeared before King Solomon, clothed in white gloves and aprons, in token of their innocence, acknowledging their premeditated guilt, and humbly imploring his pardon.

Q. What followed?

where the above-mentioned instruments were supposed to have been used with such terrible effect. In the primitive lectures—i. e., those which were used after the Revival in 1717, for the subject was never ventilated before that date—they were called "the three principal entrances to the Temple"; but subsequently it was thought expedient to particularize these entrances; and the passage was altered at first to "the east, west and south doors"; and, at the Union in 1813, the version became "*north, south, and east* entrances." In the United States they say that the first attack was made at the south door, the second at the west door, and finally at the east. In Scotland the arrangement is *east, south, and west.* In France, it was originally *south,* north, and east, but now *west,* south, and east. In the Adonhiramite Masonry, which was used there about 1767, the doors are not mentioned at all.—*The Freemason's Treasury,* p. 307.

A. King Solomon ordered them to divide in parties, and travel three east, three west, three north, and three south, with others whom he should appoint, in search of the ruffians.

Q. What followed?

A. The three, as they were passing a westerly course, coming down near the port of Joppa, met a seafaring man, of whom they inquired if he had seen any strangers pass that way. He informed them that he had seen three, who, from their appearance, were workmen from the Temple, seeking a passage into Ethiopia; but, not having King Solomon's pass, were unable to obtain one, and had returned back into the country.

Q. What followed?

A. They returned and bore this intelligence to King Solomon, who ordered them to divide themselves, and travel as before, with positive instructions to find the ruffians, and with as positive assurance, that if they did not the twelve should be deemed the murderers, and suffer severely for the crime committed.

Q. What followed?

A. They travelled as before, and, after many days of hardships and toil, on their return one of the brethren, more weary than the rest, sat down on the brow of a hill to rest and refresh himself, and on attempting to rise, accidentally caught hold of an acacia, which easily giving way, aroused his curiosity; upon which he hailed his companions, and on examination found it to be a grave.

Q. What followed? (See Note P, page 272.)

A. At this time a party arrived with the ruffians, and related that, while sitting down to rest and refresh themselves, they heard the following horrid exclamations from the clefts of an adjacent rock: the first was the voice of Jubela, exclaiming, "Oh! that my throat had been cut across," &c., &c.; the second was the voice of Jubelo, exclaiming, "Oh! that my breast had been torn open," &c., &c.; the third was the voice of Jubelum, exclaiming, "Oh! that my body had been severed in two, my bowels taken from thence," &c., &c. (See p. 112.) Upon which they rushed in, seized, bound, and brought them before King Solomon; who, after due conviction of their guilt, ordered them to be executed according to their several imprecations upon their own heads, uttered from the clefts of the rocks.[1] (See Note P, page 271.)

---

[1] The questions and answers in this lecture, relative to the disposition of the body and its discovery, &c., &c., are precisely like the historical part of this Degree, page 132, or that portion describing the conferring of the Degree, page 107.

THIRD SECTION

Q. How long was the Temple in building?

A. Seven years; during which it rained not in the daytime, that the workmen might not be obstructed in their labor.

Q. What supported the Temple?

A. Fourteen hundred and fifty-three columns, and two thousand nine hundred and six pilasters; all hewn from the finest Parian marble.

Q. What further supported it?

A. Three grand columns or pillars.

Q. What were they called?

A. Wisdom, Strength, and Beauty.

Q. What did they represent?

A. The pillar of Wisdom represented Solomon, king of Israel, whose wisdom contrived the mighty fabric; the pillar of strength, Hiram, king of Tyre, who strengthened Solomon in his grand undertaking; the pillar of Beauty, Hiram Abiff, the widow's son, whose cunning craft and curious workmanship beautified and adorned the Temple.

Q. How many were there employed in the building of King Solomon's Temple?

A. Three Grand Masters, three thousand three hundred Masters or overseers of the work, eighty thousand Fellow Crafts, and seventy thousand Entered Apprentices, &c., &c. (See p. 126).

Q. How many constitute an Entered Apprentices' Lodge?

A. Seven; one Master and six Entered Apprentices.

Q. Where did they usually meet?

A. On the Ground Floor of King Solomon's Temple.

Q. How many constitute a Fellow Crafts' Lodge?

A. Five; two Masters and three Fellow Crafts.

Q. Where did they usually meet?

A. In the Middle Chamber of King Solomon's Temple.

Q. How many constitute a Master's Lodge?

A. Three Master Masons.

Q. Where did they usually meet?

A. In the Sanctum Sanctorum, or Holy of Holies, of King Solomon's Temple.

Q. Have you any emblems in this Degree?

A. We have several, and they are divided into two classes.

Q. What are the first class?

A. The Pot of Incense, the Beehive, the Book of Constitutions guarded by the Tyler's Sword, the Sword pointing to a Naked Heart, the All-seeing Eye, the Anchor and Ark, the Forty-seventh

Problem of Euclid, the Hour-Glass, the Scythe, and the Three Steps on the Master's Carpet.

Q. How are they explained?

These answers are monitorial. (See pp. 127-130.)

Q. What are the second class of emblems?

A. The Setting-Maul, Spade, Coffin, Grave, and Sprig of Acacia; and are thus explained.[1] (See p. 130.)

Reader, I have given you the whole of the first three Degrees in Masonry. This ends the third, or Master Masons' Degree.

But few Masons take sufficient interest in Masonry to be advanced further, and consequently do not get the password which was lost by the tragical death of Hiram Abiff.

King Solomon is said to have substituted, in place of the lost one, the word now used in the Master Masons' Degree, viz.: Mah-Hah-Bone, which is given on the five points of fellowship, and in low breath.

The missing word was found, after four hundred and seventy years, and was then, and still is, used in the Royal Arch Degree, as will be seen in the ceremonies of that Degree.

CLOSING THE LODGE

The Lodge is closed in nearly the same manner that it is opened, and, in fact, all three of the Degrees are closed alike.

We will suppose the business of the Lodge finished, and that the Master proceeds to close.

W. M.—Brother Senior Warden, do you know of any thing further before this Lodge of Masons previous to closing?

S. W. (rising to his feet, and giving the sign of a Master Mason, if opened on that Degree.)—Nothing, Worshipful (some say), in the west. (Sits down.)

W. M.—Any thing in the south, Brother Junior Warden?

J. W. (makes the same sign as the Senior Warden.)—Nothing Worshipful.

W. M.—Brother Secretary, have you any thing on your desk?

Sec.—Nothing, Worshipful.

W. M.—Has any brother around the Lodge any thing to offer for the benefit of Masonry before we proceed to close?

W. M.—Reading of the present communication. (Secretary reads the minutes, &c., &c.)

---

[1] LECTURE.—In the Masters' Degree, the first section illustrates the ancient and proper mode of raising a candidate to this sublime Degree. In the second section, the historical traditions of the Order are introduced, and an important instance of

W. M.—Brother Senior Warden, have you any alterations or additions to make to the minutes?

S. W. (rising to his feet and making the sign).—I have none, Worshipful.

W. M.—Brother Junior Warden, have you any to make?

J. W.—None, Worshipful.

W. M.—Has any brother present any?

W. M.—Brethren, the minutes will stand approved, if there are no objections. (Gives one rap (•), when the Junior Deacon, at the inner door of the Lodge, rises to his feet.) Brother Junior Deacon, the last as well as the first care of Masons, when convened?

J. D. (makes sign).—To see that the Lodge is duly tyled.

W. M.—You will attend to that part of your duty, and inform the Tyler that we are about to close this Lodge, and direct him to tyle accordingly. (Deacon opens the door, and delivers his message.)

J. D.—The Lodge is tyled, Worshipful.

W. M.—How tyled?

J. D.—By a brother of this Degree within the outer door.

W. M.—His duty there?

J. D.—To keep off all cowans and eavesdroppers, and suffer none to pass or repass, except such as are duly qualified and have the Worshipful Master's permission. (Sits down.)

W. M. (one rap, Senior Warden rises to his feet).—Brother Senior Warden, at the opening of this Lodge you informed me that you were a Master Mason. What induced you to become a Master Mason?

S. W.—In order that I might travel in foreign countries, work, and receive Master's wages, being better enabled to support myself and family, and contribute to the relief of worthy distressed Master Masons, their widows and orphans.

W. M.—Have you ever travelled?

S. W.—I have; from west to east, and from east to west again.

Some Lodges use the following questions and answers, both at opening and closing:

W. M.—Why did you leave the west and travel to the east?

S. W.—In search of that which was lost.

W. M.—To what do you allude, my brother?

S. W.—The Master's word.

W. M.—Did you find it?

S. W.—I did not, but found a substitute.

Masonic virtue is exemplified. In the third section, our emblems are explained, and the construction of Solomon's Temple described.—*Lexicon.*

This is also used occasionally by some Masters in the lecture:

W. M.—The Junior Deacon's station?

S. W.—At the right hand of the Senior Warden in the west.

W. M. (two raps, all the officers rise to their feet).—Your duty there, Brother Junior Deacon?

J. D.—(See opening ceremony, p. 14.)

W. M.—The Senior Deacon's station?

J. D.—At the right hand of the Worshipful Master in the east.

W. M.—Your duty there, Brother Senior Deacon?

S. D.—(See opening ceremony, p. 14).

W. M.—The Secretary's station?

S. D.—At the left hand of the Worshipful Master in the east.

W. M.—Your duty there, Brother Secretary?

Sec.—(See opening ceremony, p. 14).

W. M.—The Treasurer's station?

S. D.—At the left hand of the Worshipful Master in the east.

W. M.—Your duty there, Brother Treasurer?

Treasurer—(See opening ceremony, p. 14.)

W. M.—The Junior Warden's station?

Treasurer— In the south, Worshipful.

W. M.—Why in the south, and your duty there, Brother Junior?

J. W.—(See opening ceremony, p. 15.)

W. M.—The Senior Warden's station?

J. W.—In the west, Worshipful Master.

W. M.—Why in the west, and your duty there, Brother Senior?

S. W.—(See opening ceremony, p. 15.)

W. M.—The Worshipful Master's station?

S. W.—In the east, Worshipful.

W. M.—Why in the east, and his duty there?

S. W.—As the sun rises in the east, to open and govern the day, so rises the Worshipful Master in the east (here the Master gives three raps (● ● ●), when all in the Lodge rise to their feet, the Master rising first), to open and govern his Lodge, set the Craft to work, and give them proper instructions.

W. M.—Brother Senior Warden, it is my orders that this Lodge be now closed, and stand closed until our next regular communication (barring emergency), when all, or a suitable number, shall have due and timely notice. In the mean time, it is hoped and expected that every brother will demean himself as becomes a man and a Mason. This you will communicate to the Junior Warden in the south, and he to the brethren about the

Lodge, that they having due and timely notice, may govern them-selves accordingly.

S. W.—Brother Junior Warden, it is the orders of the Worship-ful Master, &c., &c.

J. W.—Brethren, you have heard the orders of the Worshipful Master, as communicated to me through the Senior Warden in the west—you will take notice, and govern yourselves accord-ingly.

W. M.—Brethren, together on the signs. (The signs are just the same as at opening. See pp. 16, 17, 18; also p. 155.)

After the signs are gone through with by the whole Lodge, the Master gives one rap with his gavel, which is responded to by the Senior Warden, and then by the Junior Warden, and then again by the Master, one rap. Senior Warden, one. Junior Warden, one. Again, the Master, one. Senior Warden, one. Junior Warden, one. Rapping three times each

W. M.—Brother Senior Warden, how should Masons meet?

S. W.—On the Level.

W. M.—And how act, Brother Junior?

J. W.—On the Plumb.

W. M.—And part on the Square; and so let us ever meet, act, and part.

Master takes off his hat, and repeats the following prayer:

"May the blessing of Heaven rest upon us, and all regular Masons; may brotherly love prevail, and every moral and social virtue cement us. Amen."

Response—So mote it be.

Some Lodges sing the following, to the air of "Bonny Doon":

"Adieu! a heart-warm, fond adieu,
    Ye brothers of our mystic tie,
Ye favored and enlightened few,
    Companions of my social joy."

See *Monitors* for balance of the verses.

CHARGE AT CLOSING A LODGE

BRETHREN:—You are now about to quit this sacred retreat of friendship and virtue, to mix again with the world. Amid its concerns and temptations, forget not the duties you have heard so frequently inculcated and so forcibly recommended in this Lodge.

Be diligent, prudent, temperate, discreet. Remember that you have promised to befriend and relieve every brother who shall need your assistance; you have promised to remind him, in the most friendly manner, of his errors, and, if possible, to aid him in a reformation. These generous principles are to extend further. Every human being has a claim upon your kind offices. Do good unto all. Remember it more "especially to the household of the faithful."

Finally, brethren, be ye all of one mind, live in peace, and may the God of love and peace delight to dwell with and bless you.

W. M.—Brother Senior Warden, I now declare this Lodge duly closed. Brother Junior Deacon (turning to that officer), you will inform the Tyler.

Worshipful Master gives one rap with his gavel, when the Lodge is closed, and the brethren divest themselves of their regalia, preparatory to returning to their respective homes.[1]

---

[1] "In the performance of a ceremony so solemn and momentous as the closing of a Mason's Lodge, every member has a lively interest. At the usual report, preceded by an inquiry involving the best interests of Masonry, the brethren are again reminded *what is the chief care of a Mason.* The avenues to the Lodge are carefully inspected by the meridian officer, whose knowledge and fidelity have entitled him to the confidence of the brethren, and, after he had publicly proclaimed the security of the Lodge, the business of closing proceeds. The particular duties of the leaders of the respective bands of craftsmen are rehearsed. At the command of the Worshipful Master, the Senior Warden performs his duty, after seeing that the brethren have received their due proportion of Masonic instruction and improvement; and the whole concludes with an impressive address to the brethren on their respective duties as men and Masons, when pursuing their accustomed avocations in the world; and with a fervent petition to the Deity, supplicating his blessing on the fraternity wheresoever dispersed under the wide canopy of heaven."—*Theo. Phil.,* p. 297.

"This Degree has a reference to the Christian dispensation, when the day of salvation is more fully revealed; atonement is made for sin; and *the resurrection from the dead* plainly communicated and confirmed by the resurrection of Christ from the grave. The Jewish law had degenerated into a mass of *rottenness* and corruption:—piety, which planned the Temple at Jerusalem, was expunged; the reverence and adoration due to the Divinity *was buried in the filth and rubbish* of the world; and religion and morality were scattered to the four winds of heaven. *Three ruffian* nations *from the south, the west, and the east*—the Syrians, the Chaldeans and the Romans—gave in succession this temporary dispensation its *death-blow;* those who sought religion through the wisdom of the ancients *were not able to raise her; she eluded their grasp,* and the polluted hands were also stretched forth in vain for her restoration. Her tomb *was in the rubbish and filth cast forth from the Temple, and acacia waved its branches over her monument. In this state of darkness and despair* she lay until the Saviour came, *instituted the five points of Christian fellowship,* and *raised her from the dust, in which she had been indecently interred,* to a more glorious inheritance."—*Theo. Phil.,* p. 30?.

This interpretation is borne out in the higher Degrees of sublime Masonry. Thus, in the thirty-second, or Degree of Prince of the Royal Secret, according to the Continental nomenclature, the following analogies are explained: "The symbolical

The "work," or rather the lectures in the several degrees of Masonry, more especially in the first three degrees (masonically termed the Blue Degrees, or Blue Lodge), differ so much in each State that it would be a difficult thing to get exactly at the proper responses to some of the Masonic interrogatories. No three States in the Union "work" alike. Each Grand Lodge has a "work" of its own, which is taught the subordinate Lodges annually by its Grand Lecturer.[1]

It is generally known among Masons, that in the Northwestern States the lectures and "work" are those as taught by Barney. There is a great degree of uniformity in Michigan, Illinois, and Wisconsin—also in Indiana and Iowa. The Barney "work" is that adopted by the Baltimore Convention. The "work" in Minnesota and New York is strongly impregnated with what is called, among Masons, "Morganry"—very similar to the disclosures of Morgan and Richardson—so much so, that many Masters purchase these publications for their instruction in their duties and in the ritual. Masonry has but little changed, and a knowledge of the alterations which have been made since Morgan's exposure was written is all that is requisite to make a "bright Mason." The only alterations which occur in the lectures of each degree are in the commencement. A concise sketch of Brother Barney, the author of the three lectures introduced in this work, would not be out of place, as it will account to the

mystery of the death of (Hiram Abiff) represents that of the Messiah; for the three (blows) which were given to him at the three gates of (the Temple) allude to the three points of condemnation against Christ at three separate places, viz.: before Caiaphas, Herod, and Pilate. It was from the last that he was led to that most violent and excruciating death. The three (blows) were given with the three (tools, i. e., gauge, square, and gavel). These are symbols of the blow on the cheek of Christ, the flagellation, and the blow with the spear. Some substitute for the latter, but with less propriety, the crown of thorns. The brethren assembled around the grave of (Hiram Abiff) is a representation of the disciples lamenting the death of Christ. The Word, which was said to be lost, was pronounced upon the cross, which the Jews could not comprehend. The false brethren are represented by Judas, who proved false to his Master; and the sprig of cassia represented the cross, of which wood it is said to have been composed."—*Historical Landmarks*, vol. II. p. 176.

I am decidedly of opinion that our tradition is merely allegorical; for there can be no doubt but the Chief Architect was present at the dedication of the Temple. Thus we find that "Hiram made an end of doing all the work that he made King Solomon for the house of the Lord." (1 Kings vii. 40.) To place the fact of Hiram's being alive at the finishing of the Temple beyond all doubt, it is said (2 Chron. iv. 11), "And Hiram finished the work that he was to make for King Solomon for the house of God."—*Historical Landmarks*, vol. II. p. 168.

[1] A Grand Lecturer is elected annually at the session of the Grand Lodge of each State. His business is to teach the subordinate Lodges the Ritual of Freemasonry, and he is paid generally by salary, or so much from each Lodge before whom he may lecture.

reader for the difference existing between Masonic "works" in the several States, and in Europe:

"In the year 1817, Brother John Barney, formerly of Charlotte, Vermont, went to Boston, and obtained possession of the Preston Lectures, taught there by Gleason, and approved by the Grand Lodge of Massachusetts. With these lectures he returned to Vermont, and submitted them to the Grand Lodge, at its annual session in October, 1817. The subject was there referred for examination to a committee, which reported that these lectures were according to the most approved method of 'work' in the United States, and proposed to give Brother Barney letters of recommendation to all Lodges and brethren in all parts as a brother well qualified to give Masonic information to any desirous of his services.

"This report of the committee was accepted and adopted by the Grand Lodge, and Brother Barney, provided with the recommendation thus obtained, visited many of the Lodges of the State, and imparted to them a knowledge of these lectures. At this time Brother Barney wrote a portion of them in cipher. Subsequently to 1818, Brother Barney went to the Western and Southwestern States, and, being in delicate health, adopted the profession of Masonic lecturing as a means of subsistence.

"A few years afterward, on his return to his brethren in Vermont, he stated to them, as I have been credibly informed and believe, that he found in the Western and Southwestern States different systems of lecturing prevailing, and that, upon presenting Gleason's Lectures to them, they were objected to by the different Grand Masters, who would not sanction his lecturing in their respective jurisdictions, unless he would adopt the lectures then in use among them; that, desiring to pursue his occupation there, he learned the different systems of lecturing existing among them, and made use of his newly acquired knowledge under the sanction of the respective Grand Masters." (See Note Q, Appendix.)

These facts will account for the want of agreement between the East and the West and Southwest, as to what are the *true* Barney Lectures.

From the foregoing remarks, it will be seen that the essential points of Masonry are identical the world over, and that the differences, which are of minor importance, may be gathered by comparing the present work with Richardson's *Monitor* or Allyn's *Ritual*.

The "work" known among Masons as the "Webb Work,"

and inculcated by Robert Morris,[1] is generally accepted as the "Work" of ancient origin, and there is not much doubt but that it will be adopted by the Grand Lodges throughout the United States.

[1] See Robert Morris's *Freemason's Monitor*, 1860.

THE LODGE.

A LODGE is understood to be the room or place in which a regularly constituted body of Freemasons assembles for work and the transaction of business connected with the Institution. The term is also used to designate the collection of Masons thus assembled, just as we use the word "church" to signify the building in which a congregation of worshippers meet, as well as the congregation itself.

A Lodge is defined to be an assembly of Masons, *just*, *perfect*, and *regular*, who together meet to expatiate on the beauties and mysteries of the Order, and to add new material to the sacred work. It is *just*, because it contains the volume of the Sacred Law unfolded, together with the square and compasses; *perfect*, having the required number of members present to transact business in a regular and constitutional manner, and *regular*, from its warrant of constitution, which implies that it meets and works under the sanction of the legal Masonic authority of the jurisdiction in which the Lodge is held, subject to its by-laws and the general regulations. It is either particular or general, and will be best understood by attending it.—*Charges of* 1722.

FORMATION OF LODGES.

No Lodge is recognized at the present day unless it has emanated from a Grand Lodge, and works in obedience to the regulations of its parent. Whatever may be the status of a Mason irregularly made, no countenance is given to an irregular (clandestine) Lodge.

Lodges, according to the American system, are recognized of two kinds, distinct in their character, and working under distinct and separate authority : the first, *Under Dispensation* from the Grand Master; the second, *Under Warrant* (charter) from the Grand Lodge. Their powers and authority will be separately considered.

LODGE UNDER DISPENSATION.

In the formation of a new Lodge, which is technically termed a *Lodge under Dispensation*, a petition signed by not less than seven Master Masons in good standing is presented to the Grand Master, or other officer having authority to grant dispensations. There must be good reason for the organization of the Lodge at that time and place. The place of meeting must be designated, and the names of the first three officers stated. The petition must be recommended by the nearest chartered Lodge (in some States all the Lodges whose territory would be reduced), which must certify that the officers proposed are qualified to confer the degrees and give the lectures, etc.

POWERS OF A LODGE UNDER DISPENSATION.

The powers of a Lodge under dispensation are such as may be prescribed by the local regulations in force in the jurisdiction where it is located. The petitioners for the new Lodge must give notice to the old Lodge that they have signed such petition, and pay all dues to that time ; but (in the most of States) they are not required to dimit from the Lodge until the charter is granted. This, however, like other rules, is subject to local regulations. Usually a Lodge U. D. has the same authority as a warranted Lodge except holding elections and installing officers.

CHARTERED LODGES.

The powers, duties and privileges of a subordinate Lodge are such as are defined by its charter. by the constitutions and general regulations of the Grand Lodge, and the ancient landmarks. They are divided into—

I. EXECUTIVE.—In the direction and performance of its work under the control of its Master, and in all other matters in sustaining the Master, who has the primary executive power of the Lodge.

II. LEGISLATIVE.—Embracing all matters relating to its internal concerns not in derogation of the ancient landmarks, the constitutions and general regulations of the Grand Lodge, or of its own particular by-laws; and

III. JUDICIAL.—Embracing the exercise of discipline and settlement of controversies between and over all its members (except the Master), and over all Masons and non-affiliated brethren within its jurisdiction, subject to an appeal to the Grand Lodge.

The powers of a chartered Lodge are divided into IN-HERENT and CORPORATE.

A Lodge by virtue of its inherent rights, as defined by ancient landmarks, established usages of Masonry, and when recognized by a Grand Lodge, has the power: 1. To retain its charter until lawfully surrendered, suspended, or revoked; 2. To fix its time and place (if not outside of the place named in the charter) of meetings; 3. To meet and do all the work of craft Masonry; 4. To elect and initiate members, and reject any application for membership; 5. To elect and install its officers; 6. To make laws requiring its members to contribute to its funds; 7. To instruct its representatives, for their government, at all communications of the Grand Lodge; 8. To place on trial, for cause, its own members, sojourners, and unaffiliated Masons living within its jurisdiction; 9. To appeal to the Grand Master or Grand Lodge from the decision of the Master; 10. To make by-laws for its local government.

The corporate rights of a Lodge are conferred by its charter, and by the powers thereof they are entitled: 1. To representation in all communications of the Grand Lodge; 2. To protection while in the lawful exercise of its inherent rights; and 3. To the enjoyment of all powers conferred by the Grand Lodge upon any constituent Lodge.

FORFEITURE OF CHARTER.

The acts for which a charter may be forfeited and the Lodge dissolved are: 1. Contumacy to the authority of the Grand Master or Grand Lodge; 2. Departure from the original plan of Masonry, and a violation of the ancient landmarks; 3. Disobedience of the constitutions; 4. Ceasing to meet for one year or more; 5. Admitting clandestine Masons, or initiating known immoral candidates.

SURRENDERING THE CHARTER.

A Lodge may be dissolved by the voluntary surrender of its charter by its members, after special summons for that purpose, unless the minority opposed to such surrender consist of seven or more members, that number being the constitutional complement to *receive*, hence that number may *retain* the charter. This rule is now of almost universal practice in the United States.

SUSPENDING THE CHARTER.

The Grand Master may, for cause, arrest the charter of a Lodge, not to extend beyond the next annual communication of the Grand Lodge. Such suspension for the time arrests the work of the Lodge and prevents its meetings, but does not affect the Masonic standing of its members nor destroy the legality of its charter.

DUTIES OF A LODGE.

A Lodge by its acceptance of a charter, and its officers and members by their several Masonic obligations, are sacredly bound to obey the laws of Masonry. The duties of a Lodge, therefore, are: 1. To observe and preserve the ancient usages of Masonry; 2. To obey the constitution and regulations of the Grand Lodge; 3. To render the Grand Master or his deputy all due respect and obedience; 4. Respectfully to hear all official communications from the Grand Lodge, the Grand Master, or any officer acting by their authority; 5. To be properly represented at the annual communications of the Grand Lodge; 6. To possess the proper jewels, clothing, etc., and a suitable seal; 7. To provide for its meetings a safe and suitable Lodge room; 8. To make, through its Secretary, the annual reports of its work and condition to Grand Lodge, and punctually to pay its annual dues.

For a persistent or inexcusable neglect by a Lodge, or of its officers, of any of the duties imposed; and for any deliberate violation of its obligations to Masonry or to the authority of the Grand Lodge or the edicts of the Grand Master, the charter thereof may be suspended or revoked.

AUTHORITY OVER SUSPENDED MASONS.

A Master Mason having been suspended for unmasonic conduct, and while under such suspension, may, upon new charges for repetition of the first offence, or for any other offence, be tried and expelled, or an additional term of suspension be inflicted if the offence so warrants, by the Lodge having personal jurisdiction over him.

GOVERNMENT OF THE LODGE.

There is no plainer or more definite law in Masonry than that the Master must preside over his Lodge; but in case of his absence, from any cause, the Senior Warden, and in the absence of both, the Junior Warden shall summon the Lodge to order, and succeed to all the powers and privileges of the Master, as though the Master himself were present, provided the warrant shall be present. In the absence of the Master or either of the Wardens the Lodge cannot be opened. A Past Master can only preside when the Master or one of the Wardens is present and opens the Lodge, after which he may call such Past Master to the chair. Whoever occupies the chair legally controls the Lodge. Even the Grand Master, if present, can exercise no authority until he has taken the chair and assumed the gavel.

OFFICERS OF A LODGE.

The prosperity, the success, and the usefulness of a Lodge, and its ability to discharge the duties and objects of Freemasonry, depend greatly upon the character and judgment of its officers.

The discipline of a Masonic Lodge, the order observed at its meetings, the obedience there exacted, and cheerfully rendered on the part of the brethren, make its government as nearly perfect as it is possible for any human institution to be. Intelligent and capable officers make good Lodges. It is the imperative duty of the officers of a Lodge to be careful, prudent, and conciliating, positive in requiring obedience to the law ; smoothing down all asperities of manner, spreading the cement of brotherly love and affection ; rendering to every one that due attention which should ever distinguish a band of brothers, and whilst by their own example they exhibit the beauties of the craft, they admonish with kindness, and reprehend with justice. Unity is the mainspring of Freemasonry. Destroy that, and the machinery will fall in pieces. It will be a difficult matter to preserve the links in the chain of unity unbroken, unless the Master pursues an accommodating policy, which may cause the brethren to be mutually pleased with each other's society, accompanied by an inflexible regard to discipline, which, while it allows freedom of action, will preserve inviolable the respectful submission that is due the Chair, as its undoubted and inalienable prerogative.

The duties, responsibilities and prerogatives of the officers of a Lodge are now well defined (see Part I.), and consist of—1. A Master, who is styled Worshipful ; 2. A Senior Warden ; 3. A Junior Warden ; 4. A Treasurer ; 5. A Secretary ; 6. A Senior Deacon ; 7. A Junior Deacon ; 8. Two Stewards, or two Masters of Ceremonies (sometimes both); 9. A Tyler. In addition to the above, many Lodges are provided with a Chaplain, Marshal, Organist, and Board of Trustees.

PAST MASTERS.

By the term Past Masters, it must be understood to allude to those who have been legally elected Masters of chartered Lodges, served their term of office, and are recognized as *Actual* Past Masters, and who are distinguished from those who have been seated in the *chair* in a Royal Arch Chapter. Their privileges are such as may be expressly given by the Constitution of the Grand Lodge, and, in addition, they are qualified to install any Master elect, when requested to do so, and to be present at the qualification of a Master elected to the chair.

A Past Master is always eligible to re-election, without further service, to any office in the Lodge of which he is a member.

He is eligible as a proxy or representative of the Grand Master to perform any duty when that officer cannot attend.

As a courtesy, a Past Master is entitled to a seat in the east on the right of the acting Master.

A Chapter or *virtual* Past Master has no rights in a subordinate Lodge, and consequently cannot install a newly elected Master, or be present at the conferring of the Past Master's degree. This rule, however, is local, limited to a portion of the State jurisdictions.

Every Master Mason in good standing is the peer of a Past Master in matters of discipline, etc.

ELECTION AND INSTALLATION OF OFFICERS.

The election and appointment of officers shall be held annually, at such time as is prescribed by the Constitution of the Grand Lodge, or the by-laws of the Lodge (usually the regular meeting next preceding the festival of St. John the Evangelist, Dec. 27), and their installation must take place on the same evening, or within a reasonable period thereafter. Until such election and installation the incumbents in office shall hold over. No officer can be installed by proxy.

Previous to the annual election (if not already provided for in the by-laws), the Master should instruct the Secretary to call together the Lodge, notify every member of the amount of his indebtedness to the Lodge, and that in default of payment he will not be entitled to vote at such election.

Some opposition has been expressed against this doctrine on the constitutional provision that every member in good standing is entitled to one vote, but it is respectfully submitted that a member who fails to comply with the conditions of good standing, is not entitled to the immunities.

A Lodge having failed to elect its officers at the constitutional time, the Grand Master may grant a dispensation to hold an election at another time to complete the work of the Lodge.

At the election two tellers are appointed, who shall receive and count the ballots, and announce the result, under the supervision of the Master. A ballot represents a brother's vote, which is the expression of whatever opinion he may entertain.

Nominations of candidates for office are in order, and the candidate must receive a majority of all the votes cast to be legally declared elected.

When the constitution or the by-laws do not otherwise provide, the election of an officer may be taken by show of hands, or by a brother, selected for the purpose, casting one ballot, if there be no opposing candidate.

Every member of a Lodge in good standing is eligible to any office in his Lodge, except that of Master.

The members of a Lodge cannot prevent the installation of the Master elect by objecting to it, but the acting Master, in his judgment, may postpone the installation until the case can be submitted to the Grand Master.

FORMS OF MASONIC DOCUMENTS.

PETITION FOR A DISPENSATION FOR A NEW LODGE.

To the M. W. Grand Master of Masons of the State of ———:

The undersigned petitioners, being Ancient Free and Accepted Master Masons, having the prosperity of the Fraternity at heart, and willing to exert their best endeavors to promote and diffuse the genuine principles of Masonry, respectfully represent—That they are desirous of forming a new Lodge in the —— of ——, county of ——, and State of ——, to be named ——, No. —. They therefore pray for letters of Dispensation, to empower them to assemble as a regular Lodge, to discharge the duties of Masonry in a regular and constitutional manner, according to the original forms of the Order, and the regulations of the Grand Lodge. They have nominated and do recommend Brother A B to be the first Master; Brother C D to be the first Senior Warden, and Brother E F to be the first Junior Warden, of said Lodge. . If the prayer of this petition shall be granted, they promise a strict conformity to the edicts of the Grand Master, and the constitution, laws, and regulations of the Grand Lodge.

(This petition must be signed by not less than seven Master Masons, recommended by one or two Lodges. The constitutional fee must be forwarded to the Grand Master or Grand Secretary. On receipt of the Dispensation, the Master, Wardens, and brethren named therein will assemble, and open a Master's Lodge in due form. The three officers named must be present. But a Lodge is not constituted, or officers installed, until a charter is granted.)

RECOMMENDATION FOR NEW LODGE.

To the M. W. Grand Master of Masons of ——:

At a regular meeting of —— Lodge, No. —, holden at ——, on the —— day of ——, 19—, the petition of several Master Masons, praying for a Dispensation to open a new Lodge at ——, in the county of ——, State of ——, was duly laid before the Lodge, when it was

Resolved, That this Lodge, being fully satisfied that the petitioners are Master Masons in good standing, and being willing to vouch for their Masonic abilities, does therefore recommend that the Dispensation prayed for be granted to them.

A true copy of the records.

—— ——, *Secretary.*

(Seal.)

FORM OF DISPENSATION FOR NEW LODGE.

Grand Lodge of Free and Accepted Masons of the State of ——.

To all to whom these presents may come, GREETING:

WHEREAS, a petition has been presented to me by Brothers ——, residing within this jurisdiction, praying, on account of the convenience of their respective dwellings, and for other good reasons, for a Dispensation to empower them to assemble as a legal Lodge, to discharge the duties of Masonry in the several degrees of Entered Apprentice, Fellow Craft, and Master Mason, in a regular and constitutional manner, according to the ancient forms of the Fraternity, and the constitution and regulations of this Grand Lodge;

And, WHEREAS, The said petitioners have been recommended to me as Master Masons in good standing by the Worshipful Master, Wardens and brethren of —— Lodge, No. —, under our jurisdiction; Therefore, I, —— ——, Grand Master of the Grand Lodge of Free and Accepted Masons of the State of ——, by virtue of the arthority in me vested, do hereby grant this my Dispensation, authorizing and empowering our trusty and well-beloved brethren aforesaid, to form and open a new Lodge in the —— of ——, in county of ——, and State of ——, to be called —— Lodge, and therein to admit and make Entered Apprentices, Fellow Crafts, and Master Masons, in accordance with the ancient usages and customs of the Fraternity, obeying in all things the constitution, laws, and edicts of this Grand Lodge, and not otherwise.

And I do hereby appoint our worthy brother, A B, to be the first Master; Brother C D to be the first Senior Warden, and Brother E F to be the first Junior Warden of said new Lodge.

And it shall be their duty, and they are hereby required to return this Dispensation with a correct transcript of all proceedings had under the authority of the same, together with an attested copy of their by-laws, to our Grand Lodge, at its next annual communication, for examination, and such further action as shall then be deemed wise and proper.

This Dispensation to continue in full force till the annual communication aforesaid, unless sooner revoked by me.

(Seal.)   In testimony whereof, I have hereunto set my hand and seal, this — day of ——, A.D. 19—.

—— ——, *Grand Master.*

COMMISSION TO CONSTITUTE A LODGE AND INSTALL ITS OFFICERS.

BY THE M. W. GRAND MASTER OF MASONS OF THE STATE OF ——.

To all to whom these presents may come, GREETING:

WHEREAS, the Most Worshipful Grand Lodge of ——, at its late annual communication, empowered, by warrant of constitution regularly issued, A B, Master, C D, Senior Warden, and E F, Junior Warden, and their successors, to assemble as a regular Lodge, at ——; and ancient Masonic usage requires that said Lodge shall be duly constituted;

Now, therefore, know ye, that I, —— ——, Grand Master of Masons of the State of ——, reposing special trust and confidence in the skill, prudence and ability of Brother ——, Past Master (or W. Master) of —— Lodge, No. —, being unable to attend in person, have authorized and empowered our said Worshipful Brother to constitute, in form, the new Lodge at ——, to be known and designated as —— Lodge, No. —, and to install the officers of said new Lodge according to the ancient usages of the craft; and for so doing this shall be his sufficient warrant.

Given under our hand and seal, at the City of ——, on the — day of ——, A.L. 59—, A. D. 19—.

—— ——, *Grand Master.* (Seal.)

This form may be readily adapted to the appointing of a proxy for any other purpose.

COMMISSION FOR REPRESENTATIVE (OTHER THAN MASTER AND WARDEN).

To all whom these presents may concern, GREETING:

KNOW YE, that we, the members of —— Lodge, No. —, reposing trust and confidence in the fidelity, skill, and Masonic abilities of our Worthy Brother ——, do hereby constitute and appoint him our representative in the Grand Lodge of ——, in case of the absence of the Worshipful Master and Wardens, at its next annual communication, to be held at —— on the — day of ——, 19—, empowering him to act in our behalf, hereby ratifying and confirming whatsoever he may do in said capacity.

(Seal.)

In testimony whereof, the Master of our said Lodge has set his hand, and caused the Secretary to affix the seal of the Lodge thereto, this — day of ——, A.L. 59—, A.D. 19—.

Attest:

—— ——, *Master.*

—— ——, *Secretary.*

COMMISSION FOR PROXY OF A MASTER, OR EITHER OF THE WARDENS OF A LODGE.

To whom these presents may concern, GREETING:

KNOW YE, that I, —— ——, Master of —— Lodge, No. —, held at —— in the county of ——, do hereby constitute and appoint our worthy Brother —— my proxy in the Grand Lodge of ——, empowering him to act in my behalf, and hereby confirming and ratifying whatsoever he may do in said capacity.

(Seal.)

Given under my hand and the seal of said Lodge, this — day of ——, A.L. 59—, A.D. 19—.

Attest:

—— ——, *Master.*

—— ——, *Secretary.*

FORMS OF MASONIC DOCUMENTS.

PETITION FOR INITIATION AND MEMBERSHIP.

*To the W. Master, Wardens and Members of —— Lodge, No. —,
F. and A. Masons:*

The petition of the undersigned respectfully represents, that entertaining a favorable opinion of your ancient and honorable institution, being unbiased by the improper solicitation of friends, and uninfluenced by mercenary or other improper motives, he is desirous of being admitted and becoming a member of your Lodge, if found worthy, promising a cheerful conformity to the usages and customs of the Order.

Place of residence is ——; age is — years; and his occupation is ——. (Signed), —— ——.

Recommended by —— ——,
—— ——.

APPLICATION FOR AFFILIATION.

To the W. Master, Wardens and Members of —— Lodge, No. —:

The undersigned, a Master Mason in good standing, and last a member of —— Lodge, No. —, located at ——, State of ——, ——, respectfully prays to be admitted to membership in your Lodge.

Dated, ——, 19—.

Signed, —— ——.
Recommended by —— ——.

REPORT OF COMMITTEE ON APPLICATION.

The Committee upon the application of ——, report favorably (or unfavorably).

Signed, —— ——,
—— ——; } Committee.
Dated, ——, 19—. —— ——.

NOTICE FOR PAYMENT OF DUES.

HALL OF —— LODGE, No. —. ——, 19.

Brother —— :

Take notice, that your Lodge dues for the present year are now due, and payable on or before the ——.

The amount is $—, on payment of which I shall be pleased to hand you a receipt.   Fraternally,
    (Seal.)
                        ——— ———, *Secretary*.

TO SHOW CAUSE WHY MEMBER SHOULD NOT PAY DUES, OR BE STRUCK FROM ROLL OF MEMBERS.

                    HALL OF —— LODGE, No. —.
                        ——, 19—.

To Brother ——:

You will take notice that you are required to pay the sum of $—, being the amount of dues owing by you to —— Lodge, No. —, or show cause at the next stated communication of the Lodge, to be held on the — day of ——, 19—, at — o'clock, P.M., why your name should not be stricken from the roll of members, as provided by sec. — of the by-laws of this Lodge.
        By order of the Lodge.
    Seal.)
                        ——— ———, *Secretary*.

APPLICATION FOR DEGREES BY A PERSON WHO HAS BEEN ELECTED BY ANOTHER LODGE, OR HAS RECEIVED ONE OR MORE DEGREES THEREIN.

To the W. Master, Wardens and Members of —— *Lodge, No.* —, *F. and A. M.:*

The undersigned respectfully shows that, on or about the — day of ——, 19—, he was duly elected as a candidate for the three degrees of Masonry by —— Lodge, No. —, located at ——, where he then resided, and thereafter duly received the first degree (or first and second degrees) of Masonry in said Lodge; that, for the sake of greater convenience (or other good cause), your petitioner prays that he may receive the remaining degrees in your Lodge.

The consent of —— Lodge is hereto annexed (or show it to be impossible to obtain consent).
    Dated, ——, 19—.
                        Signed,
    Recommender. ——— ———.   ——— ———.

APPLICATION FOR DISPENSATION TO AVOID DELAY.

HALL OF —— LODGE, No. —.
—, 19—.

To the M. W. —— Grand Master of Masons of the State of ——:

M. W. SIR: Mr. A B, having duly presented his application to be initiated, passed, and raised to the sublime degree of Master Mason in —— Lodge, No. —, and imperative circumstances [state the nature thereof], making it necessary that he should proceed without delay, respectfully asks that a dispensation be granted, empowering said Lodge to confer said degrees as soon as may be practicable.

Signed, A—— B——.

I, the Master of —— Lodge, No. —, certify that the application of A B presents a case of emergency, and recommend that the dispensation asked for be granted, and that he may receive the degrees accordingly, if found worthy.

(Seal.) Signed, —— ——, *Master.*
—— ——, *Secretary.*

DISPENSATION TO AVOID DELAY.

OFFICE OF THE GRAND MASTER OF MASONS.
—, 19—.

To whom these presents shall come, GREETING:

Application having been made to permit —— Lodge, No. —, under this jurisdiction, to initiate, pass and raise A B to the sublime degree of Master Mason, who is unable, for certain reasons, to wait the time prescribed by our regulations, and the said Lodge consenting thereto;

Now, know ye, that I, —— ——, Grand Master of Masons in and for said State, by virtue of the power and authority in me vested, do hereby authorize and empower said Lodge to proceed and confer the degrees without delay on said A B, in accordance with the ancient usages and customs of Freemasonry, and not otherwise; and for so doing these presents shall be their sufficient warrant.

(Seal.) Given under my hand, and the private seal of Grand Master, this — day of ——, 19—.
—— ——, *Grand Master.*

18

WORSHIPFUL MASTER'S ASSISTANT.

NOTICE OF APPOINTMENT OF COMMITTEE.

HALL OF —— LODGE, No. —, ——, 19—.

Brother —— ——:

Take notice, that at a stated communication of this Lodge held this date, you were appointed on a committee to examine into and report upon ——. The committee appointed consists of Bros. ——.

Report to be called for at next stated communication.

Fraternally,

——— ———, Secretary.

DISPENSATION AUTHORIZING LODGE TO CONTINUE ITS LABORS AFTER LOSS OF ITS CHARTER.

To all to whom these presents shall come, GREETING:

Know ye, that whereas it hath been represented to us by W. Brother ——, Master of —— Lodge, No. —, of said Lodge, that the charter of said Lodge has been lost (by fire or otherwise), and that the same cannot be found; and, whereas, the Master, Wardens and members are desirous of continuing the labors of said Lodge;

Now, therefore, by virtue of the power and authority in us vested, as Grand Master of Masons in the State of ——, we do hereby authorize and empower the said Master, Wardens and members of —— Lodge, No. —, to continue their Masonic labors, and to perform all the functions of a regular Lodge in as full and complete a manner as if their charter was still in existence, until the next annual communication of the M. W. Grand Lodge, to which this dispensation shall be returned.

(Seal.) Witness our hand and seal, at the city of ——, the — day of ——, A.L. 59—, A.D. 19—.

——— ———, Grand Master.

DISPENSATION TO ELECT A MASTER.

THE MOST WORSHIPFUL GRAND LODGE OF —— FREE AND AC-
CEPTED MASONS.

To whom these presents may come, GREETING .

Whereas, I have received official information that the office of

Master of —— Lodge, No. —, has become vacant by the (death
or permanent removal from the jurisdiction) of —— ——, late
Master thereof, and it is represented to me that it is important to
the welfare of said Lodge that said office shall be filled, and a
Master of said Lodge duly elected to supply said vacancy: Now,
Know Ye, that I, —— ——, Grand Master of Masons of the State
of ——, do issue this, my special dispensation, authorizing and
empowering said Lodge to proceed to fill said vacancy by the
election of a brother to serve as Master until his successor is duly
elected.

Given under my hand and private seal, at ——, this — day
of ——, A.L. 59—, A.D. 19—.

—— ——, *Grand Master.* (Seal.)

A dispensation for the above purpose is seldom called for. The
almost universal rule prevails, that in the absence of the Master, the
Senior Warden assumes the responsibilities and duties of the Master.

COMMISSION TO DEDICATE A MASONIC HALL.

THE MOST WORSHIPFUL GRAND LODGE OF —— FREE AND AC-
CEPTED MASONS.

To all to whom these presents shall come, GREETING:

Whereas, —— Lodge, No. —, in the —— of ——, has prepared
and furnished a room, in which the members thereof desire to
hold their meetings in future; and it is meet and proper that the
same should be dedicated to Masonic uses with appropriate ceremonies: Now, Know Ye, that I, —— ——, Grand Master of
Masons of the State of ——, reposing special trust and confidence
in the Masonic skill and ability of our Worshipful Brother ——,
Master (or Past Master) of —— Lodge, No. —, have thought
proper (being unable to attend in person), to nominate and appoint
him to perform the ceremonies of dedication, according to the
ancient usages of the craft, and for so doing this shall be his
sufficient warrant. And he is hereby required to report his acts
and doings in the above service to this office.

Given under my hand and the private seal of the Grand
Master, at ——, this — day of ——, A.L. 59—, A.D. 19—.

—— ——, *Grand Master.* (Seal.)

COMMISSION TO LAY A CORNER-STONE.

To whom these presents shall come, GREETING:

Whereas, —— Lodge, No. —, in the —— of ——, has undertaken to erect a building in which the members thereof propose to hold their future meetings, and having requested that the corner-stone be laid with the appropriate ceremonies of the Order:

Now, Know Ye, that I, —— ——, Grand Master of Masons in the State of ——, reposing especial trust and confidence in the Masonic skill and ability of our Worshipful Brother ——, a Past Master of —— Lodge, No. — (R. W. Brother if a Grand Officer), have thought proper, being unable to attend in person, to nominate and appoint him to lay the corner-stone of the proposed building according to the ancient usages of the craft, and for so doing this shall be his sufficient warrant. And he will report his acts and doings hereunto to this office.

Given under my hand and the private seal of Grand Master, at ——, this —— day of ——, A.D. 19—, A.L. 59—.
—— ——, *Grand Master.*　(Seal.)

PETITION FOR CHANGING LOCATION OF LODGE.

HALL OF —— LODGE, No. —.　——, 19—.

To the M. W. Grand Master of the Grand Lodge of ——:

At the last regular meeting of this Lodge, the desire was expressed, and the sense of the Lodge taken in favor of removal from the present place of meeting to ——. Your permission for such removal is therefore respectfully solicited, and the same having been obtained, the further conditions in section — of the by-laws shall be carefully complied with.

(Seal.)　　　　　　　　—— ——, *Master.*

Attest:　—— ——, *Secretary.*

APPOINTMENT OF DISTRICT DEPUTY GRAND MASTER.

THE GRAND LODGE OF —— FREE AND ACCEPTED MASONS.

To all whom it may concern, GREETING:

Know Ye, That reposing special trust and confidence in the

Masonic skill and ability of our Worthy Brother ——, a Past Master of —— Lodge, No. —, I do hereby appoint him to the office of District Deputy Grand Master of the ——, District of this Grand Jurisdiction, composed of the counties of ——, and embracing the several subordinate Lodges therein. He will be obeyed and respected accordingly.

This Commission is to continue in force (unless sooner revoked) until the next annual communication of the Grand Lodge.

Given under my hand and the private seal of the Grand Master, this — day of ——, A.L. 59—, A.D. 19—.

—— ——, *Grand Master.* (Seal.)

APPLICATION FOR A DIMIT.

To the W. Master, Wardens and Brethren of —— *Lodge, No.* —, *Free and Accepted Masons:*

The undersigned, now a member of the Lodge, and having paid all known dues and assessments, requests that he may be dimitted from the Lodge. Signed,

Dated, ——, 19—.
—— ——

DIMIT.

FREE AND ACCEPTED MASONS.

—— LODGE, No. —.

Acknowledging the jurisdiction of the Grand Lodge of the State of ——, to all whom it may concern, GREETING: This certifies that Bro. ——, whose name appears in the margin of this dimit, is a Master Mason, and was a member of this Lodge, in good standing, and having paid all dues, and otherwise complied with all legal requirements of the Lodge, we do cordially commend him to the fraternal regard of all true Free and Accepted Masons, wherever dispersed around the globe.

.... *No Variatur.*

(Seal.)

In testimony whereof, we have caused this dimit to be signed by the Master, and the seal of the Lodge to be attached, this — day of ——, A.D. 19—, A.L. 59—. —— ——, *Master.*

—— ——, *Secretary.*

DUNCAN'S
Masonic Ritual and Monitor

PART TWO

TO THE DEGREES OF MARK MASTER, PAST MASTER, MOST EXCELLENT MASTER, AND THE ROYAL ARCH

BY

MALCOLM C. DUNCAN

EXPLAINED AND INTERPRETED BY COPIOUS NOTES AND NUMEROUS ENGRAVINGS

REVISED EDITION

MARK MASTER, OR FOURTH DEGREE

THE Degree of Mark Master, which is the Fourth in the Masonic series, is, historically considered, of the utmost importance, since we are informed that, by its influence, each operative Mason, at the building of King Solomon's Temple, was known and distinguished, and the disorder and confusion which might otherwise have attended so immense an undertaking was completely prevented, and not only the craftsmen themselves, but every part of their workmanship was discriminated with the greatest nicety and the utmost facility.

It is claimed by Masonic writers,[1] that this Degree in Masonry was instituted by King Solomon, at the building of the Temple, for the purpose of detecting impostors, while paying wages to the craftsmen. Each operative was required to put his mark upon the product of his labor, and these distinctive marks were all known to the Senior Grand Warden. If any of the workmanship was found to be defective, it was a matter of no difficulty for the overseers to ascertain at once who was the imperfect craftsman, and remedy the defect. Thus the faulty workman was punished, without diminishing the wages of the diligent and faithful craftsmen. A candidate upon whom this Degree has been conferred is said to have been "advanced to the honorary Degree of Mark Master."

Eight officers are necessary to open a Lodge in this Degree, viz.: 1. R. W. Master; 2. S. G. Warden; 3. J. G. Warden; 4. Senior Deacon; 5. Junior Deacon; 6. Master Overseer; 7. Senior Overseer; 8. Junior Overseer.

[1] This Degree is said to have been instituted to detect impostors, in paying the wages to the craftsmen, as we have just seen. It is a well-known fact, that such a system of distinction was practised in the Masonry of all ages. Mr. Godwin, speaking of buildings of more modern construction than the Temple of Solomon, says: "The marks, it can hardly be doubted, were made to distinguish the work of different individuals. At the present time, the man who works a stone (being different from the man who sets it) makes his mark on the bed or other internal face of it, so that it may be identified.—*Historical Landmarks*, vol. I., p. 427.

The officers of a Chapter rank as follows, viz.: the High Priest, as R. W. Master; King, as Senior Grand Warden; Scribe, as Junior Grand Warden; Captain of the Host, as Master of Ceremonies; Principal Sojourner, as Senior Deacon; Royal Arch Captain, as Junior Deacon; Master of the Third Veil, as Master Overseer; Master of the Second Veil, as Senior Overseer; Master of the First Veil, as Junior Overseer. The Treasurer, Secretary, and Tyler, corresponding in rank with the same officers in other Degrees. These officers are filled by the officers of the Chapter under whose warrant the Lodge is held.

The symbolic color of the Mark Degree is purple. The apron is of white lambskin, edged with purple, and the collar of purple, edged with gold. But as Mark Lodges are no longer independent bodies, but always held under the warrant of a Royal Arch Chapter, the collars, aprons, and jewels of the Chapter are generally made use of in conferring the Mark Degree.

Lodges of Mark Masters are "dedicated to Hiram, the Builder."

The interior arrangements of the Lodge, and the positions of the Master, Wardens, Deacons, Secretary, and Treasurer, are the same as those in the Entered Apprentices' Degree (p. 8). The Master Overseer takes his seat on the right of the Right Worshipful Master in the east. The Senior Overseer sits on the right of the Senior Grand Warden in the west, and his Junior on the right of the Junior Grand Warden in the south.

Right Worshipful Master (giving a rap with his gavel).—Brethren, I am about to open a Lodge of Mark Master Masons in this place, for the dispatch of business. I will thank you for your attention and assistance. If there is any person present who has not taken this Degree, he is requested to retire.

To Senior Grand Warden:

Brother Senior, are you satisfied that all present are Mark Masters?

S. G. W.—Right Worshipful, I wish the pass-word might be given by the brethren.

The two Deacons thereupon go round and receive the word, which is JOPPA, in the same manner as in the Master Mason's Degree (p. 20).

R. W. M. (giving one rap).—Brother Junior Deacon, the first care of congregated Masons?

J. D. (rising on his feet, and, at the same time, giving a sign—see Fig. 20, p. 153).—To see the Lodge tyled, Right Worshipful.

R. W. M.—Perform that part of your duty, and inform the Tyler that we are about to open a Lodge of Mark Master Masons in this place, for the dispatch of business; and direct him to tyle accordingly.

The Junior Deacon then walks rapidly to the door, and gives four raps (● ● ● ●), which are answered by four without from the Tyler; the Junior Deacon gives one, which is answered by the Tyler with (●); the door is then partly opened, when the Junior Deacon delivers his message. He then returns, gives the sign (see Fig. 20, p. 153) again, and says:

The door is tyled, Right Worshipful.

R. W. M.—How tyled?

J. D.—Within the outer door, by a brother of this Degree, with a drawn sword in his hand.

R. W. M.—His duty there?

J. D.—To keep off all cowans and eavesdroppers, see that none pass or repass without due qualification, or permission from the Right Worshipful Master.

R. W. M.—Let us be clothed, brethren.

Here the officers and members put on their aprons and jewels. The Master gives two raps with his gavel, which brings all the subordinate officers on their feet; and each, standing in his place, recites his duty on being questioned.

R. W. M.—The Junior Overseer's station in the Lodge?

J. O.—At the south gate.

R. W. M.—Your duty there, Brother Junior Overseer?

J. O.—To inspect all materials brought up for the building of the Temple; and, if approved, pass them on to the Senior Overseer, at the west gate, for further inspection.

R. W. M.—The Senior Overseer's place in the Lodge?

S. O.—At the west gate.

R. W. M.—Your business there, Brother Senior Overseer?

S. O.—To inspect all materials brought up for the building of the Temple, and, if approved, pass them on to the Master Overseer, at the east gate, for further inspection.

R. W. M.—The Master Overseer's place in the Lodge?

M. O.—At the east gate.

R. W. M.—Your business there, Brother Master Overseer?

M. O.—To preside at the inspection of all materials brought up for the building of the Temple; and, if disapproved, to call a council of my brother Overseers.

R. W. M.—The Junior Deacon's place in the Lodge?

J. D.—At the right, in front of the Senior Grand Warden.

R. W. M.—Your duty there, Brother Junior?

J. D.—To carry messages from the Senior Grand Warden in the west to the Junior Grand Warden in the south, and elsewhere about the Lodge as he may direct.

R. W. M.—The Senior Deacon's place in the Lodge?

S. D.—At the right, in front of the Right Worshipful Master in the east.

R. W. M.—Your duty there, Brother Senior?

S. D.—To carry messages from the Right Worshipful Master in the east to the Senior Grand Warden in the west, and elsewhere about the Lodge, as he may direct; to assist in the preparation and initiation of candidates; and to welcome and clothe all visiting brethren.

R. W. M.—The Secretary's station in the Lodge?

Sec.—At the left hand of the Right Worshipful Master in the east.

R. W. M.—Your duty there, Brother Secretary?

Sec.—To record the doings of the Lodge, collect all money, pay it over to the Treasurer, and keep a true and correct account of the same.

R. W. M.—The Treasurer's station in the Lodge?

Treas.—At the right hand of the Worshipful Master in the east.

R. W. M.—Your duty there, Brother Treasurer?

Treas.—To receive all money from the hands of the Secretary, to keep a true and correct account of the same, and pay it out by order of the Right Worshipful Master, with the consent of the brethren.

R. W. M.—The Junior Grand Warden's place in the Lodge?

J. G. W.—In the south, Right Worshipful.

R. W. M.—Your duty there, Brother Junior?

J. G. W.—As the sun is in the south at high twelve, which is the glory and beauty of the day, so stands the Junior Grand Warden in the south, to call the crafts from labor to refreshment, and from refreshment to labor, that the Right Worshipful Master may have profit and pleasure thereby.

R. W. M.—The Senior Grand Warden's place in the Lodge?

S. G. W.—In the west, Right Worshipful.

R. W. M.—Your duty there, Brother Senior?

S. G. W.—As the sun sets in the west, to close the day, so stands the Senior Grand Warden in the west, to assist the Right Worshipful Master in opening and closing his Lodge, pay the crafts their wages, if any be due, and see that none go away dissatisfied; harmony being the strength and support of all institutions, but more especially of ours.

R. W. M. — The Right Worshipful Master's Station in the Lodge?

S. G. W.—In the east, Right Worshipful.

R. W. M.—His duty there, Brother Senior?

S. G. W.—As the sun rises in the east, to open and adorn the day, so rises the Right Worshipful Master in the east to open and adorn his Lodge, and set the craft to work, with proper instructions for their labor.

R. W. M. (rising).—After that manner so do I. It is my will and pleasure that a Lodge of Mark Master Masons be opened in this place, for the dispatch of business. Brother Senior, you will please communicate the same to the Junior Grand Warden

FIG. 19   FIG. 20

THE "HEAVE-OVER"   SIGN OF A MARK MASTER

in the south, that the brethren may have due and timely notice thereof.

S. G. W. (to Junior).—Brother Junior, it is the Right Worshipful Master's order that a Lodge of Mark Master Masons be opened in this place, for the dispatch of business. You will please inform the brethren thereof.

J. G. W. (giving three raps with the gavel (● ● ●).—Brethren, it is the Right Worshipful Master's order that a Lodge of Mark Master Masons be opened in this place, for the dispatch of business. You are ordered to take due notice thereof, and govern yourselves accordingly.

R. W. M.—Attend to the signs, brethren.

Here the Right Worshipful Master gives all the signs, in their regular order, from the Entered Apprentice to Mark Master, the brethren all imitating him. (For signs of the Entered Apprentice, or First Degree, see Figs. 1 and 2; for signs of the Fellow Craft, or Second Degree, see Figs. 3 and 4; and for signs of Master Mason, or Third Degree, see Figs. 5, 6, and 7, pp. 16, 17, and 18.)

After the duegard and sign of the Entered Apprentice, the duegard and sign of the Fellow Craft, and the duegard, sign, and grand hailing sign of the Master Mason are given in their regular order, then the Mark Master's signs are given. First, the HEAVE-OVER, which is given as follows:

Place the flat back of the *right* hand in the flat palm of the *left* hand, and hold them down in front opposite to the *right* hip, then bring them up to the left shoulder with a quick motion, as though you were throwing something over your left shoulder. In putting your hands together, do so with a sharp slap, the *palms* facing your shoulder. In old times this sign was made by interlacing the fingers. (See Richardson's *Monitor*.) This sign is called the Heave-over, and alludes to the rejection of the keystone in this Degree. (See Fig. 19.)

The second sign is made as follows:

After having made the first sign, drop the arms to each side of the body, and clinch the last two fingers of the right hand, leaving the first two and thumb open, parallel with each other, and about one inch apart. This alludes to the manner in which the candidate is directed to carry the keystone. You then raise the right hand rapidly to the right ear, still holding the thumb and first two fingers open, and with a circular motion of the hand pass the fingers around the ear, as though you were combing back your earlock, the ear passing between the two fingers and thumb. (See Fig. 20.) This sign alludes to a penalty of the obligation, to have the ear smitten off.

After having completed the sign, as just described, drop the right hand a little to the right side, about as high up as the waist, the palm open and horizontal, and, at the same time, lift up the left hand and bring it down edgewise and vertically upon the wrist of the right. (See Fig. 21.) These motions must all be made distinctly but rapidly. This sign alludes to the penalty of the obligation, and also to that of an impostor, which is to have his right hand cut off.

The sign of receiving wages is made by extending in front the right arm at full length, the thumb and two first fingers open, about one inch apart, the third and little fingers clinched, palm of the hand up. (See Fig. 22.) It alludes to the peculiar manner in which the Mark Master is taught to receive wages, so that impostors may be detected.

Here it is proper to remark that in the opening of any Lodge of Masons, they commence giving the signs of an Entered Apprentice, and go through all the signs of the different Degrees,

FIG. 21   FIG. 22

SECOND SIGN OF A MARK MASTER   SIGN OF RECEIVING WAGES

in regular gradation, until they arrive at the one which they are opening, and commence at the sign of the Degree in which they are at work, and descend to the last when closing.

The Master now reads from a text-book the following:

"Wherefore, my brethren, lay aside all malice, and guile, and hypocrisies, and envies, and all evil speaking. If so be ye have tasted that the Lord is gracious; to whom coming, as unto a living stone, disallowed indeed of men, but chosen of God, and precious; ye also, as living stones, be ye built up a spiritual house, an holy priesthood, to offer up sacrifices acceptable to God. Brethren, this is the will of God, that with well-doing ye put to silence the ignorance of foolish men. As free, and not as using your liberty for a cloak of maliciousness, but as the servants of God. Honor all men, love the brotherhood, fear God."

The Right Worshipful Master then gives two raps with his gavel, Senior Grand Warden two, and Junior Grand Warden two, which raps are then repeated.

R. W. M.—I now declare this Lodge of Mark Master Masons opened in due and ancient form, and hereby forbid all improper conduct whereby this Lodge may be disturbed, under no less penalty than the by-laws of a majority of the Lodge may see fit to inflict.

R. W. M. (to Junior Deacon).—Brother Junior, please to inform the Tyler the Lodge is open.

Junior Deacon informs the Tyler, and returns to his seat.

No business is done in a Lodge of Mark Master Masons, except to initiate a candidate in the Fourth Degree of Masonry. The Degree being under the sanction of the Royal Arch Chapter, all business, such as balloting for candidates committee reports, &c., is done in the Seventh, or Royal Arch Degree. The Lodge being opened, and ready for such business as it has authority to transact, the Right Worshipful Master directs the Senior Deacon to ascertain if there are any candidates desiring to be advanced to the honorary Degree of Mark Master Mason. The Senior Deacon then retires to the ante-room, and if he finds any candidates in waiting, he returns to the Lodge and informs the Right Worshipful Master. It is the duty of the Senior Deacon to prepare and conduct the candidate (or candidates, as the case may be), during the first part of the ceremony of initiation, and if there are any candidates for advancement, the Right Worshipful Master directs this officer to retire to the ante-room and see them duly and truly prepared. The Junior Deacon, with an assistant, then passes out of the Lodge into the ante-room, where the candidate is in waiting (we will suppose that only one is to be advanced), and requests him to divest himself of his coat and roll up his shirt-sleeves to the shoulder. The Senior Deacon and his associate do the same. When they are thus prepared, the Deacon takes in his right hand a small block of marble or painted wood, about the size of a brick, weighing five or six pounds. The Deacon's associate also takes a similar block to carry. One of

the blocks has a square engraved upon it, the other, a plumb.
(See cut.) The candidate is then furnished with a block representing a keystone, which he is requested to carry between the
thumb and two first fingers of the right hand, the other fingers
clinched with the nails tight against the palm, the arm extended
down perpendicularly at the side. The two officers carry their
blocks in the same manner. The three are styled "Workmen
from the quarries." As we have before said, the block which the
candidate carries represents a keystone, and has the initials
H. T. W. S. S. T. K. S. engraved upon it in a circle.

Sometimes this stone weighs twelve or fifteen pounds, and it
is considered a very nice job to carry a block of this weight
plumb. The blocks which the conductors carry are usually made
of wood, and are, therefore, comparatively light. The three
"workmen" now form in a line about three feet distant from each
other, the candidate being last. The door is then opened without
ceremony, and the Junior Deacon, as conductor, together with his
associate and the candidate, enter the Lodge, and march four
times around the room, halting the last time at the Junior Overseer's station, at the south gate, where the conductor gives four
raps (in couplets) on the floor with his heel (● ● ● ●).

   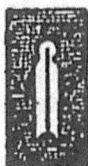   

2.   3.   9.

WORKMEN FROM THE QUARRIES

Junior Overseer—Who comes here?
Senior Deacon—Workmen from the quarries, bringing up
work.
Junior Overseer—Have you a specimen of your work?
Senior Deacon—We have.
Junior Overseer—Present your work.
The Senior Deacon presents his stone to the Junior Overseer,
who applies his small trying square to its different angles, and,
they agreeing with the angles of the square, he says:
Junior Overseer—This is good work—square work—just such
work as we are authorized to receive for the building (returning
the block to the Senior Deacon). You will pass on to the Senior
Overseer at the west gate, for further inspection.

The second workman then presents his block, and it is tried and returned the same as the conductor's.

The two workmen move on about six paces, in order to bring the candidate before the Junior Overseer's station. The Junior Deacon then instructs the candidate how to make the alarm and present his work.

Junior Overseer—Who comes here?

Candidate (prompted).—A craftsman from the quarries, bringing you work.

Junior Overseer—Have you a specimen of your work?

Candidate—I have.

Junior Overseer—Present it.

Candidate presents the keystone.

Junior Overseer (applying his square to it, and finding it does not fit).—This is a curiously wrought stone, indeed; it is neither oblong nor square; good work, true work, square work is only such as we have orders to receive; neither has it the mark of any of the craft upon it. Is that your mark? (Pointing to the letters on the keystone.)

Candidate—It is not.

Junior Overseer—Owing to its singular form and beauty, I feel unwilling to reject it; you will pass on to the Senior Overseer at the west gate for his inspection.

The conductors and the candidate pass on to the Senior Overseer's station in the west, when the same scene is repeated, and they are directed to proceed to the Master Overseer at the east gate.

The Senior Deacon here first presents his block or stone to the Master Overseer.

Master Overseer (applying his square).—This is good work, true work, and square work—just such work as I am authorized to receive and pass for the building. You are entitled to your wages—pass on.

The conductors pass on, and take their seats. The candidate then presents his keystone.

Master Overseer (applying his square).—This is a curiously wrought stone. It appears to be neither oblong nor square, and the mark upon it is not that of a craftsman. (Looking sternly at candidate.) Is this your work?

Candidate—It is not.

Master Overseer—Where did you get it?

Candidate—I picked it up in the quarry.

Master Overseer—Why do you bring another man's work to impose upon the Overseers? You will stand aside.

The Master Overseer now stamps on the floor four times with his foot, which brings up the other two Overseers.

Master Overseer—Brother Junior Overseer, did you suffer this work to pass your inspection?

Junior Overseer—I did; I observed to the young craftsman, at the time, that the stone was not such as we had orders to receive; but, owing to its singular form and beauty, I felt unwilling to reject it, and suffered it to pass to the Senior Overseer at the west gate.

Senior Overseer—I made the same observations to the young craftsman, and for the same reason permitted it to pass to the Master Overseer at the east gate.

R. W. M.—Why, you see the stone is neither oblong nor square, neither has it the mark of any of the craft upon it. Do you know this mark that is upon it?

Junior Overseer—I do not.

Senior Overseer—Neither do I.

Master Overseer—What shall I do with it?

Junior Overseer—I propose we heave it over among the rubbish. [1]

Master Overseer—Agreed.

The Master and Senior Overseers take up the keystone, and swinging it four times back and forth between them, the fourth time the Junior Overseer catches it over the left shoulder of the Master Overseer (in imitation of the sign of "heave-over," see Fig. 19), and throws it aside. At this moment all the brethren begin to shuffle around the room, leaving their seats.

R. W. M. (giving one rap with his gavel).—What is the cause of this disturbance among the workmen?

S. G. W.—It is the sixth hour of the sixth day of the week, and the craft are impatient to receive their wages.

The whole Lodge here rise to their feet and sing the following:

> "Another six days' work is done,
> Another Sabbath has begun;
> Return, my soul, enjoy thy rest,
> Improve the hours thy God hath blest."

R. W. M.—Brother Senior Grand Warden, it is my order that

[1] By the influence of the Mark Master's Degree, the work of every operative Mason was distinctly known. The perfect stones were received with acclamations; while those that were deficient, were rejected with disdain. This arrangement proved a superior stimulus to exertion, which accounts for the high finish which the Temple subsequently acquired.—*Historical Landmarks*, vol. i. p. 421.

you assemble the craft, and march in procession to the office of the Senior Grand Warden, to receive wages.

The members now form two and two (candidate behind), and march round the Lodge, singing the song:

MARK MASTER'S SONG
TUNE—"America"

Mark Masters, all appear
Before the Chief O'erseer:
   In concert move;
Let him your work inspect,
For the Chief Architect,
If there be no defect,
   He will approve.

You who have passed the square,
For your rewards prepare,
   Join heart and hand;
Each with his mark in view,
March with the just and true,
Wages to you are due,
   At your command.

Hiram, the widow's son,
Sent unto Solomon
   Our great keystone:
On it appears the name
Which raises high the fame
Of all to whom the same
   Is truly known.

Now to the westward move,
Where, full of strength and love,
   Hiram doth stand;
But if impostors are
Mixed with the worthy there,
Caution them to beware
   Of the right hand.

Now to the praise of those
Who triumphed o'er the foes
   Of Masons' arts:
To the praiseworthy three
Who founded this Degree,
May all their virtues be
   Deep in our hearts.

As they finish the second verse, each brother walks up in his turn to the Senior Warden, who stands behind a lattice-window, and thrusts his right hand, with the thumb and two first fingers open, and the third and little fingers clinched, palm up (see Fig. 22), through the hole in the window, receives his penny, withdraws his hand, and passes on, and so on until the candidate, who comes last, puts his hand through for his penny in this manner (see cut). The Senior Grand Warden seizes his hand, and, bracing his foot against the window, draws the candidate's arm through to the shoulder, and exclaims vehemently, "An impostor! an impostor!" Another person exclaims, "Strike off his hand! strike off his hand!" and at the same time runs up with a drawn sword to give the blow. The Senior Deacon now intercedes for the candidate, and says: "Spare him! spare him! he is not an impostor; I know him to be a craftsman; I have wrought with him in the quarries."

S. G. W.—He is an impostor, for he has attempted to receive wages without being able to give the token, and the penalty must be inflicted.

S. D.—If you will release him, I will take him to our Right Worshipful Master, and state his case to him, and if the penalty must be inflicted, I will see it duly executed.

S. G. W.—On those conditions I will release him, provided he can satisfy me he is a Fellow Craft Mason.

The candidate now withdraws his arm, and gives the sign of a Fellow Craft Mason. (See Fig. 4, p. 17.)

The members of the Lodge then take their seats.

S. D. (taking candidate to Master).—Right Worshipful, this young craftsman has been detected as an impostor, at the office of the Senior Grand Warden, in attempting to receive wages, which were not his due, without being able to give the token.

R. W. M. (looking sternly at the candidate).—Are you a Fellow Craft Mason?

Candidate—I am. Try me.

R. W. M.—Give me the sign of a Fellow Craft Mason.

Candidate gives the sign of a Fellow Craft.

R. W. M. (to Senior Deacon).—It is well. He is undoubtedly a Fellow Craft. (Turning to candidate.) You have attempted to receive wages without being able to give the token. I am astonished that so intelligent-looking a young craftsman should thus attempt to impose upon us. Such conduct requires severe punishment. The penalty you have incurred is to have your right hand struck off. Have you ever been taught how to receive wages?

Candidate (prompted).—I have not.

R. W. M.—Ah, this in a measure serves to mitigate your crime. If you are instructed how to receive wages, will you do better for the future?

Candidate—I will.

R. W. M.—On account of your youth and inexperience, the penalty is remitted. Brother Senior Deacon, you will take this young craftsman, and give him a severe reprimand, and take him with you to the quarries, and there teach him how to bring up a regularly wrought stone.

The reprimand thus ordered to be given to the candidate is omitted in most Lodges at the present day, but, for the satisfaction of young Masons, and the curious, we insert it here.

S. D. (taking candidate by the collar.)—Young man, it appears you have come up here this evening to impose upon us; first, by presenting work which was not fit for the building, and then by claiming wages when there was not one farthing your due. Your work was not approved; you are not entitled to any wages, and had it not been for my timely interference, you would have lost your right hand, if not your life. Let this be a striking lesson to you, never to attempt to impose upon the craft hereafter. But go with me to the quarries, and there exhibit some specimens of your skill and industry; and if your work is approved, you shall be taught how to receive wages in a proper manner. Come, I say; go with me. (Shakes the candidate severely, and hurries him off into the preparation-room.)

The Senior Deacon returns to his seat in the Lodge, and the Junior Deacon prepares the candidate for the Degree, by divesting him of his outward apparel, and all money and valuables, his breast bare, and a cable-tow four times around his body; he is also securely/blindfolded, with a hoodwink prepared for that purpose. In this condition he is conducted to the door by the Junior Deacon, who gives four distinct knocks. (● ● ● ●)

S. D.—Right Worshipful, while we are peaceably at work on the Fourth Degree in Masonry, the door of our Lodge appears to be alarmed.

R. W. M.—Brother Senior, attend to the cause of that alarm.

The Senior Deacon then steps to the door, and answers the alarm by four knocks. This is responded to from the outside by one knock, which is returned by the Senior Deacon. The door is then partly opened.

S. D.—Who comes there?

J. D.—A worthy brother, who has been regularly initiated as an Entered Apprentice Mason, served a proper time as such, passed to the Degree of a Fellow Craft, raised to the sublime Degree of a Master Mason, and now wishes for further light in Masonry, by being advanced to the honorary Degree of Mark Master Mason.

S. D.—Is it of his own free-will and accord he makes this request?

J. D.—It is.

S. D.—Is he duly and truly prepared?

J. D.—He is.

S. D.—Has he wrought in the quarries,[1] and exhibited specimens of his skill in the preceding Degrees?

J. D.—He has.

S. D.—By what further right or benefit does he expect this favor?

J. D.—By the benefit of a password.

S. D.—Has he a password?

J. D.—He has not; but I have it for him.

S. D.—Give it me.

Junior Deacon whispers in his ear the word JOPPA.

S. D.—The password is right. You will let him wait until the Right Worshipful Master is made acquainted with his request, and his answer returned.

Senior Deacon returns to the Right Worshipful Master, where the same questions are asked, and answers returned, as at the door.

R. W. M.—Since he comes endowed with the necessary qualifications, let him enter, in the name of the Lord, and take heed on what he enters.

The door is then opened—the candidate enters.

---

[1] There can be no doubt that the quarries from whence the Masons received their materials were situated very near to the Temple. Mr. Prime visited one of these quarries, situated beneath the City of Jerusalem, in 1858, and thus speaks of it: "One thing to me is very manifest. There has been solid stone taken from this excavation sufficient to build the walls of Jerusalem and the Temple of Solomon. The size of many of the stones taken from here appears to be very great. I know of no place to which the stone can have been carried but to these works, and I know of no other quarries in the neighborhood from which the great stone of the walls would seem to have come. These two connected ideas impelled me strongly toward the belief that this was the ancient quarry whence the city was built; and when the magnitude of the excavation between the two opposing hills and of this cavern is considered, it is, to say the least of it, a difficult question to answer, what has become of the stone once here, on any other theory than that I have suggested."—*Tent-Life in the Holy Land*, p. 118.

Another modern traveller, speaking of this quarry, says: "I have penetrated it for nearly half a mile, and seen there many large stones already cut, which were prepared for work but never removed. This new discovery is one of the greatest wonders of Jerusalem. It seems to extend under the Temple itself, and the stones were all finished and dressed there, and then raised up at the very spot for their appropriation."—*Christian Witness*, September 11, 1857.

S. D. (approaching candidate with a mallet and engraving chisel in his hands).—Brother, it becomes my duty to place a mark upon you which you will probably carry to your grave. As an Entered Apprentice, you were received upon one point of the compasses, pressing your naked left breast; as a Fellow Craft Mason, you were received upon the angle of a square, pressing your naked right breast; as a Master Mason, you were received upon both points of the compasses, extending from your naked left to the right breast. They were then explained to you. The chisel and mallet (placing the edge of the chisel against his breast) are instruments used by operative masons to hew, cut, carve, and indent their work; but we, as Free and Accepted Masons, make use of them for a more noble and glorious purpose. We use them to hew, cut, carve, and indent the mind. And, as a Mark Master Mason, we receive you upon the edge of the indenting chisel, and under the pressure of the mallet.

As he pronounces the last words, he braces his feet, raises his mallet, makes two or three false motions, and gives a violent blow upon the head of the chisel; throws down mallet and chisel, takes hold of the candidate's left arm.[1]

"Follow me."

They walk four times round the Lodge, and each time, as he passes the stations of the Master, and Senior and Junior Grand Wardens, they each give one loud rap with their mallet. The Master, in the mean time, reads from a text-book the following passages of Scripture: (●)

"The stone which the builders refused is become the head stone of the corner."—*Psalm* CXVIII. 22. (● ●)

Did ye never read in the Scriptures, "The stone which the builders rejected is become the head of the corner"?—*Gospel of St. Matthew* XXI. 42. (● ● ●)

And have you not read this Scripture, "The stone which the builders rejected is become the head of the corner"?—*Mark* XII. 10. (● ● ● ●)

What is this, then, that is written, "The stone which the builders rejected is become the head of the corner"?—*Luke* XX. 17.

The reading is so timed as to be completed just as the candidate arrives at the Junior Warden's post, who gives an alarm of four knocks, and the same questions are asked, and answers returned, as at the door.

The Junior Grand Warden directs him to his Senior, who, on

---

[1] The boodwink is raised from over the candidate's eyes while this scene is being enacted, after which it is replaced again, and he is marched around the room four times.

his arrival, gives four raps, and the like questions are asked and answered. From thence he is directed to the Right Worshipful Master in the east, where the same questions are asked and the same answers are given. The Master then orders that the candidate be conducted back to the Senior Warden in the west, and be taught by him to approach the east by four upright, regular steps, his feet forming a square, and body erect at the altar. The candidate then kneels, and receives the obligation, as follows:—

I, Peter Gabe, of my own free-will and accord, in the presence of Almighty God, and this Right Worshipful Lodge of Mark Master Masons, erected to him and dedicated to Hiram the Builder, do hereby and hereon, in addition to my former obligations, most solemnly and sincerely promise and swear, that I will not give the secrets of a Mark Master Mason to any one of an inferior degree, nor to any other person in the known world, except it be a true and lawful brother, or brethren, of this degree; and not unto him nor unto them whom I shall hear so to be, but unto him and them only whom I shall find so to be, after strict trial and due examination, or lawful information given. Furthermore do I promise and swear, that I will support the Constitution of the General Grand Royal Arch Chapter of the United States of America, also the Grand Royal Arch Chapter of this State, under which this Lodge is held, and conform to all the by-laws, rules, and regulations of this or any other Lodge of Mark Master Masons, of which I may at any time hereafter become a member. Furthermore do I promise and swear, that I will obey all regular signs and summonses given, handed, sent, or thrown to me from the hand of a brother Mark Master Mason, or from the body of a just and legally constituted Lodge of such, provided it be within the length of my cable-tow. Furthermore do I promise and swear, that I will not wrong this Lodge, or a brother of this Degree, to the value of his wages (or one penny), myself, knowingly, nor suffer it to be done by others, if in my power to prevent it. Furthermore do I promise and swear, that I will not sell, swap, barter, or exchange my mark, which I shall hereafter choose, after it has been recorded in the book of marks, for any other one, unless it be a dead mark, or one of an older date, nor will I pledge it a second time until it is lawfully redeemed from the first pledge. Furthermore do I promise and swear, that I will receive a brother's mark when offered to me requesting a favor, and grant him his request if in my power; and if it is not in my power to grant his request, I will return him his mark with the value thereof, which is half a shekel of silver, or quarter of a dollar. To all of which I do most solemnly and sincerely promise and swear, with a fixed and steady purpose of mind in me to keep and perform the same, binding myself under no less penalty than to have my right ear smitten off, that I may forever be unable to hear the word, and my right hand chopped off, as the penalty of an impostor, if I should ever prove wilfully guilty of violating any part of this my solemn oath, or obligation, of a Mark Master Mason. So help me God, and make me steadfast to keep and perform the same.

R. W. M.—Detach your hand and kiss the book four times.

As soon as the candidate has taken the obligation, some brother makes an alarm on the outside of the door.

J. D. (rising.)—There is an alarm at the door, Right Worshipful.

R. W. M.—Attend to the alarm, brother, and see who comes there.

Junior Deacon inquires the cause of the alarm, and returns with a letter for the Right Worshipful Master, who opens it and reads as follows, or something to this effect:—

To the Right Worshipful Master St. John's Mark Lodge:

Dear Brother—I am at present in a position where the possession of twenty-five dollars will greatly benefit me. Will you please see Brother Gabe, and ask him if he will loan me that amount? I regret to say that the only security I can offer for the loan is my *mark*, which I pledge until I refund him the money. Please see that he gets it, and send the money per the bearer.

Yours, fraternally,

John Jay.

R. W. M. (to candidate, at the same time handing him the mark.)—Well, can you accommodate Brother Jay with this money he asks the loan of?

Candidate receives the mark, says he has no money about him; he cannot grant the request.

S. G. W.—Right Worshipful, I can accommodate Brother Jay with twenty-five dollars, if he will leave his mark with me as a pledge.

R. W. M. (to candidate).—Will you return the mark, then?

Candidate hands it back.

R. W. M.—How is this? Do you return it without the price, and thus break your oath before you rise from the altar? Have you not sworn, that where you could not grant a brother's request you would return his mark, with the price thereof, viz.: half a Jewish shekel of silver, or the fourth of a dollar?

Candidate is generally embarrassed, and replies that all his money was taken from him in the preparation-room.

R. W. M.—Are you sure that you have not even a quarter-dollar about you?

Candidate—I am.

R. W. M.—Look further. Perhaps some good friend has, in pity to your destitute situation, supplied you with that amount, unknown to yourself: feel in all your pockets, and if you find, after a thorough search, that you have really none, we shall have less reason to think that you meant wilfully to violate your ob igation.

The candidate feels in his pocket and finds a quarter of a dollar, which some brother had slyly placed there. He protests he had no intention of concealing it —really supposed he had none about him, and hands it to the Master, with the mark.

R. W. M.—Brother, let this scene be a striking lesson to you: should you ever hereafter have a mark presented you by a worthy brother, asking a favor, before you deny him make diligent search, and be quite sure of your inability to serve him; perhaps, you will then find, as in the present instance, that some unknown person has befriended you, and you are really in a better situation than you thought yourself.[1]

The above is a true description of the manner in which the candidate was formerly taught his duty as a Mark Master Mason. In these *latter* days, however, very few Masters countenance this method of instruction, and it is therefore almost entirely discarded. The plan now generally adopted is as follows:—

After the candidate has taken the obligation, and while he is yet kneeling at the altar, the Right Worshipful Master presents him with a small metal mark (usually gold or silver), and requests the loan of a small sum of money upon it. The candidate takes the mark, but upon examination he finds that he has no money, all having been taken from him in the ante-room. He then attempts to give it back to the Right Worshipful Master, but the latter refuses to receive it, saying to the candidate:

I cannot, brother Gabe (or as the case may be), take it back:

---

[1] MARK.—It is a plate of gold or silver worn by Mark Masters. The form is generally that of a Mark Master's keystone, within the circular inscription there being engraved a device selected by the owner. This mark, on being adopted by a Mark Master, is recorded in the Book of Marks, and it is not lawful for him ever afterward to exchange it for any other. It is a peculiar pledge of friendship, and *its presentation by a destitute brother to another Mark Master, claims from the latter certain offices of friendship and hospitality, which are of solemn obligation among the brethren of this Degree.—Lexicon.*

were I to do so, I would violate my oath as a Mark Master, and so would you.

Here the Right Worshipful Master calls the candidate's attention to that part of the obligation.

The Right Worshipful Master now requests one of the brethren present to let the newly made brother Mark Master have the price of the Mark (usually twenty-five cents). Some brother here hands the candidate that sum, and he in turn hands it, together with the Mark, to the Right Worshipful Master. The Right Worshipful Master then administers the caution to candidate, beginning as follows:—

Brother, let this scene, &c. (See line 16, page 168.)

The Right Worshipful Master now takes the candidate by the hand, and says:

Arise, brother, and I will invest you with the pass-grip and word, and also the real grip and word of a Mark Master Mason.

The pass-grip of this Degree is made by extending the right arms and clasping the fingers of the right hands, as one would naturally do to assist another up a steep ascent. It is said to have originated from the fact that the banks of the river at Joppa were

Fig. 23

PASS-GRIP OF A MARK MASTER MASON

so steep that the workmen on the Temple had to assist each other up them while conveying the timber from the forests of Lebanon. The pass-word is JOPPA.[1]

Fig. 24

REAL GRIP OF A MARK MASTER MASON

[1] Yesterday morning at daybreak, boats put off and surrounded the vessel to take us to the town (JOPPA), *the access to which is difficult, on account of the numerous*

R. W. M. (to candidate).—Will you be *off*, or *from?*

Candidate (prompted).—From.

R. W. M.—From what?

Candidate—From the pass-grip to the true grip of a Mark Master Mason.

R. W. M.—Pass on.

The grip is made by locking the little fingers of the right hands, turning the backs of them together, and placing the ends of the thumbs against each other; its name is SIROC, or MARK WELL, and, when properly made, forms the initials of those two words: Mark well.

The Right Worshipful Master, after admonishing the candidate never to give the words in any way but that in which he received them, resumes his seat, when the brethren shuffle about their feet.

R. W. M.—What means this disturbance among the workmen, Brother Senior?

S. G. W. (rising).—Right Worshipful, the workmen are at a stand for the want of a certain keystone to one of the principal arches, which no one has had orders to make.

R. W. M.—A keystone to one of the principal arches? I gave our Grand Master, Hiram Abiff, strict orders to make that keystone, previous to his assassination. (Gives two raps with his gavel, which brings the three Overseers before him.) Brother Overseers, has there been a stone of this description brought up for inspection? (Exhibiting the figure of a keystone.)

Master Overseers—There was a stone of that description brought up for inspection, but it being neither oblong nor square, nor having the mark of any of the craft upon it, and we not knowing the mark that was upon it, supposed it unfit for the building, and it was thrown over among the rubbish.

R. W. M.—Let immediate search be made for it; the Temple cannot be finished without it; it is one of the most valuable stones in the whole building. (The brethren then shuffle about the Lodge again, and find the keystone, and bring it up to the east.)

---

rocks that present to view their bare flanks. The walls were covered with spectators, attracted by curiosity. The boats being much lower than the bridge, upon which one is obliged to climb, and having no ladder, the landing is not effected without danger. More than once it has happened, that passengers in springing out have broken their limbs, and we might have met with the like accident if several persons had not hastened to our assistance.—Lexicon.

There is an old tradition among Masons, that the banks of the river at Joppa were so steep as to render it necessary for the workmen to assist each other up by means of a *peculiar locking of the right hand*, which is still preserved in the Mark Master's Degree.—Historical Landmarks, vol. I. p. 438.

The Senior Warden takes the stone from the hands of the brethren, and then reports to the Right Worshipful Master as follows:—

Right Worshipful Master, the stone has been found; it was discovered buried in the rubbish of the Temple, and I herewith transmit it to you, by trusty brothers. (Two or three of the brethren carry it to the Right Worshipful Master in the east.

The Right Worshipful Master receives the keystone and places it in front of him, on the desk, upright and plumb, with the initials on it facing the whole Lodge, but more especially the candidate, who is seated in a chair in front of the Right Worshipful Master.[1]

The Right Worshipful Master gives four raps with the gavel (● ● ● ●), when all rise to their feet. (Some Lodges do not do so, but keep their seats.) When he reads the following passages of Scripture, at the end of each passage he strikes the keystone on the top with his gavel—first, one rap; second, two raps; and so on to the fourth passage, viz.:

Right Worshipful Master strikes the keystone once. (●)

"The stone which the builders refused is become the head stone of the corner."—*Ps.* CXVIII. 22.

Right Worshipful Master strikes the keystone twice. (● ●)

Did ye never read in the Scriptures, "The stone which the builders rejected is become the head of the corner"?—*Matt.* XXI. 42.

Right Worshipful Master strikes the keystone thrice. (● ● ●)

And have you not read this Scripture, "The stone which the builders rejected is become the head of the corner"?—*Mark* XII. 10.

Right Worshipful Master strikes the keystone four times. (● ● ● ●)

What is this, then, that is written, "The stone which the builders rejected is become the head of the corner"?—*Luke* XX. 17.

Master reads to candidate from text-book: "To him that overcometh will I give to eat of the hidden manna, and I will give him a white stone, and in the stone a new name written, which no man knoweth, saving him that receiveth it." (*Rev.* XI. 17.) Come forward, and receive the new name.

Candidate steps forward.

Master—Brother? I will now invest you with the new name that

---

[1] Some Lodges here call the candidate's attention to the indenting chisel and mallet, before reading the Scripture relative to the stone.

none but a Mark Master can receive. It is a circle of letters which are the general mark of this Degree.

Here the Right Worshipful Master calls the candidate's attention to the keystone before him, by pointing out to him the initials on the stone, which he is informed read as follows:—

HIRAM, TYRIAN, WIDOW'S SON, SENDETH TO KING SOLOMON

The candidate is here instructed how to read the words when challenged by any stranger, which is as follows:—

R. W. M.—Hiram.
Candidate—Tyrian.
R. W. M.—Widow's.
Candidate—Son.
R. W. M.—Sendeth.
Candidate—To.
R. W. M.—King.
Candidate—Solomon.

R. W. M. (pointing to the centre within the circle of these letters). —Within this circle of letters every Mark Master Mason must place his own private mark, which may be any device he may choose to select; and when you have selected your mark, and it is once regularly recorded in the Book of Marks of this or any other Lodge of which you may be chosen a member, you have no more right to change it than you have to change your own name.

Marks are not generally recorded; this duty is very much neglected—it should be done, and strictly enforced in every Lodge.

Master reads to candidate: "He that hath an ear to hear, let him hear."—*Rev.* III. 13.

The Master further instructs the candidate in the signs of the penalties of this Degree (see Figs. 19, 20, 21, and 22), and then presents, or points out to him on the chart, the working-tools of a Mark Master Mason, viz.: a *mallet* and *chisel*, the use of which he explains as follows:—

The *chisel* morally demonstrates the advantages of discipline and education. The mind, like the diamond in its original state, is rude and unpolished, but as the effect of the chisel on the external coat soon presents to view the latent beauties of the diamond, so education discovers the latent beauties of the mind, and draws them forth to range the large field of matter and space, to display the summit of human knowledge, our duty to God and

TOOLS OF A MARK MASTER

man. The *mallet* morally teaches to correct irregularities, and to reduce man to a proper level; so that by quiet deportment he may, in the school of discipline, learn to be content. What the mallet is to the workman, enlightened reason is to the passions: it curbs ambition, it depresses envy, it moderates anger, and it encourages good dispositions, whence arises among good Masons that comely order,

"Which nothing earthly gives, or can destroy,
The soul's calm sunshine, and the heartfelt joy."

R. W. M. (to candidate).—Brother, in taking this Degree, you have represented one of the Fellow Craft Masons who wrought at the building of King Solomon's Temple. It was their custom on the eve of the sixth day of the week to carry up their work for inspection. This young craftsman discovered in the quarries the keystone to one of the principal arches that had been wrought by the Grand Master, Hiram Abiff, and, throwing away his own work, he took it up to the Temple, where it was inspected by the Overseers, rejected as of no account, and thrown over among the rubbish. He then repaired to the office of the Senior Grand Warden to receive his wages; but not being able to give the token, he was detected as an impostor, which like to have cost him his right hand; but King Solomon pardoned him, and after a severe reprimand he was taken back to the quarries. Previous to the completion of the Temple, the progress of the work was interrupted for want of the keystone, which circumstance being communicated to King Solomon, he gave orders that search should be made for it among the rubbish, where it was found, and afterward applied to its intended use.

On the sixth hour of the sixth day of every week, the craft, being eighty thousand in number, formed in procession, and repaired to the office of the Senior Grand Wardens, to receive their wages; and in order to prevent the craft being imposed upon by unskilful workmen, each craftsman claiming wages was made to thrust his hand through a lattice window, and at the same time give this token, holding under the two last fingers of his hand a copy of his mark. (See Fig. 22, p. 156.)

The Senior Grand Warden casts his eye upon the corresponding mark in the book (where all the marks of the craft, eighty thousand in number, were recorded), and, seeing how much money was due to that particular mark, placed it between the thumb and two fore-fingers of the craftsman, who withdrew his hand and passed on; and so on, each in his turn, until all were paid off. If any person attempted to receive wages without being able to give the token, the Senior Grand Warden seized him by the hand, drew his arm through the window, held him fast, and exclaimed immediately, "An impostor!" Upon this signal, an officer, who was stationed there for that purpose, would immediately strike his arm off.

The following charge is then given to the candidate by the Right Worshipful Master:

Brother, I congratulate you on having been thought worthy of being advanced to this honorable Degree of Masonry. Permit me to impress it on your mind, that your assiduity should ever be commensurate with your duties, which become more and more extensive as you advance in Masonry. In the honorable character of Mark Master Mason, it is more particularly your duty to endeavor to let your conduct in the Lodge and among your brethren be such as may stand the test of the Grand Overseer's square; that you may not, like the unfinished and imperfect work of the negligent and unfaithful of former times, be rejected and thrown aside, as unfit for that spiritual building, that house not made with hands, eternal in the heavens. While such is your conduct should misfortunes assail you, should friends forsake you, should envy traduce your good name, and malice persecute you, yet may you have confidence that among Mark Master Masons you will find friends who will administer to your distresses, and comfort your afflictions: ever bearing in mind, as a consolation under the frowns of fortune, and as an encouragement to hope for better prospects, that the stone which the builders rejected, possessing merits to them unknown, became the chief stone of the corner.

The brethren shuffle round the Lodge again, as before.

R. W. M. (giving one rap).—Brother Senior, what is the cause of this disturbance?

S. G. W.—Right Worshipful, it is the sixth hour of the sixth day of the week, and the crafts are impatient to receive their wages.

R. W. M.—You will form them in procession, and let them repair to the office of the Senior Grand Warden and receive their wages.

Members form two and two and march around the Lodge against the sun, and sing from the text-book the last three verses of the Mark Master's Song. The Ceremony of paying the wages is gone through at the Master's seat in the east, the Master acting as Senior Grand Warden, and paying "every man a penny."

The members then inquire, each of the other, "How much have you?" The answer is given, "A penny." Some one asks the candidate the question, and he replies, "A penny." At this information, all the brethren pretend to be in a great rage, and hurl their pennies on the floor with violence, each protesting against the manner of paying the craft.

R. W. M. (giving one rap).—Brethren, what is the cause of this confusion?

S. D.—The craft are dissatisfied with the manner in which you pay them. Here is a young craftsman, who has just passed the square, and has received as much as we, who have borne the burden and fatigue of the day; and we don't think it is right and just, and we will not put up with it.

R. W. M.—This is the law, and it is perfectly right.

J. D.—I don't know of any law that will justify any such proceeding. If there is any such law, I should be glad if you would show it.

R. W. M.—If you will be patient, you shall hear the law. (Reads.) "For the kingdom of heaven is like unto a man that is an householder, which went out early in the morning, to hire laborers into his vineyard. And when he had agreed with the laborers for a penny a day, he sent them into his vineyard. And he went out about the third hour, and saw others standing idle in the market-place, and said unto them, Go ye also into the vineyard; and whatsoever is right, I will give you. And they went their way. And he again went out, about the sixth and ninth hour, and did likewise; and about the eleventh hour, he went out and found others standing idle, and saith unto them, Why stand ye here all the day idle? They say unto him, Because no man hath hired us. He saith unto them, Go ye also into the vineyard, and whatsoever is right, that shall ye receive. So when even was come, the lord of the vineyard saith unto his steward, Call the laborers, and give them their hire, beginning from the last unto the first. And when they came that were hired about the eleventh hour, they received every man a penny. But when the first came, they supposed that they should have received more; and they likewise received every man a penny. And when they had received it, they murmured against the good man of the house, saying, These last have wrought but one hour, and thou hast made them equal unto us, which have borne the burden and heat of the day. But he answered one of them, and said, Friend, I do thee no wrong: didst thou not agree with me for a penny? Take that thine is, and go thy way: I will give unto this last, even as unto thee. Is it not lawful for me to do what I will with my own? Is thine eye evil, because I am good? So the last shall be first, and the first last; for many are called, but few chosen."— *Matthew* xx. 1 to 16.

R. W. M.—Are you content?

Brethren (picking up their pennies).—We are satisfied.

LECTURE ON THE FOURTH, OR MARK MASTER'S DEGREE —
SECTION FIRST

Question. Are you a Mark Master Mason?

Answer. I am; try me.

Q. How will you be tried?

A. By the chisel and mallet.

Q. Why by the chisel and mallet?

A. Because they are the proper Masonic implements of this degree.

Q. Where were you advanced to the degree of Mark Master Mason?

A. In a regular and duly constituted Lodge of Mark Master Masons.

Q. What were the preparatory circumstances attending your advancement to this degree?

A. I was caused to represent one of the fellow crafts employed at the building of King Solomon's Temple, whose custom it was, on the eve of the sixth day of each week, to carry up their work for inspection.

Q. By whom was it inspected?

A. By three Overseers appointed by King Solomon, and stationed at the South, West, and East gates.

Q. How many fellow crafts were employed at the building of King Solomon's Temple?

A. Eighty fellow crafts.

Q. Among so large a number was not our Grand Master liable to be imposed upon by unskillful workmen presenting work unfit for use?

A. They were not, for King Solomon took the precaution that each craftsman should choose for himself a mark, and place it upon his work, so it should be readily known and distinguished when brought up promiscuously for inspection.

Q. What were the wages of a fellow craft whose work had been approved?

A. One penny a day.

Q. Among so large a number was not our Grand Master liable to be imposed upon by unskillful workmen demanding wages not their due?

A. They were not, for King Solomon took the further precaution that each craftsman demanding wages should thrust his right hand into the apartments of the Senior Grand Warden, with a copy of his mark in the palm thereof, at the same time giving this token (see page 156).

Q. To what does this token allude?

A. To the way and manner in which each fellow craft received his wages.

Q. Of what further use is it?

A. To distinguish a true craftsman from an impostor.

Q. When an impostor is discovered, what should be his penalty?

A. To have his right hand chopped off.

SECOND SECTION

Q. Where were you prepared to be advanced to the degree of Mark Master Mason?

A. In a room adjoining a regularly and duly constituted Lodge of Mark Master Masons.

Q. How were you prepared?

A. I was deprived of all metals, divested of my outward apparel, in a working posture, with a cable-tow four times around my body, in which situation I was conducted to the door of the Lodge, where a regular demand was made by four (4) distinct knocks.

Q. To what do the four (4) distinct knocks allude?

A. To the fourth (4th) degree of Masonry, it being that upon which I was about to enter.

Q. What was said to you from within?

A. Who comes here.

Q. Your answer?

A. A worthy brother who has been duly initiated, passed the degree of Fellow Craft, raised to the sublime degree of Master Mason, and now wishes for further promotion in Masonry by being advanced to the degree of Mark Master Mason.

Q. What were you then asked?

A. If it was an act of my own free will and accord, and if I was worthy and well qualified, duly and truly prepared; if I had wrought in the quarries and exhibited suitable specimens of skill in the preceding degree, and was properly vouched for; all of which being answered in the affirmative, I was then asked by what further right or benefit I expected to gain this important privilege.

Q. Your answer?

A. By the benefit of the pass.

Q. Give the pass. (Joppa!)

Q. To what does it allude?

A. To the ancient city of Joppa, where the materials for the Temple were landed when brought down from Mount Lebanon. Masonic tradition informs us that the sea-coast at that place was so nearly perpendicular it was difficult for workmen to ascend without the assistance from above, which assistance was afforded them, given by guards stationed there for that purpose. It has since been adopted as a proper pass to be given before gaining admission to any regular and well governed Lodge of Mark Master Masons.

Q. What was then said to you?

A. I was directed to wait until the Right Worshipful Master could be informed of my request, and his answer returned.

Q. What was his answer?

A. Let the candidate enter and be received in due and ancient form.

Q. How were you received?

A. On the edge of the engraver's chisel, applied to my naked left breast, and under the impression of the mallet, which was to teach that the moral precepts of this degree should make a deep and lasting impression upon my mind and future conduct.

Q. How were you then disposed of?

A. I was conducted four (4) times regularly around the Lodge to the Worshipful Junior Warden in the South, where the same questions were asked and answers returned as at the door.

Q. How did the Worshipful Junior Warden dispose of you?

A. He directed me to be conducted to the Worshipful Senior Warden in the West, where the same questions were asked and answers returned as before.

Q. How did the Worshipful Senior Warden dispose of you?

A. He directed me to be conducted to the Right Worshipful Master in the East, where the same questions were asked and answers returned as before.

Q. How did the Right Worshipful Master dispose of you?

A. He ordered me to be re-conducted to the Worshipful Senior Warden in the West, who taught me to approach to the East, advancing by four (4) upright regular Masonic steps, my feet forming a square and my body erect, to the Right Worshipful Master.

Q. How did the Right Worshipful Master dispose of you?

A. He made me a Mark Master Mason.

Q. How?

A. In due form?

Q. What is that due form?

A. Kneeling upon both knees, both hands covering the Holy Bible, square and compasses, in which due form I took upon myself the solemn oath or obligation of a Mark Master Mason.

Q. Have you that obligation?

A. I have.

Q. Will you give it?

A. I will, with your assistance.

Q. Proceed. I, A. B., &c., &c.

Q. Have you a sign in this degree?

A. I have several.

Q. Show me a sign? (Chopping off the right ear.)

Q. What is that called?

A. The dueguard.

Q. To what does it allude?

A. To the penalty of my obligation, that I should suffer my right ear to be smote off sooner than divulge any of the secrets of this degree unlawfully.

Q. Show me another sign? (Chopping off right hand.)

Q. What is that called?

A. The sign.

Q. To what does it allude?

A. To the additional portion of the penalty of my obligation, that I would sooner have my right hand striken off as the penalty of an impostor than divulge any of the secrets of this degree unlawfully.

Q. Show me another sign? (Carrying the key-stone.)

Q. What is that called?

A. The grand hailing sign of distress of a Mark Master Mason.

Q. To what does it allude?

A. To the way and manner each brother is obliged to carry his work while being advanced to this degree.

Q. Show me another sign? (Heave over.)

Q. What is that called?

A. The principal sign.

Q. To what does it allude?

A. To the principal words of this degree.

Q. What are they?

A. Heave over.

Q. To what does it further allude?

A. To the rejection of the "Key Stone" by the Overseers.

Q. How happened that circumstance?

A. Just before the completion of the Temple, our Grand Master, Hiram Abiff, was slain, as we have had an account in the preceding degree. It so happened on the eve of the sixth day of a certain week, when the craftsmen were bringing up their work for inspection, a young fellow craft seeing this piece of work, and concluding it designed for some portion of the Temple, brought it up.

Q. What followed?

A. On presenting it to the Junior Overseer at the south gate, he observed that it was neither a regular oblong nor a square, nor had it the mark of any of the workmen upon it; but, from its singular form and beauty, he was unwilling to reject it, and suffered it to pass to the Senior Overseer at the west gate.

Q. What followed?

A. He, for similar reasons, suffered it to pass to the Master Overseer at the east gate for his inspection.

Q. What followed?

A. The Master Overseer called together his brother Overseers and held a consultation, observing that it was neither a regular oblong nor a square; neither had it the mark of any of the workmen upon it; nor did they know that which was upon it, and concluding it unfit for use, agreed to heave it over among the rubbish.

Q. What followed?

A. The Senior Grand Warden informed King Solomon that the Temple was nearly completed, but the workmen were nearly at a stand for the want of a certain "key-stone," which none of them had had orders to furnish.

Q. What followed?

A. King Solomon observed that that particular piece of work had been assigned to one Grand Master Hiram Abiff; and, from his known skill and punctuality, he no doubt had completed it agreeable to the original design; ordered inquiry to be made of the Overseers, to see if any piece of work bearing a certain mark had been presented for inspection.

Q. What followed?

A. On inquiry being made it was found that there had; but it being neither a regular oblong nor a square, nor had it the mark of any of the workmen upon it; and they, not knowing that which was upon it, and concluding it unfit for use, agreed to heave it over among the rubbish.

Q. What followed?

A. King Solomon ordered strict search to be made in and about the several apartments of the Temple, and among the rubbish, to see if it could be found.

Q. What followed?

A. Search was accordingly made, the stone found, and afterwards applied to its intended use.

Q. Have you a grip to this degree?

A. I have several.

Q. Communicate it to me. (Give grip.)

Q. Has that a name?

A. It has.

Q. Give it? (Mark Well.)

Q. On what is this degree founded?

A. The key-stone to a certain arch in King Solomon's Temple.

Q. By whom was it wrought?

A. Our Grand Master, Hiram Abiff; but before he had given orders to have it carried up, he was slain, as we have had an account of it in the preceding degree.

Q. What was its color?

A. White; and to it alludes a certain passage of Scripture, which says: "To him that overcometh will I give to eat of the hidden manna, and I will give him a white stone, and in that stone a new name written, which no man knoweth save him that receiveth (or receives it).

Q. What is that new name?

A. It is composed of the words of which the letters on the "key-stone" are the initials.

Q. What are they?

A. "Hiram, Tyrian, Widow's, Son, Sendeth, To, King, Solomon."

Q. Of what use is this circle of letters?

A. It was the mark of our G. M., H. A.; it is now a general mark of this degree, in the centre of which each brother places his own private mark, to which the tie in the obligation particularly alludes.

Q. What is the price of a brother's mark?

A. A Jewish half shekel of silver, equal in value to one-quarter of a dollar.

Q. Were you, at any time during your advancement to this degree, called upon with this portion of your obligation?

A. I was.

Q. At what time?

A. While on my bended knees at the altar.

Q. Why at that particular time?

A. To impress upon my mind in the most solemn manner that I should never hastily reject the application of a worthy brother, especially when accompanied by so sacred a pledge as his mark, but grant him his request if in my power; if not, return him his mark with the price thereof, which will enable him to procure the common necessaries of life.

Q. By whom was this degree founded?

A. Our three Grand Masters—Solomon King of Israel, Hiram King of Tyre, and Hiram Abiff.

Q. For what purpose was it founded?

A. To be conferred upon all those who should be found worthy and well qualified, not only as an honorary reward for their zeal, fidelity and attachment to Masonry, but to render it impossible that any brother who should be found worthy of being advanced to this degree should ever be reduced to such extreme indigence as to suffer for the common necessities of life, when the price of his mark would procure the same.

Q. Who does a brother represent, presenting a mark and receiving assistance?

A. Our Grand Master, Hiram Abiff, who was a poor man, but for his regular and upright deportment, his great skill in architecture and the sciences, became eminently distinguished among the craftsmen.

Q. Who does a brother represent, receiving a mark and granting assistance?

A. Our Grand Master, Solomon, King of Israel, who was a rich man and eminently distinguished for his great liberality.

Q. What are the working tools of a Mark Master Mason?

A. The chisel and mallet.

Q. What is the use of the chisel?

A. It is used by operative Masons to cut, carve, mark and engrave their work.

Q. What does it Masonically teach?

A. The chisel morally demonstrates the advantage of discipline and education. (See *Monitors, it is Monitorial.*)

Q. What is the use of the mallet?

A. It is used by operative Masons to knock off excrescences and smooth surfaces.

Q. What does it Masonically teach?

A. The mallet morally teaches to correct irregularities and to reduce man to a proper level, so that by quiet deportment he may, in the school of discipline, learn to be content. (See *Monitor, it is Monitorial.*)

PRAYER AT THE CLOSING OF A MARK MASTER'S LODGE

Supreme Grand Architect of the Universe, who sittest on the throne of mercy, deign to view our labors in the cause of virtue and humanity with the eye of compassion; purify our hearts, and cause us to know and serve thee aright. Guide us in the paths of rectitude and honor; correct our errors by the unerring square of thy wisdom, and enable us so to practise the precepts of Masonry, that all our actions may be acceptable in thy sight. So mote it be. Amen.[1]

[1] The legend of the Degree is in substance as follows: "A young Craftsman found in the quarries of Tyre a stone of peculiar form and beauty, which was marked with a double circle, containing certain mysterious characters that greatly excited his curiosity. He had the ambition to produce this stone to the inspecting Mark Master as a work of his own. But as it was neither a single nor a double cube, nor of any other prescribed form, it was rejected, notwithstanding the beauty of its execution, and cast forth among the rubbish. The young man then frankly told the Master that the work was not his own, but that he was induced to bring it up on account of its perfect workmanship, which he thought could not be equalled. Some time afterward, when one of the arches in the foundations of the Temple was nearly completed, the keystone was missing. It had been wrought in the quarries by H. A. B. (*Hiram Abiff*) himself, and was marked with his mark. Search was made for it in vain, when the adventure of the young Fellow Craft was recollected, and among the rubbish the identical stone was found, which completed the work."—*Historical Landmarks*, vol. II. p. 126.

MARK OF A MARK MASTER MASON

PAST MASTER, OR FIFTH DEGREE

THIS degree in Masonry was instituted to try the qualifications of a Master Mason before becoming Master of a Lodge, and no Mason can constitutionally preside over a Lodge of Master Masons unless he has been admitted to this Degree. A Mason usually takes this Degree before offering himself as a candidate for presiding in a Master's Lodge; but should it so happen that a Mason is elected Master of a Lodge who is not a Past Master, the Past Master's Degree may be conferred upon him without any other ceremony than that of administering the obligation. In such a case it is usually done by Royal Arch Masons, acting by order of a Grand Master.

The Past Master's Lodge consists of seven officers, as follows:—

1. Right Worshipful Master; 2. Senior Warden; 3. Junior Warden; 4. Secretary; 5. Treasurer; 6. Senior Deacon; 7. Junior Deacon.[1]

The interior arrangement is the same as in the first degree, and the officers are similarly seated. (See p. 8.)

---

[1] The regular officers of a Past Masters' Lodge correspond exactly with those of a Lodge of Master Masons.

The officers of a Chapter take rank in a Past Masters' Lodge as follows, viz.: the High Priest as Master; the King as Senior Grand Warden; the Scribe as Junior Grand Warden; the Treasurer and Secretary occupy the corresponding stations; the Principal Sojourner as Senior Deacon; the Royal Arch Captain as Junior Deacon, and the Tylor at his proper station.

The symbolic color of the Past Master's Degree is purple. The apron is of white lambskin, edged with purple, and should have the jewel of the Degree inscribed upon it. The collar is of purple, edged with gold. But, as Past Masters' Lodges are held under the warrants of Royal Arch Chapters, the collars, aprons, and jewels of the Chapter are generally made use of in conferring the Past Master's Degree.

When a Lodge of Past Masters is opened in due form, the ceremony is similar to that of a Master's Lodge. If there is a candidate in waiting he is usually introduced into the Lodge as though it were open on the Mark Master's Degree, and he is made a Past Master before he is aware of it. Since the many disclosures of this and other Degrees in Masonry, it requires a great deal of tact and ingenuity to confer this Degree so. as to produce the effect desired. The candidate is elected to, the Degree in the Royal Arch Chapter, as no business is permitted to be done in this Degree except that of initiation. Formerly it was the custom for all the members to wear their hats while conferring this Degree, but now no member wears his hat except the Right Worshipful Master. We will now proceed to give the manner of conferring this Degree "in old times," as described by Richardson, and, at the close, will give the reader an idea of the modern way of conferring it. By comparing this with Richardson's work, the initiated will perceive that we have made some trifling alterations, and corrected several errors which occur in that book.

A Master Mason wishing to enter on the Degree of Past Master, petitions the Chapter, and is balloted for in the same way that a candidate would be in one of the first Degrees; but he is received very differently. Having had the requisite ballot, the Junior Deacon conducts him into the Lodge, places him on a seat, and then repairs to his own station near the Senior Warden in the west. Soon after, a heavy alarm is given at the outer door.

J. D. (to the Master, rising).—There is an alarm at the outer door, Right Worshipful.

R. W. M.—Attend to the alarm, and see who comes there.

Junior Deacon goes to the door, and soon returns, bringing a letter to the Master, who opens it, and reads aloud to the Lodge as follows:—

DEAR BROTHER—Our dear mother has been taken suddenly very ill, and the physician despairs of saving her live. Come home immediately; do not lose a moment in delay.

Your affectionate sister,
ALICE.

R. W. M. (addressing the Lodge).—Brethren, you see by the tenor of this letter to me that it is necessary I should leave immediately. You must appoint some one to fill the chair, for I cannot stay to confer this Degree.

J. W.—Right Worshipful, I certainly sympathize with you for the afflicting calamity which has befallen your family, and am sorry that it seems so urgently necessary for you to leave; but could you not stop a few moments? Brother Gabe has come on purpose to receive this Degree, and expects to receive it. I believe he is in the room, and can speak for himself; and unless he is willing to put off the ceremony, I do not see how you can avoid staying.

The candidate, sympathizing with the Master, says he consents to wait, and by no means desires the Right Worshipful to stay one moment on his account.

J. W.—I thank our brother for his courtesy, but I have other reasons, Right Worshipful, why I desire you should stay to confer this Degree to-night. In the first place, it is uncertain when I myself shall be able to attend again—then we might not get so many brethren together at another meeting; and as this is a very difficult Degree to confer, I feel that you ought to stay.

R. W. M.—Brethren, it is impossible for me to stay. You will therefore appoint some one to fill the chair. There are a number of brethren present who are well qualified to confer the degree; you will therefore please to nominate.

J. W.—I nominate our Brother Senior Warden to fill the chair.

R. W M.—Brethren, it is moved and seconded that Brother Senior Warden fill the chair this evening, to confer this Degree on Brother Gabe. All those in favor will signify it by saying aye. (Two or three of the members respond by saying aye.) Those opposed will say no. (Nearly all the members exclaim, No!) It is not a vote. Brethren will please nominate a new Master.

S. W.—I nominate Brother Junior Warden to fill the chair.

The Master puts the question with a similar result, when some member nominates Brother Gabe (the candidate), who is unanimously voted for and declared duly elected.

R. W. M.—Brother Gabe, you are elected Master of this Lodge. Will you please to step this way and take the chair?

The candidate goes forward to take the chair, when the Right Worshipful Master pushes him back, and says:

R. W. M.—Before you occupy the Master's chair, you must first assent to the ancient regulations, and take an obligation to discharge with fidelity the duty of Master of the Lodge.

The candidate having no objection, the Master addresses him as follows:—

1. You agree to be a good man and true, and strictly to obey the moral law?

2. You agree to be a peaceful subject, and cheerfully to conform to the laws of the country in which you reside?

3. You promise not to be concerned in any plots or conspiracies against government; but patiently to submit to the dicisions of the supreme legislature?

4. You agree to pay a proper respect to the civil magistrates, to work diligently, live creditably, and act honorably by all men?

5. You agree to hold in veneration the original rules and patrons of Masonry, and their regular successors, supreme and subordinate, according to their stations, and to submit to the awards and resolutions of your brethren, when convened, in every case consistent with the Constitution of the Order?

6. You agree to avoid private piques and quarrels, and to guard against intemperance and excess?

7. You agree to be cautious in carriage and behavior, courteous to your brethren, and faithful to your Lodge?

8. You promise to respect genuine brethren, and discountenance impostors, and all dissenters from the original plan of Masonry?

9. You agree to promote the general good of society, to cultivate the social virtues, and to propagate the knowledge of the arts?

10. You promise to pay homage to the Grand Master for the time being, and to his office when duly installed, strictly to conform to every edict of the Grand Lodge, or general assembly of Masons, that is not subversive to the principles and groundwork of masonry?

11. You admit that it is not in the power of any man, or body of men to make innovations in the body of Masonry?

12. You promise a regular attendance on the committees and communications of the Grand Lodge, on receiving proper notice, and to pay attention to the duties of Masonry on all convenient occasions?

13. You admit that no new Lodge can be formed without permission of the Grand Lodge, and that no countenance be given to any irregular Lodge, or to any person clandestinely initiated therein, being contrary to the ancient charges of the Order?

14. You admit that no person can be regularly made a Mason in, or admitted a member of, any regular Lodge, without previous notice, and due inquiry into his character?

15. You agree that no visitors shall be received into your Lodge

without due examination, and producing proper vouchers of their having been initiated into a regular Lodge?

Do you submit to these charges, and promise to support these regulations, as Masters have done in all ages before you?

Candidate—I do.

R. W. M.—You will now take upon yourself the obligation of this Degree. Please to kneel at the altar.

The candidate is conducted to the altar, kneels on both knees, lays both hands on the Holy Bible, square, and compasses, and takes the following oath:

I, Peter Gabe, of my own free-will and accord, in presence of Almighty God, and this Worshipful Lodge of Past Master Masons, erected to him, and dedicated to the Holy Saints John, do hereby and hereon, most solemnly and sincerely promise and swear, in addition to my former obligations, that I will not give the secrets of a Past Master Mason, or any of the secrets pertaining thereto, to any one of an inferior Degree, nor to any person in the known world, except it be to a true and lawful brother, or brethren, Past Master Masons, or within the body of a just and lawfully constituted Lodge of such; and not unto him or unto them whom I shall hear so to be, but unto him and them only whom I shall find so to be, after strict trial and examination, or lawful information.

Furthermore do I promise and swear, that I will obey all regular signs and summonses sent, thrown, handed, or given from the hand of a brother of this Degree, or from the body of a just and lawfully constituted Lodge of Past Masters.

Furthermore do I promise and swear, that I will support the constitution of the General Grand Royal Arch Chapter of the United States; also, that of the Grand Chapter of the State in which this Lodge is located, and under which it is held, and conform to all the by-laws, rules, and regulations of this, or any other Lodge of which I may at any time become a member, so far as in my power.

Furthermore do I promise and swear, that I will not assist or be present at the conferring of this Degree upon any person who has not, to the best of my knowledge and belief, regularly received (in addition to the Degrees of Entered Apprentice, Fellow Craft, and Master Mason) the Degree of Mark Master, or been elected Master of a regular Lodge of Master Masons.

Furthermore do I promise and swear, that I will aid and assist all poor and indigent Past Master Masons, their widows and orphans, wherever dispersed around the globe, they applying to me as such, and I finding them worthy, so far as is in my power without material injury to myself or family.

Furthermore do I promise and swear, that the secrets of a brother of this Degree, delivered to me in charge as such, shall remain as secure and inviolable in my breast, as they were in his own before communicated to me, murder and treason excepted, and those left to my own election.

Furthermore do I promise and swear, that I will not wrong this Lodge, nor a brother of this Degree, to the value of one cent, knowingly, myself, nor suffer it to be done by others, if in my power to prevent it.

FIG. 25   FIG. 26

DUEGARD AND STEP OF A PAST MASTER
SIGN OF A PAST MASTER

Furthermore do I promise and swear, that I will not govern this Lodge, or any other over which I may be called to preside, in a haughty and arbitrary manner; but will, at all times, use my utmost endeavors to preserve peace and harmony, among the brethren.

Furthermore do I promise and swear, that I will never open a

Lodge of Master Masons unless there be present three regular Master Masons, besides the Tyler; nor close the same without giving a lecture, or some section or part of a lecture, for the instruction of the Lodge.

Furthermore do I promise and swear, that I will not sit in a Lodge where the presiding officer has not taken the degree of Past Master Mason.

To all of which I do most solemnly and sincerely promise and swear, with a fixed and steady purpose of mind to keep and perform the same; binding myself under no less penalty than (in addition to all my former penalties) to have my tongue split from tip to root, that I might forever thereafter be unable to pronounce the word, should I ever prove wilfully guilty of violating any part of this my solemn oath, or obligation, of a Past Master Mason. So help me God, and make me steadfast to keep and perform the same.

FIG. 37

PAST MASTER'S GRIP

R. W. M. (to candidate).—Kiss the Book five times.

The obligation having been administered, the candidate rises, when the Master proceeds to give him the sign, word, and grip of this Degree, as follows:

R. W. M. (to candidate).—You now behold me approaching you from the east, under the step, sign, and duegard of a Past Master Mason.

The Master now steps off with his left foot, and then places the heel of his right foot at the toe of the left, so as to bring the two feet at right angles, and make them the right angle of a square. He then gives the sign, placing the thumb of his right hand (fingers clinched) upon his lips. It alludes to the penalty of having his tongue split from tip to root. (See Fig. 25, p. 189.)

The Master then gives a second sign by placing his right hand upon the left side of his neck, and drawing it edgewise downward toward the right side, so as to cross the three former penalties. (See Fig. 26, p. 180.)

R. W. M.—Brother, let me now have the pleasure of conducting you into the *oriental chair* of King Solomon. (Places a large cocked hat on his head, and seats him in a chair in front of the Master's chair.) That wise king, when old and decrepit, was attended by his two friends, Hiram, King of Tyre, and Hiram Abiff, who raised and seated him in his chair by means of the Past Master's grip. (See Fig. 27.)

The Master and Senior Warden now take the candidate by this grip, and raise him on his feet several times, each time letting him sit back in the chair again. The Senior Warden then goes back to his seat, the candidate rises, and the Right Worshipful Master instructs him in the grip and word of a Past Master Mason. They first take each other by the Master Mason's grip (see Fig. 17, p. 120), and, putting the insides of their feet together, the Master whispers GIBLEM[1] in the ear of the candidate. At that moment they slip their right hands so as to catch each other just above the wrist of the left arm, and raise their left hands, catching each other's right elbow, the Master saying, and the candidate repeating (in union with these motions), "From a grip to a span, from a span to a grip," afterward (almost at the same instant) letting the left hand slip up the right arm to the back of each other, the Master saying, "A threefold cord is strong," and the candidate (prompted) replying. "A fourfold cord is not easily broken." (See Fig. 27.)

The Right Worshipful Master seats the candidate in the Master's chair, places a hat on his head, and then comes down in front, and says:

Worshipful brother, I now present you with the furniture and various Masonic implements of our profession; they are emblematical of our conduct in life, and will now be enumerated and explained as presented.

The Holy Writings, that great light in Masonry, will guide you

[1] The Giblemites, or, as they are called in Scripture, the Giblim, were inhabitants of the city and district of Gebal, in Phœnicia, near Mount Lebanon, and were, therefore, under the dominion of the King of Tyre. The Phœnician word *"gibal,"* which makes *"giblim"* in the plural, signifies a mason or stone-squarer. In the Second Book of Kings, v. 17, 18, we read that "the King commanded, and they brought great stones, costly stones, and hewed stones, to lay the foundation of the house. And Solomon's builders and Hiram's builders did hew them, and the stone-squarers," which last word is, in the original, *giblim*. Gesenius says that the inhabitants of Gebal were seamen and builders, and Sir William Drummond asserts that "the Giballim were Master Masons, who put the finishing hand to Solomon's Temple." In this sense the word is also used in the Book of Constitutions, which records that John de Spoulee, who, as one of the deputies of Edward III., assisted in rebuilding Windsor Castle, was called the "Master of the Giblim." The Giblim, or the Giblimites, were, therefore, stone-squarers or Master Masons.—*Book of the Chapter*, p. 56.

to all truth; it will direct your path to the temple of happiness, and point out to you the whole duty of man.

The Square teaches to regulate our actions by rule and line, and to harmonize our conduct by the principles of morality and virtue.

The Compasses teach to limit our desires in every station; thus rising to eminence by merit, we may live respected and die regretted.

The Rule directs that we should punctually observe our duty, press forward in the path of virtue, and neither inclining to the right nor to the left, in all our actions have eternity in view.

The Line teaches the criterion of moral rectitude; to avoid dissimulation in conversation and action, and to direct our steps to the path that leads to immortality.

The Book of Constitutions you are to search at all times; cause it to be read in your Lodge, that none may pretend ignorance of the excellent precepts it enjoins.

Lastly, you receive in charge the By-laws of your Lodge, which you are to see carefully and punctually executed. I will also present you with the Mallet; it is an emblem of power. One stroke of the mallet calls to order, and calls up the Junior and Senior Deacons; two strokes call up all the subordinate officers; and three, the whole Lodge.

R. W. M.—Brethren, please to salute your new Master.

All the brethren present, headed by the Master, now walk in front of the chair, give the sign of an Entered Apprentice, and pass on. This is repeated, with the sign of each Degree in Masonry up to that of Past Master.

R. W. M. (to candidate).—I now leave you to the government of your Lodge. (Master takes his seat with the brethren.)

The Senior Warden now steps forward and delivers up his jewel and his gavel to the new Master, and each of the other officers of the Lodge does the same, taking his turn according to rank. Presently the retired Master rises.

Retired Master (addressing the Chair).—Right Worshipful, in consequence of my resignation, and the election of a new Master, the seats of the Wardens have become vacant. It is necessary you should have Wardens to assist you in the government of your Lodge. I presume the brethren who have held these stations will continue to serve, if you so request.

The new Master requests the Senior Warden to resume his jewel and gavel, when the other officers (who had left their places) also resume their seats.

Retired Master—Right Worshipful, I would respectfully suggest to you, that as the office of Treasurer is one of considerable responsibility—he holding all the funds and property of the Lodge —you should direct that he be nominated and elected by the members present. This has been customary, and if you .order a nomination to be made in this manner, I have no doubt that we shall select some one who will be satisfactory to you.

Candidate (acting as Master).—The brethren will please nominate a Treasurer for this Lodge.

Here a scene of confusion takes place, which is not easily described. The newly installed Worshipful is made the butt for every worthy brother to exercise his wit upon. Half-a-dozen are up at a time, soliciting the Master to nominate them, urging their several claims, and decrying the merits of others with much zeal; crying out, "Order, Worshipful! keep order!" Others propose to dance, and request the Master to sing for them; others whistle, or sing, or jump about the room; or scuffle and knock down chairs or benches. One proposes to call from labor to refreshment; another makes a long speech, advocating the reduction of the price of the Chapter Degrees from twenty dollars to ten, and recommending that it be permitted to pay for them in flour, or any other produce. His motion is seconded, and the new Master is pressed on all sides to put the question. If the question is put, the brethren all vote against it, and accuse the new Master of breaking his oath, when he swore he would support the Constitution of the General Grand Royal Arch Chapter, which establishes the price of the four Chapter Degrees at twenty dollars. If the Master attempts to exercise the power of the gavel, it often has the contrary effect; for if he gives more than one rap, and calls to order, every one obeys the signal with the utmost promptness, and drops on the nearest seat. The next instant, before the Master can utter a word, all are on their feet again, and as noisy as ever. Some brother now proposes that the Lodge be closed; another one hopes it will be closed in a short way.

Retired Master (to candidate).—Right Worshipful, it is moved and seconded that this Lodge be closed. You can close it as you please. You can merely declare the Lodge closed, or in any other way.

The candidate, being much embarrassed, will often attempt to close the Lodge by rapping with his gavel, and declaring it closed. Should he do so, the retired Master stops him as follows:

Retired Master—Right Worshipful, you swore in your obligation, that you would not close this or any other Lodge over which you should be called to preside, without giving a lecture or some part thereof. Do you intend to break your oath?

Candidate—I had forgotten that in this confusion. I hope the brethren will excuse me.

A brother goes and whispers to the candidate, telling him that he can resign the chair to the old Master, and have him close the Lodge, if he so prefers. The candidate is very glad to do this, and cheerfully abdicates his seat.

R. W. M. (resuming the chair).—Brother, the lesson we have just given, notwithstanding its apparent confusion, is designed to convey to you, in a striking manner, the necessity of at all times abstaining from soliciting, or accepting any office or station that you do not know yourself amply qualified to fill.

The Master now delivers the lecture in this Degree. It is divided into five sections. The first treats of the manner of constituting a Lodge of Master Masons. The second treats of the ceremony of installation, including the manner of receiving candidates to this Degree, as given above. The third treats of the ceremonies observed at laying the foundation-stones of public structures. The fourth section, of the ceremony observed at the dedication of Masonic Halls. The fifth, of the ceremony observed at funerals, according to the ancient custom, with the service used on the occasion. The lecture is usually read from a Monitor, which is kept in every Lodge. (See Lecture, page 107.)

The foregoing includes all the ceremonies ever used in conferring the Degree of Past Master; but the ceremonies are frequently shortened by the omission of some part of them; the presenting of the various implements of the profession, and their explanations, are often dispensed with; and, still more often, the charge.

Such is the manner in which this Degree was formerly conferred; but, as we have previously said, the ceremonies are now much abridged. The method of initiation to this Degree now usually adopted is as follows: The candidate for the Degree of Past Master is invited into a Lodge of Mark Masters, and as soon as he is seated, some one of the brethren rises and moves that the Lodge be closed. Another brother immediately gets up and proceeds to call the Master's attention to some unfinished business or the report of some committee. This action is all a *ruse*, and only intended to mislead the candidate from their real design. He (the candidate) sits there, thinking all the while that he is witnessing the regular business of a Mark Lodge, whereas he is in reality passing the preliminary steps of initiation. One of the brethren now moves an adjournment, another rises and opposes the motion, while a third asks the Chapter to help him with a loan of money. Some one of the members will oppose the loan, and high words frequently pass between the brethren (all for effect). Finally, the Right Worshipful Master will attempt to put to vote some resolutions on the subject, and a lengthy debate ensues as to the legality of this disposition of the funds of the Chapter. After the debate has proceeded for some time, one of the brethren rises and accuses the Right Worshipful Master of corruption, and charges him in plain terms with being interested in obtaining the loan. Upon this the Right Worshipful Master indignantly repels the insinuation, and demands to be relieved from serving an,· longer as Master of the Lodge. Another scene of excitement then ensues—some of the brethren favor the removal of the Right Worshipful Master, while others advocate his retaining his position. Finally, the Right Worshipful Master refuses to serve under any consideration, and peremptorily resigns. Some of the members now urge the pretended late Right Worshipful Master to assist in instating his successor to office. This he consents to do. The candidate is then nominated, elected, and placed in the Oriental chair, etc. The balance of the Degree, from the election of the Master, is correct, as given by Richardson in the foregoing pages, only the candidate is very seldom treated so badly as is represented there. The candidate is usually relieved from embarrassment in good season by the retired Master, who resumes his seat and reads the following charge to him:—

BROTHER—The conferring at this time of a Degree which has no historical connection with the other capitular Degrees is an apparent anomaly, which, however, is indebted for its existence to the following circumstances:

Originally, when Royal Arch Masonry was under the government of symbolic Lodges, in which the Royal Arch Degree was then always conferred, it was a regulation that no one could receive it unless he had previously presided as the Master of that or some other Lodge; and this restriction was made because the Royal Arch was deemed too important a Degree to be conferred only on Master Masons.

But, as by confining the Royal Arch to those only who had been actually elected as the presiding officers of their Lodges, the extension of the Degree would have been materially circumscribed, and its usefulness greatly impaired, the Grand Master often granted, upon due petition, his dispensation to permit certain Master Masons (although not elected to preside over their Lodges) "to pass the chair," which was a technical term, intended to designate a brief ceremony, by which the candidate was invested with the mysteries of a Past Master, and, like him, entitled to advance in Masonry as far as the Royal Arch, or the perfection and consummation of the Third Degree.

When, however, the control of the Royal Arch was taken from the symbolic Lodges and intrusted to a distinct organization—

that, namely, of Chapters—the regulation continued to be observed, for it was doubtful to many whether it could legally be abolished; and, as the law still requires that the august Degree of Royal Arch shall be restricted to Past Masters, our candidates are made to pass the chair simply as a preparation and qualification toward being invested with the solemn instructions of the Royal Arch.

The ceremony of passing the chair, or making you in this manner a Past Master, does not, however, confer upon you any official rank outside of the Chapter, nor can you in a symbolic Lodge claim any peculiar privileges in consequence of your having received in the Chapter the investiture of the Past Master's Degree. Those who receive the Degree in symbolic Lodges as a part of the installation service, when elected to preside, have been properly called "Actual Past Masters," while those who pass through the ceremony in a Chapter, as simply preparatory to taking the Royal Arch, are distinguished as "Virtual Past Masters," to show that, with the investiture of the secrets, they have not received the rights and prerogatives of the Degree.

With this brief explanation of the reason why this Degree is now conferred upon you, and why you have been permitted to occupy the chair, you will retire, and suffer yourself to be prepared for those further and profounder researches into Masonry, which can only be consummated in the Royal Arch Degree.[1]

If there is no further business, the lecture is delivered by the Right Worshipful Master, and the Lodge closed with the following prayer:[2]

---

[1] See Mackey's "Book of the Chapter."

[2] The chief object of this Degree in the United States is to exemplify the necessity of government, and to enforce upon the minds of those who are called to govern, the importance of qualifying themselves for the skilful and efficient discharge of their duties. The ceremonies of the Degree extend to no great length; but they are such as strongly to impress upon the newly elected Master a sense of his own deficiencies in the matter of government, and the need he has of promptness and energy in preserving the discipline of the Society over which he is to preside. The process of conferring the Degree, teaching by practical illustration, is apparently grave, though withal rather amusing. After the Lodge is opened upon the Third Degree, the Master receives intelligence from without that some sudden emergency demands his presence in another place. He therefore resigns the chair, and desires the brethren to elect a successor. The new Master is placed in the chair; but from various causes, too long to be enumerated here, he finds himself utterly unable to keep order, when the old Master reappears and kindly relieves him from his embarrassment, by teaching him how to command obedience; for it frequently happens that, in the plenitude of his power, a scrupulous compliance with his own ignorant and inopportune mandates has occasioned the very confusion which had appalled him.—*Historical Landmarks,* vol. II. p. 128.

PAST MASTERS—An honorary Degree conferred on the W. (Worshipful) Master, at his installation into office. In this Degree, the necessary instructions are conferred

Supreme Architect of the Universe, accept our humble praises for the many mercies and blessings which Thy bounty has conferred on us, and especially for this friendly and social intercourse. Pardon, we beseech Thee, whatever Thou hast seen amiss in us since we have been together, and continue to us Thy presence, protection and blessing. Make us sensible of the renewed obligations we are under to love Thee supremely, and to be friendly to each other. May all our irregular passions be subdued, and may we daily increase in Faith, Hope, and Charity, but more especially in that Charity which is the bond of peace, and the perfection of every virtue. May we so practise Thy precepts that we may finally obtain Thy promises, and find an entrance through the gates into the temple and city of our God. So mote it be. Amen.

LECTURE ON THE FIFTH, OR PAST MASTER'S DEGREE.—PART OF THE SECOND SECTION[1]

Question. Are you a Past Master?

Answer. I have the honor so to be.

Q. How gained you this distinguished honor?

A. By having been regularly elected and duly installed to preside over and govern a Lodge of Free and Accepted Masons. Previous to my installation I was caused to kneel at the altar in due form, and take upon myself a solemn oath or obligation to keep and conceal the secrets belonging to the chair.

Q. What is that due form?

A. Kneeling upon both knees, both hands covering the Holy Bible, square and compasses, my body erect; in which due form I took upon myself the solemn oath or obligation of a Past Master.

Q. Have you that obligation?

A. I have.

Q. Will you give it?

A. I will, with your assistance.

Q. Proceed. I, A. B., &c., &c. (See obligation of a Past Master.)

respecting the various ceremonies of the Order, such as installations, processions, the laying of corner-stones, etc. The ceremonies of the Degree, when properly conferred, inculcate a lesson of diffidence in assuming the responsibilities of an office without a due preparation for the performance of its duties.—*Lexicon.*

[1] This portion of the second section of the Lecture on the Fifth Degree relates to the induction of candidates, and is not given in the Monitors. With the exception of this, the Lecture may be found in "Webb's Monitor."

Q. Have you a sign belonging to the Chair?

A. I have several.

Q. Show me a sign? (Give sign, thumb to mouth.)

Q. What is that called?

A. The duegard.

Q. To what does it allude?

A. To the penalty of my obligation, that I would sooner have my tongue cleave to the roof of my mouth, than divulge any of the secrets belonging to the chair unlawfully.

Q. Show me another sign? (Give sign, drop your hand in from mouth in a circular manner down over your breast to your right side.)

Q. What is that called?

A. The sign.

Q. To what does it allude?

A. To the additional portion of the penalty of my obligation, that I would sooner suffer the severest inflictions of all my former penalties, than divulge any of the secrets belonging to the chair unlawfully.

Q. Have you a grip belonging to the chair?

A. I have.

Q. Communicate it to a brother. (Give the Past Master's grip. See the grip.)

Q. Has it a name?

A. It has.

Q. Give it. (Give the word. See word of Past Master.)

Q. What does it signify?

A. Stone squarer.

Q. What were you presented with?

A. The jewel of my office—which is a square, and it was hoped I would prepare a square stone in the Temple of Masonry.

Q. What were you next presented with?

A. The three great lights in Masonry, the Holy Bible, square and compasses. Within that sacred volume I would find all that was necessary for my counsel and guidance, these three great lights I was always to see in proper position when the lodge was open. If in the E. A. degree, that both points of the compasses are beneath the square; if in the F. C. degree, one point is elevated above the square; if in the Master's degree, both points are elevated above the square.

Q. What were you next presented with?

A. The charter or warrant, which would empower me to do all regular Masonic work.

Q. What were you next presented with?

A. The constitution, which I was carefully to search, and see that it was not infringed.

Q. What were you next presented with?

A. The By-laws, which I was to carefully search and see that they were strictly enforced.

Q. What were you next presented with?

A. The records, which I was to see carefully kept, that nothing improper be transmitted to paper, and have a general supervision over the duties of the secretary.

Q. What were you next presented with?

A. I, as Master should be covered; [1] while the rest of the brethren remained uncovered.

Q. What were you next presented with?

A. Last, but not least, I was presented with the gavel, which I was informed was an emblem of power, one blow of which would call the Lodge to order; and in opening and closing, the deacons would arise; two blows would call up the rest of the subordinate officers, on three blows, the whole Lodge; one blow would again seat them and call the Lodge to order.

Q. How were you then disposed of?

A. I was conducted to the chair, once so ably filled by our Grand Master Solomon, King of Israel, and it was hoped that a portion of his wisdom would rest upon and abide with me.

Q. What are the duties of the chair?

A. They are many and various.

Q. Of what do they consist?

A. In opening, instructing and closing Lodges; of initiating, crafting, and raising Masons; presiding at consecrations, dedications and installations; at the laying of corner stones of public edifices; presiding at funeral obsequies, and all other duties corresponding thereunto and connected therewith.

[1] A hat.

PAST MASTER'S JEWEL

MOST EXCELLENT MASTER, OR SIXTH DEGREE

No Mason can receive the Degree of Most Excellent Master until after he has become a Past Master, and presided in a Lodge, or, in other words, been inducted into the Oriental Chair of King Solomon. When the Temple of Jerusalem was finished,[1] those who had proved themselves worthy, by their virtue, skill, and fidelity, were installed as Most Excellent Masters, and, even at this date, none but those who have a perfect knowledge of all preceding Degrees are (or should be) admitted.[2]

[1] The Masonic tradition upon which the Degree is founded is described in the ancient Book of Constitutions, in the following words:

"The Temple was finished, in the short space of seven years and six months, to the amazement of all the world; when the cope-stone was celebrated by the fraternity with great joy. But their joy was soon interrupted by the sudden death of their dear Master, Hiram Abiff, whom they decently interred in the Lodge near the Temple, according to ancient usage.

"After Hiram Abiff was mourned for, the tabernacle of Moses and its holy relics being lodged in the Temple, Solomon, in a general assembly, dedicated or consecrated it by solemn prayer and costly sacrifices past number, with the finest music, vocal and instrumental, praising Jehovah upon fixing the holy ark in its proper place, between the cherubim; when Jehovah filled his own Temple with a cloud of glory."

[2] It is an established doctrine of the Order, that while three form a Lodge, and five may hold it, seven only can make it perfect. In such a case there requires an intermediate Degree to complete the series; for the Mark and Past Masters have been already admitted into the Craft Lodges. This Degree, as used by our transatlantic brethren, who are zealous and intelligent Masons, is called the Excellent Master, and the routine is thus stated: 1. E. A. P.; 2. F. C.; 3. M. M.; 4. Mark Master;

A Lodge of Most Excellent Masters is opened in nearly the same manner as Lodges in the preceding Degrees. The officers are, a Master, Senior and Junior Wardens and Deacons, Secretary and Treasurer, and of course a Tyler.

The officers of a Chapter rank as follows:—

The High Priest, as Right Worshipful Master; King, as Senior Warden; Scribe, as Junior Warden; Principal Sojourner, as Senior Deacon; Royal Arch Captain, as Junior Deacon. The Treasurer, Secretary, and Tyler corresponding in rank with the same officers of other Degrees.

The symbolic color of the Most Excellent Master's Degree is purple. The apron is of white lambskin, edged with purple. The collar is of purple, edged with gold. But, as Lodges of this Degree are held under warrants of Royal Arch Chapters, the collars, aprons, and jewels of the Chapter are generally made use of in conferring the Degree.

The Right Worshipful Master represents King Solomon, and should be dressed in a crimson robe, wearing a crown, and holding a sceptre in his hand.

A candidate receiving this Degree is said to be "received and acknowledged as a Most Excellent Master."

Lodges of Most Excellent Masters are "dedicated to King Solomon."

The officers of the Lodge are stationed as in the Entered Apprentice's Degree, described on Page 8. The Master presiding calls the Lodge to order, and says:

Master (to the Junior Warden).—Brother Junior, are they all Most Excellent Masters in the south?

J. W.—They are, Right Worshipful.

Master (to the Senior Warden).—Brother Senior, are they all Most Excellent Masters in the west?

S. W.—They are, Right Worshipful.

Master—They are also in the east.

Master gives one rap, which calls up the two deacons.

Master (to Junior Deacon).—Brother Junior, the first care of a Mason?

J. D.—To see the door tyled, Most Excellent.

Master—Attend to that part of your duty, and inform the Tyler that we are about to open this Lodge of Most Excellent Masters, and direct him to tyle accordingly.

Junior Deacon goes to the door and gives six knocks, which the Tyler from without answers by six more. He then gives one

5. Past Master; 6. Excellent Master; 7. Royal Arch.—*Historical Landmarks,* vol. II. p. 669.

knock, which the Tyler answers with one, and he then partly opens the door, and informs the Tyler that by order of the Most Excellent Master a Lodge of Most Excellent Masters is now about to be opened in this place, and he must tyle accordingly. He then returns to his place and addresses the Master:

J. D.—The Lodge is tyled, Most Excellent.

Master—By whom?

J. D.—By a Most Excellent Master Mason without the door, armed with the proper implements of his office.

Master—His duty there?

J. D.—To keep off all cowans and eavesdroppers, and see that none pass or repass without permission of the Right Worshipful Master.

The Master now questions each officer of the Lodge as to his duties, which are recited by them as in the other Degrees.

Master (to Senior Warden).—Brother Senior, you will assemble the brethren around the altar for our opening.

S. W.— Brethren, please to assemble around the altar, for the purpose of opening this Lodge of Most Excellent Master Masons.

The brethren now assemble around the altar, and form a circle, and stand in such a position as to touch each other, leaving a space for the Right Worshipful Master; they then all kneel on their left knee, and join hands, each giving his right-hand brother his left hand, and his left-hand brother his right hand; their left arms uppermost, and their heads inclining downward: all being thus situated, the Right Worshipful Master reads the following verses from Psalm XXIV:

"The earth is the Lord's, and the fulness thereof; the world, and they that dwell therein. For he hath founded it upon the seas, and established it upon the floods. Who shall ascend into the hill of the Lord? and who shall stand in his holy place? He that hath clean hands, and a pure heart: who hath not lifted up his soul unto vanity, nor sworn deceitfully. He shall receive the blessing from the Lord, and righteousness from the God of his salvation. This is the generation of them that seek him, that seek thy face, O Jacob. Selah. Lift up your heads, O ye gates (here the kneeling brethren alternately raise and bow their heads as the reading proceeds); and be ye lifted up, ye everlasting doors; and the King of glory shall come in. Who is this King of glory? The Lord, strong and mighty; the Lord, mighty in battle. Lift up your heads, O ye gates; even lift them up, ye everlasting doors; and the King of glory shall come in. Who is this King of glory? The Lord of hosts; he is the King of glory. Selah."

While reading these verses, the Right Worshipful Master advances toward the circle of kneeling brethren, taking his steps only when reading those passages relative to the King of glory. The reading being ended the Right Worshipful Master then kneels, joins hands with the others, which closes the circle, and they all lift their hands, as joined together, up and down, six times, keeping time with the words as the Right Worshipful Master repeats them: "One, two, three; one, two, three." This is Masonically called balancing. They then rise, disengage their hands, and lift them up above their heads, with a moderate and somewhat graceful motion, and cast up their eyes; turning at the same time to the right, they extend their arms, and then suffer them to fall loose and somewhat nerveless by their sides. This sign is said by Masons, to represent the sign of astonishment made by the Queen of Sheba, on first viewing Solomon's Temple. (See Fig. 30.)

The Right Worshipful Master resumes his seat and says: "Brethren, attend to the signs." He himself then gives all the signs, from an Entered Apprentice up to this Degree, and the brethren join and imitate him.

Master (to the Senior Warden).—Brother Senior, it is my will and pleasure that this Lodge of Most Excellent Masters be now opened for dispatch of business, strictly forbidding all private committees, or profane language, whereby the harmony of the same may be interrupted, while engaged in their lawful pursuits, under no less penalty than the by-laws enjoin, or a majority of the brethren may see cause to inflict.

The Senior Warden repeats this to his Junior, and the Junior announces it to the Lodge, as follows:

J. W.—Brethren, you have heard our Right Worshipful Master's will and pleasure, as just communicated to me—so let it be done.

The Lodge being opened, the ordinary business of the evening in gone through with, as in the former Degrees. If a candidate is to be initiated, the Junior Deacon goes to the preparation-room, where he is in waiting, and prepares him. He takes off the candidate's coat, puts a cable-tow six times round his body, and conducts him to the door of the Lodge, where he gives six distinct knocks (which are answered by the Senior Deacon from within), and then one knock, which is answered in the same manner.

S. D. (partly opening the door).—Who comes there?

J. D.—A worthy brother, who has been regularly initiated as an Entered Apprentice Mason; passed to the Degree of Fellow Craft; raised to the sublime Degree of Master Mason; advanced to the honorary Degree of a Mark Master Mason; presided in the chair as Past Master; and now wishes for further light in Masonry, by being received and acknowledged as a most Excellent Master.

S. D.—Is it of his own free-will and accord he makes this request?

J. D.—It is.

S. D.—Is he duly and truly prepared?

J. D.—He is.

S. D.—Is he worthy and well qualified?

J. D.—He is.

S. D.—Has he made suitable proficiency in the preceding Degrees?

J. D.—He has.

S. D.—By what further right or benefit does he expect to obtain this favor?

J. D.—By the benefit of a pass-word.

S. D.—Has he a pass-word?

J. D.—He has it not; but I have it for him.

S. D.—Give it to me.

Junior Deacon whispers in the ear of the Senior Deacon the word RABBONI. (In many Lodges, the Past Master's word, GIBLEM, is used as pass-word for this Degree, and the word RABBONI,[1] as the real word.)

S. D.—The word is right. You will wait until the Most Excellent Master is made acquainted with your request, and his answer returned.

Senior Deacon repairs to the Right Worshipful Master in the east, and gives six raps at the door.

Master—Who comes there?

S. D.—A worthy brother, who has been regularly initiated as an Entered Apprentice; passed to the Degree of a Fellow Craft; raised to the sublime Degree of a Master Mason; advanced to the honorary Degree of a Mark Master; presided as Master in the chair, and now wishes for further light in Masonry, by being received and acknowledged as a Most Excellent Master.

Master—Is it of his own free-will and accord he makes this request?

S. D.—It is.

Master—Is he duly and truly prepared?

S. D.—He is.

Master—Is he worthy and qualified?

S. D.—He is.

_____

[1] "She turned herself, and saith unto him, RABBONI; which is to say Master."—St. John, xx. 16.

Master—Has he made suitable proficiency in the preceding Degrees?

S. D.—He has.

Master—By what further right or benefit does he expect to obtain this favor?

S. D.—By the benefit of a pass-word.

Master—Has he a pass-word?

S. D.—He has not; but I have it for him.

Master—Give it.

Senior Deacon whispers in his ear the word RABBONI.

Master—The pass is right. Since he comes endowed with all these necessary qualifications, let him enter this Lodge of Most Excellent Masters, in the name of the Lord.

The door is then flung open, and the Senior Deacon receives the candidate upon the keystone. The candidate is then walked six times around the Lodge by the Senior Deacon, moving with the sun. The first time they pass around the Lodge, when opposite the Junior Warden, he gives one rap with the gavel; when opposite the Senior Warden, he does the same, and likewise when opposite the Right Worshipful Master. The second time around each gives two blows; the third, three, and so on, until they arrive to six. (See Note K, Appendix.)

During this time the Right Worshipful Master reads the following verses from Psalm CXII:

"I was glad when they said unto me, Let us go into the house of the Lord. (● ●)

"Our feet shall stand within thy gates, O Jerusalem. Jerusalem is builded as a city that is compact together. (● ● ●)

"Whither the tribes go up, the tribes of the Lord, unto the testimony of Israel, to give thanks unto the name of the Lord. (● ● ● ●)

"For there are set thrones of judgment, the thrones of the house of David. (● ● ● ● ●)

"Pray for the peace of Jerusalem: they shall prosper that love thee. Peace be within thy walls, and prosperity within thy palaces. (● ● ● ● ● ●)

"For my brethren and companions' sakes, I will now say, Peace be within thee. Because of the house of the Lord our God, I will seek thy good."

The reading of the foregoing is so timed as not to be fully ended until the Senior Deacon and candidate have performed the sixth revolution. Immediately after this the Senior Deacon and candidate arrive at the Junior Warden's station in the south, where the same questions are asked and the same answers returned as at the door. (Who comes there? &c.) The Junior Warden then directs the candidate to pass on to the Senior Warden in the west, for further examination; where the same questions are asked and answers returned as before. The Senior Warden directs him to be conducted to the Right Worshipful Master in the east, for further examination. The Right Worshipful Master asks the same questions and receives the same answers as before.

Master (to Senior Deacon).—Please to conduct the candidate back to the west, from whence he came, and put him in the care of the Senior Warden, and request him to teach the candidate how to approach the east, by advancing upon six upright regular steps to the sixth step, and place him in a position to take upon him the solemn oath, or obligation, of a Most Excellent Master Mason.

The candidate is conducted back to the west, and the Senior Warden teaches him how to approach the east in this Degree. First, by taking the first step in Masonry, as in the Entered Apprentice's Degree, that is, stepping off with the left foot, and bringing up the right foot so as to form a square; then taking the steps as directed in the Fellow Craft Degree, and so on up to this one—beginning always with the Entered Apprentice's step. (See Fig. 14, p. 93.)

On arriving at the altar the candidate kneels on both knees, and places both hands on the Bible, square, and compasses. The Master then comes forward and addresses him:

Master—Brother, you are now placed in a proper position to take upon you the solemn oath or obligation of a Most Excellent Master Mason, which I assure you, as before, is neither to affect your religion nor politics. If you are willing to take it, repeat your name and say after me:

I, Peter Gabe, of my own free-will and accord, in presence of Almighty God and this Lodge of Most Excellent Master Masons, erected to Him and dedicated to King Solomon, do hereby and hereon, most solemnly and sincerely promise and swear, in addition to my former obligations, that I will not give the secrets of Most Excellent Master to any one of an inferior Degree, nor to any person in the known world, except it be to a true and lawful brother of this Degree, and within the body of a just and lawfully constituted Lodge of such; and not unto him nor them whom I shall hear so to be, but unto him and them only whom I shall find so to be, after strict trial and due examination, or lawful information.

Furthermore do I promise and swear, that I will obey all regular signs and summonses handed, sent, or thrown to me from a brother of this Degree, or from the body of a just and lawfully constituted Lodge of such; provided it be within the length of my cable-tow.

Furthermore do I promise and swear, that I will support the Constitution of the General Grand Royal Arch Chapter of the United States; also, that of the Grand Chapter of this State, under which this Lodge is held, and conform to all the by-laws, rules, and regulations of this, or any other Lodge of which I may here-after become a member.

Furthermore do I promise and swear, that I will aid and assist all poor and indigent brethren of this Degree, their widows and orphans, wheresoever dispersed around the globe, as far as in my power, without injuring myself or family.

Furthermore do I promise and swear, that the secrets of a

Fig. 28

SIGN OF A MOST EXCELLENT MASTER

brother of this Degree, given to me in charge as such, and I knowing them to be such, shall remain as secret and inviolable in my breast as in his own, murder and treason excepted, and the same left to my own free-will and choice.

Furthermore do I promise and swear, that I will not wrong this

Lodge of Most Excellent Master Masons, nor a brother of this Degree, to the value of any thing, knowingly, myself, nor suffer it to be done by others if in my power to prevent it.

Furthermore do I promise and swear, that I will dispense light and knowledge to all ignorant and uninformed brethren at all times, as far as is in my power, without material injury to myself or family. To all which I do most solemnly swear, with a fixed and steady purpose of mind in me to keep and perform the same; binding myself under no less penalty than to have my breast torn open, and my heart and vitals taken from thence, and exposed to rot on the dunghill, if ever I violate any part of this, my solemn oath, or obligation, of a Most Excellent Master Mason. So help me God, and keep me steadfast in the due performance of the same.

Master (to the candidate).—Detach your hands and kiss the book six times.[1] (Candidate obeys.) You will now rise and

FIG. 39

GRIP OF A MOST EXCELLENT MASTER

receive from me the sign, grip, and word of a Most Excellent Master Mason.

[1] We have seen in the Masonic ceremonies a constant reiteration of the number *three*, and sometimes thrice repeated, which is called giving the grand honors of Masonry. There must have been some cause or reason for this custom, now unknown. And I will venture to say, that its original intention was in honor and out of reverence to the ancient Trinity. The practice seems to be kept up by the Church of Rome, which goes to corroborate this opinion. One of the rules established by the reverend mother abbess of the Ursuline Convent at Charlestown, as reported by Miss Reed, one of the novices in that institution, is, "before entering the room, to give *three knocks* on the door, accompanied with some religious ejaculation, and wait until they are answered by *three* from within." The Mason will see that this is an exact copy of his rules and practice.

The reader has observed that the number *six*, in the Degree under consideration, is particularly respected. In the opening scene of initiations, not noticed above, the candidate is prepared with a rope wound six times round his body, and is then conducted to the door of the Lodge, against which he gives six distinct knocks, which are answered by the same number from within; and, when admitted, he is walked six times around the Lodge, *moving with the sun*. On the contrary, the brethren more advanced form a procession, as above stated, and march six times around the Lodge, *against* the course of the sun. Masons from habit pass through these ceremonies, without stopping to examine into their meaning and original intention.

The Druids also paid great veneration to the number six. "As to what remains," says Mayo (vol. II. p. 289), "respecting the superstitions of the Druids, I know not

The sign is given by placing your two hands, one on each breast, the fingers meeting in the centre of the body, and jerking them apart as though you were trying to tear open your breast. It alludes to the penalty of the obligation. (See Fig. 28.)

The grip is given by taking each other by the right hand, and clasping them so that each compress the third finger of the other with his thumb. (If one hand is large and the other small, they cannot both give the grip at the same time.) It is called the grip of all grips, because it is said to cover all the preceding grips. (See Fig. 29.)

Master (holding candidate by his hand and placing the inside of his right foot to the inside of candidate's right foot) whispers in his ear—RABBONI.

Should there be more than one candidate for initiation, the ceremony stops here until the others are advanced thus far, and then they all receive the remainder together.

A noise of shuffling feet is now heard in the Lodge, which is purposely made by some of the members.

Master (to Senior Warden).—What is the cause of all this confusion?

S. W.—Is not this the day set apart for the celebration of the cope-stone, Right Worshipful?

Master—Ah, I had forgotten. (To Secretary.) Is it so, Brother Secretary?

Sec. (looking at his book).—It is, Right Worshipful.

Master (to Senior Warden).—Brother Senior, assemble the brethren and form a procession, for the purpose of celebrating the cope-stone.

The candidate now stands aside, while the brethren assemble and form a procession, double file, and march six times around the Lodge, against the course of the sun, singing from the text-book the first three verses of the Most Excellent Master's Song:

All hail to the morning that bids us rejoice;
The Temple's completed, exalt high each voice;
The cope-stone is finished, our labor is o'er;
The sound of the gavel shall hail us no more.

what was the foundation of the religious respect which they had for the number six; but it is certain they preferred it to all other numbers. It was the sixth day of the moon that they performed their principal ceremonies of religion, and that they began the year. They went six in number to gather the mistletoe; and in monuments now extinct we often find six of these priests together."—*Fellow's Inquiry into the Origin, History, and Purport of Freemasonry*, p. 818.

To the power Almighty, who ever has guided
   The tribes of old Israel, exalting their fame;
To Him who hath governed our hearts undivided,
   Let's send forth our voices to praise His great name.

Companions assemble on this joyful day
(The occasion is glorious) the keystone to lay;
Fulfilled is the promise, by the Ancient of Days,
To bring forth the cope-stone with shouting and praise.

The keystone is now brought forward and placed in its proper place; that is, two pillars or columns, called Jachin and Boaz (see pp. 71 und 83), each about five feet high, are set up, and an arch placed on them, made of planks or boards, in imitation of block-work, in the centre of which is a mortise left for the reception of a keystone; the Most Excellent Master takes the keystone and steps up into a chair, and places it into the arch, and drives it down to its place by giving it six raps with his gavel.[1]
As soon as this ceremony is through, all the brethren move around as before, continuing the song:

There is no more occasion
For level or plumb-line,
For trowel or gavel,
For compass or square.

As they come to these words, all the brethren divest themselves of their jewels, aprons, sashes, &c., and hang them on the arch as they pass round.

Our works are completed,
The ark safely seated,
And we shall be greeted
As workmen most rare.

The Ark, which all this time has been carried round by four of the brethren, is brought forward and placed on the altar, and a pot of incense[2] is placed on the ark.

---

[1] During the ceremonies two pillars are erected, each of about five feet high, and an arch placed over them, made in imitation of block-work, in the centre of which a mortise is left for the reception of a keystone; the Most Excellent Master, taking the keystone in his hand, places it in the arch, and drives it home with six raps of his gavel.—*Historical Landmarks*, vol. II. p. 128.
[2] This pot contains gum camphor or other inflammable matter.

Now those that are worthy,
    Our toils who have shared,
And proved themselves faithful,
    Shall meet their reward;
Their virtue and knowledge,
    Industry and skill,
Have our approbation—
    Have gained our good-will.

The brethren now all halt, and face inward to the altar, and beckon the candidate to come forward and join in the ceremonies, which he does.

We accept and receive them,
    Most Excellent Masters,
Invested with honor
    And power to preside
Among worthy craftsmen,
    Wherever assembled,
The knowledge of Masons
    To spread far and wide.

As they begin the next verses, each one throws up his hands and rolls his eyes upward—giving a sign of admiration or astonishment like that described (see p. 203) as having been expressed by the Queen of Sheba on first viewing Solomon's Temple —and keeps them in that position while singing these two verses of the song: (See Fig. 30.)

Almighty Jehovah,
    Descend now, and fill
This Lodge with thy glory,
    Our hearts with good-will;
Preside at our meetings,
    Assist us to find
True pleasure in teaching
    Good-will to mankind.

Thy wisdom inspired
The great institution;
Thy strength shall support,
    Till Nature expire;
And when the creation
Shall fall into ruin,
Its beauty shall rise
    Through the midst of the fire.

The brothers now all join hands as in opening, and while in this attitude the Right Worshipful Master reads the following passage of Scripture, 2 Chron. VII. 1, 4.

FIG. 80

SIGN OF ADMIRATION, OR ASTONISHMENT

"Now when Solomon had made an end of praying, the fire came down from heaven, and consumed the burnt-offering and the sacrifices; and the glory of the Lord filled the house. And the priests could not enter into the house of the Lord, because the glory of the Lord had filled the Lord's house. And when all the children of Israel saw how the fire came down, and the glory of the Lord upon the house, they bowed themselves with their faces to the ground upon the pavement, and worshipped and praised the Lord, saying, For he is good (here the Master, who is high-priest of the Chapter, kneels and joins hands with the rest), for his mercy endureth forever."

They all then repeat in concert the words, "*For he is good* (here one of the brethren, standing behind the candidate, throws a piece of blazing gum-camphor or other combustible matter into the *pot of incense* standing on the altar, around which the brethren are kneeling), *for his mercy endureth forever*," six times, each time bowing their heads low toward the floor. The members now balance six times, as in opening (see page 203), rise and balance six times more, then, disengaging themselves from each other, take their seats.

Master (to candidate.)—Brother, your admission to this Degree of Masonry is a proof of the good opinion the brethren of this Lodge entertain of your Masonic abilities. Let this consideration induce you to be careful of forfeiting, by misconduct and inattention to our rules, that esteem which has raised you to the rank you now possess. It is one of your great duties, as a Most Excellent Master, to dispense light and truth to the uninformed Mason; and I need not remind you of the impossibility of complying with this obligation without possessing an accurate acquaintance with the lectures of each degree. If you are not already completely conversant in all the Degrees heretofore conferred on you remember that an indulgence, prompted by a belief that you will apply yourself with double diligence to make yourself so, has induced the brethren to accept you. Let it, therefore, be your unremitting study to acquire such a degree of knowledge and information as shall enable you to discharge with propriety the various duties incumbent on you, and to preserve unsullied the title now conferred upon you of a Most Excellent Master.

This charge closes the initiation, and a motion is generally made to adjourn, and close the Lodge.

Master (to J. W.)—Brother Junior, you will please assemble the brethren around the altar, for the purpose of closing this Lodge of Most Excellent Masters.

The brethren immediately assemble around the altar in a circle, and kneel on the right knee, put their left arms over, and join hands as before. While kneeling in this position, the Master reads the following verses from the one hundred and thirty-fourth Psalm:

"Behold, bless ye the Lord, all ye servants of the Lord, which by night stand in the house of the Lord.

"Lift up your hands in the sanctuary, and bless the Lord.

"The Lord, that made heaven and earth, bless thee out of Zion."

The Master then closes the circle as in opening, when they balance six times, rise and balance six times more, disengaging their hands, and giving the signs from this Degree downward. The Lodge is then closed as in the preceding Degrees. The following is read at closing:—

"The Lord is my shepherd; I shall not want. He maketh me to lie down in green pastures; he leadeth me beside the still waters. He restoreth my soul; he leadeth me in the paths of righteousness for his name's sake. Yea, though I walk through the valley of the shadow of death, I will fear no evil; for thou art with me; thy rod and thy staff they comfort me. Thou preparest a table before me in the presence of mine enemies; thou anointest my head with oil; my cup runneth over. Surely goodness and mercy shall follow me all the days of my life; and I will dwell in the house of the Lord forever."—*Psalm XXIII.*[1]

LECTURE ON THE SIXTH, OR MOST EXCELLENT MASTER'S DEGREE

Question. Are you a Most Excellent Master?

Answer. I am. Try me.

Q. How will you be tried?

A. By the cap stone.

Q. Why by the cap stone?

A. Because it completed King Solomon's Temple, upon the ceremonies of the dedication of which this Degree is founded.

Q. Where were you received and acknowledged as a Most Excellent Master?

A. In a regular and duly constituted Lodge of Most Excellent Masters.

Q. How gained you admission?

A. By six distinct knocks. (● ● ● ● ● ●)

Q. To what do the six distinct knocks allude?

A. To the Sixth Degree of Masonry, it being that upon which I was about to enter.

Q. What was said to you from within?

A. Who comes here?

Q. Your answer?

A. A worthy brother who has been duly initiated, passed to the degree of Fellow Craft, raised to the sublime degree of Master Mason, advanced to the degree of Mark Master, and regularly passed the chair, now wishes for further promotion in Masonry, by being received and acknowledged as a Most Excellent Master.

Q. What were you then asked?

A. If it was an act of my own free will and accord; if I was worthy and well qualified; if I had made suitable proficiency in the preceding degree, and was properly vouched for, all of which

[1] "Recent discoveries in Ethiopia have brought to light," says a writer on the Egyptian antiquities in the British Museum, "arches regularly constructed with the *keystone.* The same arch is also found in the vaulted roof of a small building or portico in the Egyptian style, which is attached to one of the sides of the largest pyramids at Assour. At Jebel Barkal, Mr. Waddington observed an arched roof in a portico attached to a pyramid." These pyramids are supposed to be of higher antiquity than the building of King Solomon's Temple.—*Theo. Phil.*, p. 203.

being answered in the affirmative, I was asked by what right or benefit I expected to gain this important privilege.

Q. Your answer?

A. By the benefit of the pass.

Q. Give it. (Word—Mark Well.)

Q. What was then said to you?

A. I was directed to wait until the Right Worshipful Master could be informed of my request, and his answer returned.

Q. What was his answer?

A. Let the candidate enter.

Q. How were you then disposed of?

A. I was conducted *six* times round the Lodge, to the Worshipful Senior Warden in the West, where the same questions were asked and answers returned as at the door.

Q. How did the Worshipful Senior Warden dispose of you?

A. He directed me to be conducted to the Right Worshipful Master in the East, where the same questions were asked and answers returned as before.

Q. How did the Right Worshipful Master dispose of you?

A. He ordered me to be conducted to the Worshipful Senior Warden in the West, who taught me to approach to the altar, advancing by six upright Masonic steps, my feet forming a square and my body erect, to the Right Worshipful Master.

Q. What did the Right Worshipful Master do with you?

A. He made me a Most Excellent Master.

Q. How?

A. In due form.

Q. What is that due form?

A. Kneeling upon both knees, both hands covering the Holy Bible, square and compasses, my body erect, in which due form I took upon myself the solemn oath of a Most Excellent Master.

Q. Have you that obligation?

A. I have.

Q. Will you give it?

A. I will with your assistance.

Q. Proceed. (I, A. B., etc., etc. See obligation.)

Q. Have you a sign belonging to this degree?

A. I have several.

Q. Show me a sign. (Give sign.)

Q. What is that called?

A. A duegard.

Q. Show me another sign. (Gives sign.)

Q. What is that called?

A The sign.

Q. To what does it allude?

A. To the penalty of my obligation, that I would have my breast torn open—my heart torn out and exposed to rot upon the dung hill, sooner than divulge any of the secrets of this degree unlawfully.

Q. Show me another sign. (Give sign of admiration.)

Q. What is that called?

A. The sign of admiration.

Q. To what does it allude?

A. To the wonder and admiration of our ancient brethren who were present and permitted to view the interior of that magnificent edifice which King Solomon had erected, and was about to dedicate to the service of the Supreme Being.

Q. Have you a grip?

A. I have.

Q. Communicate it to a brother? (Give grip.)

Q. Has it a name?

A. It has.

Q. Give it. (Rabboni.)

Q. What does it signify?

A. Good Master or Most Excellent Master.

Q. What is it otherwise called?

A. The cover grip.

Q. Why?

A. Because as this covers grips of preceding degrees, so should we as Most Excellent Masters, considering that man in his best estate is subject to frailties and errors, endeavor to cover his faults and imperfections with the broad mantle of charity and brotherly love.

Q. When originated this grip?

A. At the completion of the temple. When King Solomon entered he was so well pleased with the master builder that he took him by the right hand and exclaimed, Hail, Rabboni, which signifies Good Master and Most Excellent Master.

Q. What followed?

A. A procession was formed, the ark safely seated, the cap stone placed in the principal arch, and Lodge closed with solemn invocations to Deity.

KEYSTONE

ROYAL ARCH, OR SEVENTH DEGREE

THE Royal Arch Degree seems not to have been known to what are called *modern* Masons as late as about 1750. That portion of the old Freemasons who met at the famous Apple-Tree Tavern, in 1717, and formed the society upon somewhat new principles, that is, so far as to admit into fellowship, indiscriminately, respectable individuals of all professions, were denominated, by the non-adherents to this plan, *modern* Masons. This affair caused the division of the Masonic Society into two parties, which continued till 1813, nearly one hundred years. To the rivalry occasioned by this schism, Masonry, it is presumed, is mainly indebted for the great celebrity it has obtained in the world.

It appears that the non-conformists to this new scheme, who considered themselves the orthodox party, by rummaging among the old records of the Order, first discovered the Royal Arch Degree, which had probably lain dormant for centuries; during which time, it would appear, the society had been confined almost exclusively to operative masons; who continued the ceremonies only of the apprentice, fellow-craft or journeyman, and master mason, these being deemed appropriate to their occupation.

A society of Royal Arch Masons is called a Chapter, and not a Lodge, as in the previous Degrees. All Chapters of Royal Arch Masons are "dedicated to Zerubbabel," and the symbolic color of this Degree is scarlet. The several Degrees of Mark Master, Present or Past Master, and Most Excellent Master, are given only under the sanction of the Royal Arch Chapter; and a Master Mason who applies for these Degrees usually enters the Chapter also, and sometimes the four degrees are given at once. If he takes the four, he is only balloted for once, viz.: in the Mark Master's Degree. Candidates receiving this Degree are said to be "exalted to the most sublime Degree of the Royal Arch."

It is a point of the Royal Arch Degree not to assist, or be present, at the conferring of this Degree upon more or less than three candidates at one time. If there are not three candidates present, one or two companions, as the case may be, volunteer to represent candidates, so as to make the requisite number, or a "team," as it is technically styled, and accompany the candidate or candidates through all the stages of exaltation.

At the destruction of Jerusalem by Nebuchadnezzar, three Most Excellent Masters were carried captives to Babylon, where they remained seventy years, and were liberated by Cyrus, King of Persia. They returned to Jerusalem to assist in rebuilding the Temple, after travelling over rugged roads on foot. They arrived at the outer veil of the Tabernacle, which was erected near the ruins of the Temple. This Tabernacle was an oblong square, enclosed by four veils, or curtains, and divided into separate apartments by four cross veils, including the west end veil or entrance. The veils were parted in the centre, and guarded by four guards, with drawn swords.

At the east end of the Tabernacle, Haggai, Joshua, and Zerubbabel usually sat in grand council, to examine all who wished to be employed in the noble and glorious work of rebuilding the Temple. Since that time, every Chapter of Royal Arch Masons, if properly formed, represents the Tabernacle erected by our ancient brethren, near the ruins of King Solomon's Temple, and our engraving shows the interior arrangement of a Chapter of the Royal Arch Degree.[1] (See Fig. 31.)

These three Most Excellent Masters, on their arrival, were introduced to the Grand Council, and employed, furnished with tools, and directed to commence their labors at the northeast corner of the ruins of the old Temple, and to clear away and remove the rubbish, in order to lay the foundation of the new. The Grand Council also gave them strict orders to preserve whatever should fall in their way (such as specimens of ancient architecture, &c.,) and bring it up for their inspection.

Among the discoveries made by the three Masters was a secret vault in which they found treasures of great benefit to the craft, &c. The ceremony of exalting companions to this Degree, is a recapitulation of the adventures of these three Most Excellent Masters, and hence it is that three candidates are necessary for an initiation.

---

[1] In America, we find an essential variation from any other system of the Royal Arch. The names of the officers vary materially, as also do the ceremonies. As in Ireland, it constitutes the Seventh Degree, although the intermediate steps are different. In Ireland they are: 1. E. A. P.; 2. F. C.; 3. M. M.; 4. P. M.; 5. Excellent; 6. Super-Excellent; 7. Royal Arch: while in America the Fourth is Mark Master; 5. P. M.; 6. Most Excellent Master; 7. Royal Arch.—*Origin of the English Royal Arch*, p. 58.

The Grand Council consists of the Most Excellent High Priest, King, and Holy Scribe. The High Priest is dressed in a white robe, with a breastplate of cut glass, consisting of twelve pieces, an apron, and a mitre. The king wears a scarlet robe, apron, and crown. The mitre and crown are generally made of pasteboard; sometimes they are made of most splendid materials, gold and silver velvet; but these are kept for public occasions. The mitre has the words, "Holiness to the Lord," in gold letters, across the forehead. The scribe wears a purple robe, apron, and turban.

A Chapter of Royal Arch Masons consists of nine officers, as follows:

1. High Priest, or Master. (Joshua.)
2. King, or Senior Grand Warden. (Zerubbabel.)
3. Scribe, or Junior Grand Warden. (Haggai.)
4. Captain of the Host (as Marshal, or Master of Ceremonies), or Senior Deacon.
5. Principal Sojourner, who represents the Junior Deacon.
6. Royal Arch Captain, who represents the Master Overseer.
7. Grand Master of the Third Veil, or Senior Overseer.
8. Grand Master of the Second Veil, or Junior Overseer.
9. Grand Master of the First Veil.

In addition to these, three other officers are usually present, viz., Secretary, a Treasurer, and a Tyler, or sentinel.

The officers and companions of the Chapter being stationed as in the engraving (see Fig. 31), the High Priest proceeds to business as follows:

High Priest—Companions,[1] I am about to open a Chapter of Royal Arch Masons in this place, for the dispatch of business, and will thank you for your attention and assistance. If there is any person present who is not a companion Royal Arch Mason, he is requested to retire from the room.

After waiting for any stranger or brother not of this degree to retire, he gives one rap with the gavel, which brings up the Captain of the Host.

High Priest—Companion Captain, the first care of congregated Masons?

[1] The members of this Degree are denominated companions, and are "entitled to a full explanation of the *mysteries* of the Order"; whereas in the former Degrees they are recognized by the common, familiar appellation of brothers, and kept in a state of profound ignorance of the *sublime secret* which is disclosed in this Chapter. This accords with the custom of Pythagoras, who thus distinguished his pupils. After a probation of five years, as before stated, they were admitted into the presence of the preceptor, called his companions, and permitted freely to converse with him. Previously to the expiration of that term he delivered his instructions to them from behind a screen.—*Fellows's Enquiry into the Origin, History, and Purport of Freemasonry,* p. 331.

Fig. 81

ROYAL ARCH CHAPTER

1. Treasurer. 2. Secretary. 3. King. 4. High Priest. 5. Scribe. 6. Captain of the Host. 7. Principal Sojourner. 8. Royal Arch Captain. 9. Grand Master of the Third Veil. 10. Grand Master of the Second Veil. 11. Grand Master of the First Veil. 12. Burning Bush. 13. Altar.

Captain (placing the palm of his right hand to his forehead, as if to shade his eyes).—To see the Tabernacle duly guarded, Most Excellent. (For this sign, see Fig. 36.)

High Priest—Attend to that part of your duty, and inform the Guard that we are about to open a Chapter of Royal Arch Masons in this place for the dispatch of business; direct him to guard accordingly.

The Captain of the Host stations the Guard at the outside of the door, gives him his orders, closes the door, and makes an alarm of three times three (● ● ● ● ● ● ● ● ●) on the inside, to ascertain that the Guard is on his post: the Guard answers by nine corresponding raps. The Captain of the Host then gives one, and Guard does the same. The Captain then returns to his post.

Captain (to High Priest).—The Chapter is duly guarded, Most Excellent.

High Priest—How guarded?

Captain—By a companion of this Degree at the outer avenue, with a drawn sword in his hand.

High Priest—His duty there?

Captain—To observe the approach of all cowans and eavesdroppers, and see that none pass or repass but such as are duly qualified.

High Priest—Companions, we will be clothed.

The companions place the furniture of the Chapter in proper order, clothe with their various jewels, robes, and badges of this Degree, and draw aside the veils, which brings the hall into one apartment, and resume their seats. The High Priest then gives two raps with the gavel, which brings all the officers on their feet, while the following lecture is given, or questions asked, by the High Priest, and answered by the Captain of the Host.

High Priest—Companion Captain of the Host, are you a Royal Arch Mason?

Captain—I am, that I am.

High Priest—How shall I know you to be a Royal Arch Mason?

Captain—By three times three.

High Priest—Where were you made a Royal Arch Mason?

Captain—In a just and legally constituted Chapter of Royal Arch Masons, consisting of Most Excellent High Priest, King and Scribe, Captain of the Host, Principal Sojourner, Royal Arch Captain, and the three Grand Masters of the veils, assembled in a room or place representing the Tabernacle erected by our ancient brethren near the ruins of King Solomon's Temple.

High Priest—Where is the High Priest stationed, and what are his duties?

Captain—He is stationed in the sanctum sanctorum. His duty, with the King and Scribe, is to sit in the Grand Council, to form plans, and give directions to the workmen.

High Priest—The King's station and duty?

Captain—Station, at the right hand of the High Priest; duty, to aid him by his advice and counsel, and in his absence to preside.

High Priest—The Scribe's station and duty?

Captain—Station, at the left hand of the High Priest; duty, to assist him and the King in the discharge of their duties, and to preside in their absence.

High Priest—The Captain of the Host's station and duty?

Captain—Station, at the right hand in front of Grand Council; duty, to receive orders, and see them duly executed.

High Priest—The Principal Sojourner's station and duty?

Captain—Station, at the left hand in front of Grand Council; duty, to bring the blind by a way that they know not; to lead them in paths they have not known; to make darkness light before them, and crooked things straight.

High Priest—The Royal Arch Captain's station and duty?

Captain—Station, at the inner veil, or entrance to the sanctum sanctorum; duty, to guard the same, and see that none pass but such as are duly qualified, and have the proper pass-words, and the signet of truth.

High Priest—What is the color of his banner?

Captain—White, and is emblematical of that purity of heart and rectitude of conduct which are essential to obtain admission into the divine sanctum sanctorum above.

High Priest—The stations and duties of the three Grand Masters of the veils?

Captain—Station, at the entrance of their respective veils; duty, to guard the same, and see that none pass but such as are duly qualified, and in possession of the proper pass-words and tokens.

High Priest—What are the colors of their banners?

Captain—That of the third, scarlet; which is emblematical of fervency and zeal, and the appropriate color of the Royal Arch Degree. It admonishes us to be fervent in the exercise of our devotions to God, and zealous in our endeavors to promote the happiness of men. Of the second, purple; which being produced by a due mixture of blue and scarlet, the former of which is the characteristic color of the symbolic, or three first Degrees, it teaches us to cultivate and improve that spirit of harmony between the brethren of the symbolic Degrees and the companions of the sublime Degrees, which should ever distinguish the members of a society founded upon the principles of everlasting truth and universal philanthropy. Of the first, blue; the peculiar color of the three ancient, or symbolical Degrees. It is an emblem of universal friendship and benevolence, and instructs us that in the mind of a Mason those virtues should be as expansive as the blue arch of heaven itself.

High Priest—The Treasurer's station and duty?

Captain—Station, at the right hand in rear of the Captain of the Host; his duty, to keep a just and regular account of all the property and funds of the Chapter placed in his hands, and exhibit them to the Chapter when called upon for that purpose.

High Priest—The Secretary's place in the Chapter?

Captain—Station, at the left in rear of the Principal Sojourner; his duty, to issue the orders and notifications of his superior officers, record the proceedings of the Chapter proper to be written, to receive all moneys due the Chapter, and pay them over to the Treasurer.

High Priest—Guard's place and duty?

Captain—His station is at the outer avenue of the Chapter; his duty, to guard against the approach of cowans and eavesdroppers, and suffer none to pass or repass, but such as are duly qualified.

High Priest (addressing the Chapter).—Companions, you will assemble round the altar, for the purpose of assisting me in opening a Chapter of Royal Arch Masons.

All the members present (except the Grand Council) approach the altar, and, forming a circle, kneel, each upon his right knee. An opening in the circle is left for the High Priest, the King, and the Scribe. The High Priest rises and reads from the Second Epistle of Paul to the Thessalonians, chap. III., vs. 6 to 18:—

"Now we command you, brethren, in the name of our Lord Jesus Christ, that ye withdraw yourselves from every brother that walketh disorderly, and not after the tradition which ye have received of us. For yourselves know how ye ought to follow us; for we behaved not ourselves disorderly among you; neither did we eat any man's bread for naught; but wrought with labor and travail night and day, that we might not be chargeable to any of you; not because we have not power, but to make ourselves an example unto you to follow us." &c.

After the reading, the High Priest, the King, and the Scribe approach the altar and take their places in the circle, kneeling with the rest, the King on the right, and the Scribe on the left of the High Priest. Each one now crosses his arms and gives his right hand to his left-hand companion, and his left hand to his right-hand companion. This constitutes the living arch under which the Grand Omnific Royal Arch Word must be given, but it must also be given by three times three, as hereafter explained.

The High Priest now whispers in the King's ear the pass-word RABBONI.

The King whispers it to the companion on his right, and he to the next one, and so on until it comes round to the Scribe, who whispers it to the High Priest.

High Priest—The word is right.

The companions now all balance three times three with their arms; that is, they raise their arms and let them fall upon their knees three times in concert—after a short pause, three times more, and after another pause, three times more. They then rise and give all the signs, from the Entered Apprentice up to this Degree, after which they join in squads of three for giving the Grand Omnific Royal Arch Word, as follows:

Each one takes hold with his right hand of the right wrist of his companion on the left, and with his left hand takes hold of the left wrist of his companion on the right. Each one then places his right foot forward with the hollow in front, so that the toe touches the heel of his companion on the right. This is called "three times three;" that is, three right feet forming a triangle, three left hands forming a triangle, and three right hands forming a triangle. In this position each repeats the following:

> As we three did agree,
> In peace, love, and unity,
> The Sacred Word to keep,
> So we three do agree,
> In peace, love, and unity,
> The Sacred Word to search;
> Until we three,
> Or three such as we, shall agree
> To close this Royal Arch.

They then balance three times three, bringing the right hand with some violence down upon the left. The right hands are then raised above their heads, and the words, Jah-buh-lun, Je-ho-vah, G-o-d,[1] are given at low breath, each companion pronouncing the syllables or letters alternately, as follows:

[1] Cole adopts the following sentiment of a brother Mason: "In the R. A. (Royal Arch) Mason's Degree I beheld myself exalted to the top of *Pisgah*, an extensive scene opened to my view of the glory and goodness of the M. E. H. P. (Most Excellent High Priest) of our salvation. I dug deep for *hidden treasures*, found them, and *regained* the *omnific word*."

"If we pass on to the Royal Arch," says the Rev. G. Oliver, in his Lectures on

FIG. 32

THREE TIMES THREE

1st.	2nd.	3d.
Jah	buh	lun.
. . . .	Jah	buh
lun	. . . .	. . .
. . . .	. . . .	Jah
buh	lun.	
Je	ho	vah.

Freemasonry, "we receive a wonderful accession of knowledge, and find every thing *made perfect;* for this is the *ne plus ultra* of Masonry, and can never be exceeded by any human institution."—*Fellows's Inquiry into the Origin, History, and Purport of Freemasonry,* p. 322.

A Degree indescribably more august, sublime, and important than any which precede it, and is, in fact, the summit and perfection of ancient Masonry. It impresses on our minds a belief in the being of a God, without beginning of days or end of years, the great and incomprehensible Alpha and Omega, and reminds us of the reverence which is due to His Holy NAME.—*Historical Landmarks,* vol. I. p. 86.

. . . . Je . . . . ho
vah. . . . .
. . . . Je
ho . . . . vah.
G . . . . o . . . . d.
. . . . G . . . . o
d. . . . .
. . . . G
o. . . . . d.¹

After the word is thus given, the High Priest inquires if the word is right.

Each squad replies that it is right.

The officers and companions resume their seats. The High Priest raps three times with his gavel, the King repeats it, as also the Scribes; this is done three times (●●● ●●● ●●●).

High Priest (rising).—I now declare this Chapter of Royal Arch Masons opened in due and ancient form; and I hereby forbid all improper conduct whereby the peace and harmony of this Chapter may be disturbed, under no less penalties than·the by-laws, or a majority of the Chapter, may see fit to inflict.

High Priest (to Captain of the Host).—Companion Captain, please to inform the Guard that the Chapter is open.

The Captain proceeds on this duty, while the Secretary reads the minutes of the last meeting. Should there be any candidates to be balloted for, this is the first business in order. If one or more candidates are waiting without, the Principal Sojourner goes to the preparation-room to get them ready. If there are not three of them, a companion or companions volunteer to make the trio, as not less than three can perform the ceremonies. The three take off their coats, when the Principal Sojourner ties bandages over their eyes, and, taking a long rope, coils it seven times round the body of each, leaving about three feet slack between.

¹ This ineffable name (in INDIA) was *Aum*, which, in its triliteral form, was significant of the creative, preservative, and destroying power, that is, of Brahma, Vishnu, and Siva.—*Lexicon*, p. 146.

JEHOVAH. Of the varieties of this sacred name in use among the different nations of the earth, three particularly merit the attention of Royal Arch Masons:

1. JAH. This name of God is found in the 68th Psalm, v. 4.

2. BAAL OR BEL. This word signifies a *lord, master, or possessor*, and hence it was applied by many of the nations of the East to denote the Lord of all things, and the Master of the world.

3. ON. This was the name by which JEHOVAH was worshipped among the Egyptians.

I have made these remarks on the three names of God in Chaldaic, Syriac and Egyptian, *Baal, Jah*, and *On*, in the expectation that my Royal Arch Companions will readily recognize them in a corrupted form.—*Lexicon*.

Principal Sojourner—Three worthy brothers, who have been initiated, passed, and raised to the sublime Degree of Master Masons, advanced to the honorary Degree of Mark Master, presided as Master in the chair, and, at the completion and dedication of the Temple, were received and acknowledged Most Excellent Masters; and now wish for further light in Masonry, by being exalted to the august sublime Degree of the Holy Royal Arch.

—Captain (to candidates).—Is it of your own free-will and accord you make this request?

First Candidate (prompted).—It is.

Captain (to Principal Sojourner).—Are they duly and truly prepared?

Principal Sojourner—They are.

Captain—Have they made suitable proficiency in the preceding Degrees?

Principal Sojourner—They have.

Captain—By what further right or benefit do they expect to gain admission to this Chapter of Royal Arch Masons?

Principal Sojourner—By the benefit of a pass.

Captain—Have they that pass?

Principal Sojourner—They have it not; but I have it for them.

The Captain of the Host goes to the door, opens it, and says:

Captain—It is our Most Excellent High Priest's order, that the candidates enter this Chapter of Royal Arch Masons, and be received under a Living Arch.

Principal Sojourner (leading the candidates by the rope).—Companions, you will follow me. (Leads them in.) I will bring the blind by a way they know not: I will lead them in paths they have not known; I will make darkness light before them, and crooked things straight. These things will I do unto them, and will not forsake them. Stoop low, brethren: he that humbleth himself shall be exalted.

Meantime the brethren, or companions of the Chapter, form two lines facing each other, from the door to the centre of the room, and each one takes hold and locks his fingers with those of his opposite companion. As the candidates pass under this Living Arch, each couple place their knuckles upon the necks and backs of the candidates, kneading them pretty hard sometimes, and prostrating them on the floor. Thus they have a good deal of difficulty in forcing their way through. When they do get through, they are first conducted round the Chapter, and then to the altar, where they must kneel to receive the obligation.

Principal Sojourner (to the candidates).—Brethren, as you advance in Masonry, your obligation becomes more binding. You are now kneeling at the altar for the seventh time; and about to take a solemn oath, or obligation, which, like your former obligations, is not to interfere with the duty you owe to your country, or Maker. If you are willing to proceed, you will repeat your Christian and surname, and say after me:

I, Peter Gabe, of my own free-will and accord, in presence of Almighty God, and this Chapter of Royal Arch Masons, erected to God, and dedicated to Zerubbabel, do hereby and hereon most solemnly and sincerely promise and swear, in addition to my former obligations, that I will not reveal the secrets of this Degree to any of an inferior Degree, nor to any being in the known world, except it be to a true and lawful Companion Royal Arch Mason, or within the body of a just and legally constituted Chapter of such and never unto him, or them, whom I shall hear so to be, but to him and them only whom I shall find so to be, after strict trial and due examination, or lawful information given.

I furthermore promise and swear, that I will not wrong this Chapter of Royal Arch Masons, or a companion of this Degree, out of the value of any thing, myself, nor suffer it to be done by others, if in my power to prevent it.

I furthermore promise and swear, that I will not reveal the key to the ineffable characters of this Degree, nor retain it in my possession, but will destroy it whenever it comes to my sight.

I furthermore promise and swear, that I will not speak the Grand Omnific Royal Arch Word, which I shall hereafter receive, in any manner, except in that in which I shall receive it, which will be in the presence of three Companions Royal Arch Masons, myself making one of the number; and then by three times three, under a Living Arch, and at low breath.

I furthermore promise and swear, that I will not be at the exaltation of candidates in a clandestine Chapter, nor converse upon the secrets of this Degree with a clandestine-made Mason, or with one who has been expelled or suspended, while under that sentence.

I furthermore promise and swear, that I will not assist or be present at the exaltation of a candidate to this Degree, who has not received the Degrees of Entered Apprentice, Fellow Craft, Master Mason, Mark Master, Past Master, and Most Excellent Master.

I furthermore promise and swear, that I will not be at the exaltation of more nor less than three candidates at one and the same time.

I furthermore promise and swear, that I will not be at the forming or opening of a Chapter of Royal Arch Masons unless there be present nine Royal Arch Masons, myself making one of that number.

I furthermore promise and swear, that I will not speak evil of a Companion Royal Arch Mason, behind his back nor before his face, but will apprise him of all approaching danger, if in my power.

I furthermore promise and swear, that I will support the Constitution of the General Grand Royal Arch Chapter of the United States of America; together with that of the Grand Chapter of this State, under which this Chapter is holden; that I will stand to and abide by all the by-laws, rules, and regulations of this Chapter, or of any other Chapter of which I may hereafter become a member.

I furthermore promise and swear, that I will answer and obey all due signs and summonses handed, sent, or thrown to me from a Chapter of Royal Arch Masons, or from a Companion Royal Arch Mason, if within the length of my cable-tow.

I furthermore promise and swear, that I will not strike a Companion Royal Arch Mason, so as to draw his blood, in anger.

I furthermore promise and swear, that I will employ a Companion Royal Arch Mason in preference to any other person of equal qualifications.

I furthermore promise and swear, that I will assist a Companion Royal Arch Mason when I see him engaged in any difficulty, and will espouse his cause so far as to extricate him from the same, whether he be right or wrong.

I furthermore promise and swear, that I will keep all the secrets of a Companion Royal Arch Mason (when communicated to me as such, or I knowing them to be such), without exceptions.

I furthermore promise and swear, that I will be aiding and assisting all poor and indigent Companions Royal Arch Masons, their widows and orphans, wheresoever dispersed around the globe; they making application to me as such, and I finding them worthy, and can do it without any material injury to myself or family.

To all which I do most solemnly and sincerely promise and swear, with a firm and steadfast resolution to keep and perform the same, without any equivocation, mental reservation, or self-evasion of mind in me whatever; binding myself under no less penalty, than to have my skull smote off, and my brains exposed to the scorching rays of the meridian sun, should I knowingly or wilfully violate or transgress any part of this my solemn oath or obligation of a Royal Arch Mason. So help me God, and keep me steadfast in the due performance of the same.

Principal Sojourner—Kiss the book seven times.

The candidate kisses the book as directed.

Principal Sojourner—Companions, you will arise and follow me. For although you are obligated Royal Arch Masons, yet, as the secrets of this Degree are of infinitely more importance than any that precede it, it is necessary that you should travel through rough and rugged ways, and pass through many trials, in testimony of your fidelity to the Order, before you can be instructed in the more important secrets of this Degree.

The candidates are conducted once around the Chapter, and then again directed to kneel, while the Principal Sojourner reads the following prayer:

Supreme and inscrutable Architect of universal Nature, who, by thine Almighty word didst speak into being the stupendous arch of heaven, and, for the instruction and pleasure of thy rational creatures, didst adorn us with greater and lesser lights, thereby magnifying thy power, and endearing thy goodness unto the sons of men, we humbly adore and worship thine unspeakable perfection. We bless thee, that, when man had fallen from his innocence and his happiness, thou didst leave him the powers of reasoning, and capacity of improvement and pleasure. We thank thee, that, amid the pains and calamities of our present state, so many means of refreshment and satisfaction are reserved to us, while travelling the rugged path of life; especially would we, at this time, render thee our thanksgiving and praise for the institution, as members of which we are at this time assembled, and for all the pleasures we have derived from it. We thank thee, that the few here assembled before thee have been favored with new inducements, and been laid under new and stronger obligations of virtue and holiness. May these obligations, O blessed Father! have their full effect upon us. Teach us, we pray thee, the true reverence of thy great, mighty, and terrible Name. Inspire us with a firm and unshaken resolution in our virtuous pursuits. Give us grace diligently to search thy word in the book of nature, wherein the duties of our high vocation are inculcated with Divine authority. May the solemnity of the ceremonies of our institution be duly impressed on our minds, and have a happy and lasting effect on our lives! O Thou, who didst aforetime appear unto thy servant Moses in a flame of fire out of the midst of a bush, enkindle, we beseech thee, in each of our hearts, a flame of devotion to thee, of love to each other, and of charity to all mankind! May all thy miracles and mighty works fill us with thy dread, and thy goodness impress us with a love of thy holy name! May holiness to the Lord be engraven upon all our thoughts, words, and actions! May the incense of piety ascend continually unto thee from the altar of our hearts, and burn day and night, as a sacrifice of a sweet-smelling savor, well-pleasing unto thee! And since sin has destroyed within us the first temple of purity and innocence, may thy heavenly grace guide and assist us in rebuilding a second temple of reformation, and may the glory of this latter house be greater than the glory of the former! Amen, so mote it be.

Principal Sojourner—Companions, arise and follow me.

He now conducts them once around the Chapter, during which time he reads from the text-book the first six verses of the third chapter of Exodus:—

"Now Moses kept the flock of Jethro his father-in-law, the priest of Midian; and he led the flock to the back side of the desert, and came to the mountain of God, even to Horeb. And the angel of the Lord appeared unto him in a flame of fire out of the midst of a bush; and he looked, and behold, the bush burned with fire, and the bush was not consumed." &c.

The reading of these verses is so timed, that just when they are finished the candidates have arrived in front of a representation of the burning bush, placed in a corner of the Chapter; when the Principal Sojourner directs them to halt, and slips up the bandages from their eyes.

One of the members now personates the Deity, behind the bush, and calls out, Moses! Moses!

Principal Sojourner (answering for candidates).—Here I am.

Companion behind the bush—Draw not nigh hither: put off thy shoes from off thy feet, for the place whereon thou standest is holy ground. I am the God of thy fathers, the God of Abraham, the God of Isaac, and the God of Jacob.

Principal Sojourner directs the candidates to kneel, and he covers their faces again, and then says—And Moses hid his face, for he was afraid to look upon God.

Principal Sojourner (to candidates).—Arise, and follow me.

He then leads them three times around the Chapter, during which time he reads from the text-book 2 Chronicles, ch. XXXVI., vs. 11 to 20

"Zedekiah was one-and-twenty years old when he began to reign, and he reigned eleven years in Jerusalem. And he did that which was evil in the sight of the Lord his God, and humbled not himself before Jeremiah the prophet, speaking from the mouth of the Lord. And he also rebelled against King Nebuchadnezzar, and stiffened his neck, and hardened his heart from turning unto the Lord God of Israel. Moreover, all the chief of the priests and the people transgressed very much, after all the abominations of the heathen, and polluted the house of the Lord, which he had hallowed in Jerusalem. And the Lord God of their fathers sent to them by his messengers, because he had compassion on his people, and on his dwelling-place. But they mocked the messengers of God, and despised his Word, and misused his prophets, until the wrath of the Lord arose against his people, till there was no remedy. Therefore he brought upon them the King of the Chaldees, who slew their young men with the sword, in the house of their sanctuary, and had no compassion upon young men or maidens, old men, or him that stooped for age; he gave them all into his hand. And all the vessels of the house of God, great and small, and the treasures of the house of the Lord, and the treasures of the king, and his princes; all these he brought to Babylon. And they burnt the house of God, and brake down the wall of Jerusalem, and burnt all the palaces thereof with fire, and destroyed all the goodly vessels thereof. And them that had escaped from the sword carried he away to Babylon; where they were servants to him and his sons, until the reign of the kingdom of Persia."

When the Principal Sojourner arrives at that part of the above reading which alludes to the Chaldees killing the young men with the sword, the companions of the Chapter begin to make all sorts of queer and unearthly noises, such as rolling cannon-balls on the floor, clashing old swords, shouting, groaning, whistling, stamping, throwing down benches, &c. This noise continues during the remainder of the reading, the object being to represent the siege and destruction of Jerusalem. During this confusion the three candidates are seized, thrown upon the floor, bound hand and foot, and carried bodily into the preparation-room, when the door is closed.

In a few minutes the companions begin to shout: "Hurra for the captives!" repeating it several times.

Captain of the Host goes and opens the door, and says—Come forth! you are at liberty to return! for Cyrus has issued his proclamation to build a second Temple at Jerusalem.

Principal Sojourner (who is with the candidates).—Will you read the proclamation?

Captain of the Host reads the first three verses of the first chapter of Ezra, as follows:

"Now in the first year of Cyrus, King of Persia, the Lord stirred up the spirit of Cyrus, King of Persia, that he made a proclamation throughout all his kingdom, and put it also in writing, saying:

PROCLAMATION

"Thus saith Cyrus, King of Persia, the Lord God of heaven hath given me all the kingdoms of the earth, and he hath charged me to build him an house at Jerusalem, which is in Judah. Who is there among you of all his people? His God be with him, and let him go up to Jerusalem, which is in Judah, and build the house of the Lord God of Israel, which is in Jerusalem."

Captain of the Host—What say you to the proclamation? Are you willing to go up to Jerusalem?

Principal Sojourner (consulting candidates). — Yes, we are willing to go, but we have no pass-word whereby to make ourselves known to the brethren when we get there. What shall we say to them?

Captain of the Host reads verses 13 and 14 of the third chapter of Exodus:

"And Moses said unto God, Behold! when I come unto the children of Israel, and shall say unto them, The God of your fathers hath sent me unto you, and they shall say to me, What is his name? What shall I say to them?

"And God said unto Moses, I AM THAT I AM: and thus thou shalt say unto the children of Israel, I AM hath sent me unto you."

We were directed to use the words, "I AM THAT I AM," as a pass-word.

Principal Sojourner—We will go up. Companions, you will follow me; our pass-word is, I AM THAT I AM.

As they enter the Chapter, they again pass under the Living Arch.

Principal Sojourner—Stoop low, brethren. He that humbleth himself shall be exalted.

On one side of the hall or Chapter, the Living Arch is formed, as before described; on the other side is what is called the rugged road. This is generally made of blocks and logs of wood, old chairs, benches, &c.

The companions who form the Living Arch press harder on the candidates each time they go through, and they now go through three times. While passing through, the Principal Sojourner says:

Principal Sojourner—This is the way many great and good men have travelled before you, never deeming it derogatory to their dignity to level themselves with the fraternity. I have often travelled this road from Babylon to Jerusalem, and generally find it rough and rugged. However, I think I never saw it much smoother than it is at the present time.

The candidates, after passing the Living Arch, stumble over the rugged road, and arrive again at the entrance of the arch.

Principal Sojourner—Companions, here is a very difficult and dangerous place ahead, which lies directly in our way. Before we attempt to pass it, we must kneel down and pray. (Reads Psalm CXLI.)

"Lord, I cry unto thee; make haste unto me; give ear unto my voice.

"Let my prayer be set forth before thee as incense, and the lifting up of my hands as the evening sacrifice.

"Set a watch, O Lord, before my mouth; keep the door of my lips.

"Incline not my heart to any evil thing, to practice wicked works with men that work iniquity.

"Let the righteous smite me; it shall be a kindness: and let him reprove me; it shall be an excellent oil.

"Mine eyes are unto thee, O God the Lord: in thee is my trust; leave not my soul destitute.

"Keep me from the snare which they have laid before me, and the gins of the workers of iniquity.

"Let the wicked fall into their own nets, whilst that I withal escape."

The candidates rise and again pass under the Living Arch and over the rugged road. They then kneel again.

Principal Sojourner—Let us pray. (Reads from text-book Psalm CXLII.)

"I cried unto the Lord with my voice; with my voice unto the Lord did I make my supplication," &c.

They then pass round the third time as before, when the candidates again kneel.

Principal Sojourner reads Psalm CXLIII. from the text-book:

"Hear my prayer, O Lord, give ear to my supplications; in thy faithfulness answer me, and in thy righteousness," &c.

Principal Sojourner—We have now arrived in sight of the ruins of the old Temple, near the outer veil of the Tabernacle.

The veils are now pushed apart to admit the candidates, but as soon as they enter, the veils are closed again, and the officers (except the Principal Sojourner) take their seats.

Principal Sojourner makes an alarm by stamping nine times on the floor, which brings out the Master from the First Veil. (See Note O, Appendix.)

Master of First Veil—Who comes there? Who dares approach this outer Veil of our sacred Tabernacle? Who are you?

Principal Sojourner—Three weary travellers from Babylon.

Master of First Veil—What are your intentions?

Principal Sojourner—We have come to assist in the noble and glorious work of rebuilding the house of the Lord, without the hope of fee or reward. (See Note M, Appendix.)

Master of First Veil—How do you expect to enter here?

Principal Sojourner—By a pass-word that we received in Babylon.

Master of First Veil—Give it to me.

Principal Sojourner—I AM THAT I AM.

Master of First Veil—The pass is right. You have my permission to enter.

The candidates now enter the First Veil, when the bandages are removed from their eyes.

Master of First Veil—You surely could not have come thus far unless you were three Most Excellent Masters; but farther you cannot go without my words, sign, and word of exhortation. My words are Shem, Ham, and Japhet; my sign is this (holding out a cane), in imitation of one given by God to Moses, when he commanded him to cast his rod upon the ground thus (casting down the cane), and it became a serpent; but putting forth his hand

and taking it up by the tail, it became a rod in his hand as before.
My word of exhortation is explanatory of this sign, and is to be
found in the writings of Moses, viz.: the first verses of the fourth
chapter of Exodus. (See Note N, Appendix.)

"And the Lord said unto Moses, What is that in thy hand?
And he said, A rod. And the Lord said, Cast it on the ground;
and he cast it, and it became a serpent, and Moses fled from
before it," &c.

Fig. 33

SIGN OF THE MASTER OF THE FIRST VEIL

Principal Sojourner—Companions, we have passed the first
guard, and will make an alarm at the Second Veil. (Stamps on
the floor, as before)

Master of Second Veil—Who comes there? Who dares approach
this Second Veil of our sacred Tabernacle?

Principal Sojourner—Three weary sojourners from Babylon, who
have come to assist in rebuilding the house of the Lord, without
the hope of fee or reward.

Master of Second Veil—How do you expect to enter the Second
Veil?

Principal Sojourner—By the words, sign, and word of exhortation of the Master of the First Veil.

Master of Second Veil—Give them.

Principal Sojourner—Shem, Ham, and Japhet. (Gives the sign of casting down a cane and taking it up by the end, as before explained.)

Master of Second Veil—They are right. You have my permission to enter the Second Veil.

The candidates, led by the Principal Sojourner, pass in.

Fig. 34

Fig. 35

SIGN OF THE MASTER OF THE
SECOND VEIL

SIGN OF THE MASTER OF THE
THIRD VEIL

Master of Second Veil—Three Most Excellent Masters you must have been, or thus far you could not have come; but farther you cannot go without my words, sign, and word of exhortation. My words are Shem, Japhet, and Adoniram; my sign is this: (thrusting his hand in his bosom); it is in imitation of one given by God to Moses, when He commanded him to thrust his hand into his bosom, and, taking it out, it became as leprous as snow. My word of exhortation is explanatory of this sign, and is found in the writings of Moses, viz., fourth chapter of Exodus:

"And the Lord said unto Moses, Put now thine hand into thy

bosom. And he put his hand into his bosom; and when he took it out, behold, his hand was leprous as snow," &c.

Principal Sojourner—Companions, we will pass on, and make an alarm at the Third Veil. (Stamps nine times.)

Master of the Third Veil—Who comes there? Who dares approach this Third Veil of our sacred Tabernacle?

Principal Sojourner—Three weary sojourners from Babylon, who have come to assist in the rebuilding of the house of the Lord, without the hope of fee or reward.

Master of Third Veil—How do you expect to enter?

Principal Sojourner—By the words, sign, and word of exhortation of the Master of the Second Veil.

Master of Third Veil—Give them.

Principal Sojourner—Shem, Japhet, and Adoniram. (Thrusts his hand into his bosom as Master of Second Veil had done.)

Master of Third Veil—They are right. You can enter the Third Veil.

The candidates enter.

Master of Third Veil (to candidates).—Three Most Excellent Masters you must have been, or thus far you could not have come. But you cannot go farther without my words, signs, and word of exhortation. My words are, Haggai, Joshua, and Zerubbabel. My sign is this: (holds out a tumbler of water, and pours out a little on the floor.) It is in imitation of one given by God to Moses, when he commanded him to pour water upon the dry land, and it became blood. My word of exhortation is explanato y of this sign, and is found in the writings of Moses, viz., the fourth chapter of Exodus:

"And it shall come to pass, if they will not believe in the two former signs, thou shalt take of the water of the river and pour it upon the dry land; and the water shall become blood upon the dry land."

Master of Third Veil—I also present you with the Signet of Truth, which is that of Zerubbabel. (Presents a triangular piece of metal, with ZER-UBBA-BEL engraved on it.)

Principal Sojourner (to candidates).—Companions, we have now passed the Third Veil: let us make an alarm at the Fourth. (Stamps as before.)

Royal Arch Captain—Who comes there? Who dares approach the Fourth Veil of our sacred Tabernacle, where incense burns, day and night, upon the holy altar? Who are you, and what are your intentions?

Principal Sojourner—Three weary sojourners from Babylon, who have come up thus far to aid and assist in the noble and glorious work of rebuilding the house of the Lord, without the hope of fee or reward.

Royal Arch Captain—How do you expect to enter this Fourth Veil of our sacred Tabernacle?

Principal Sojourner—By the words, sign, and word of exhortation of the Master of the Third Veil.

Royal Arch Captain—Give them.

Principal Sojourner—Haggai, Joshua, and Zerubbabel. (Pours a little water from a tumbler, or cup, upon the floor, for the sign.)

Royal Arch Captain—They are right. You have my permission to enter the Fourth Veil.

The Veils are now drawn aside, and the candidates enter amid a dazzling light, and behold the High Priest, King, and Scribe sitting in Grand Council. The light is usually made by igniting gum camphor in an urn upon the altar.

Royal Arch Captain—Three Most Excellent Masters you must have been, or thus far you could not have come. I will present you to the Grand Council. (Stamps his foot nine times.)

High Priest—Who comes here?

Principal Sojourner—Three weary sojourners from Babylon, who have come up thus far to aid and assist in rebuilding the house of the Lord, without the hope of fee or reward.

High Priest—Have you the signet of Zerubbabel?

Principal Sojourner—We have. (Presents the signet given him by Master of Third Veil.)

High Priest takes it, and reads from the second chapter of Haggai:

"In that day will I take thee, O Zerubbabel, my servant, the son of Shealtiel, saith the Lord, and will make thee a signet: for I have chosen thee."

High Priest (to King, showing him the signet).—Companion, are you satisfied that this is the signet of Zerubbabel?

King (taking the signet, and scrutinizing it).—I am satisfied, Most Excellent, that it is.

High Priest (showing signet to Scribe).—Companion Scribe, think you this is the true signet of Zerubbabel?

Scribe (looking shrewdly at it).—I am satisfied that it is, Most Excellent.

High Priest (drawing signet across his forehead, in imitation of the penalty, see Fig. 36).—Signet of Truth, and Holiness to the Lord!

The King and the Scribe, each in turn, puts his hand to his forehead, repeating—Holiness to the Lord.

High Priest (to candidates).—It is the opinion of the Grand

Council, that you have presented the true signet of Zerubbabel. But, owing to difficulties having arisen from the introduction of strangers among the workmen, none are allowed to undertake in the noble and glorious work, but the true descendants of the twelve tribes. It is necessary you should be very particular in tracing your genealogy. Who are you, and what are your intentions?

Principal Sojourner—We are your own kindred, the descendants of those noble families of Giblemites, who wrought so hard at the building of the first Temple. We have been regularly initiated as Entered Apprentice Masons, passed to the Degree of Fellow Craft, raised to the sublime Degree of Master Mason, advanced to the honorary Degree of Mark Master, presided as Master in the chair, and at the completion and dedication of the Temple were acknowledged as Most Excellent Masters. We were present at its destruction by Nebuchadnezzar, and by him were carried away captives to Babylon; where we remained servants to him and his successors until the reign of Cyrus, King of Persia, by whose proclamation we were liberated, and have come up thus far to aid and assist in the noble and glorious work of rebuilding the house of the Lord, without the hope of fee or reward.

High Priest—Let the captives be unbound, and brought to light. Companion King, I think we had better employ these sojourners. They look like good hardy men; just such men as we want about the building. What say you?

King—It is my opinion, Most Excellent, that they are very expert workmen. I wish they might be examined.

High Priest—What is your opinion, Companion Scribe?

Scribe—If they can satisfy us they are Free Masons, I shall be in favor of employing them immediately.

High Priest—You say you are Entered Apprentice Masons. Satisfy the Grand Council.

The three candidates give the signs of Entered Apprentice. (See Figs. 1 and 2, pp. 17, 18.)

High Priest (to King and Scribe).—Companions, are you satisfied?

The King bows gracefully, and the Scribe answers, We are satisfied, Most Excellent.

High Priest (to candidates).—The Grand Council are satisfied that you are Entered Apprentice Masons. Have you been advanced to the Fellow Craft's Degree?

Candidates give the Fellow Craft signs (see Figs. 3 and 4, p. 17), when the High Priest asks his companions of the Grand Council if they are satisfied, as before, and then informs the candidates that the Grand Council approves them as true Fellow Crafts, &c.

The same questions and answers are given in like manner as to each Degree, up to and including that of Most Excellent Master, and the candidates give all the signs of those Degrees to the Grand Council in detail.

High Priest (after consultation with the King and Scribe).— Companions, we are satisfied that you are three worthy Most Excellent Masters. As such, we will employ you on the Temple. What part of the work will you undertake?

Principal Sojourner—We will take any service, however servile or dangerous, for the sake of forwarding so great and noble an undertaking.

High Priest (to Royal Arch Captain).—You will furnish them with the working tools, and direct them to repair to the northeast corner of the ruins of the old Temple, with orders to remove the rubbish, preparatory to laying the foundation of the new Temple. Advise them to carefully preserve every thing of service to the craft that falls in their way, and bring it to the Grand Council.

The candidates are presented, one with a pickaxe, one with a crow, and the other with a shovel, which are generally made of wood, and kept for the purpose in the Lodge or Chapter.

WORKING TOOLS OF A ROYAL ARCH MASON

Principal Sojourner (to the candidates).—Follow me.

Each candidate shoulders his working tools and follows the Principal Sojourner, going single file to a corner of the room where a quantity of blocks or bricks are scattered around. These they stir up a little, when they come to a ring in a trap-door, which they pull up, and find it shaped like a keystone of an arch. Each one examines it, and then looks down the trap, when the Principal Sojourner suggests that it be at once taken up to the Grand Council. He then leads the candidates back.

High Priest—Companion King, have you further business to lay before this Grand Council?

King—I have nothing, Most Excellent.

High Priest (to Scribe).—Have you any thing, worthy companion?

Scribe—I know of nothing, Most Excellent.

High Priest—I know of nothing, unless the workmen from the ruins have articles for inspection. The workmen will please come forward and give an account of their labors.

Principal Sojourner—Most Excellent, in pursuance of orders of this Grand Council, we repaired to the ruins and commenced our labors. After laboring several days, we discovered what seemed a rock, but on striking it with a crow it gave a hollow sound, and upon closer examination we discovered in it an iron ring, by help of which we succeeded in removing it from its place, when we found it to be the keystone of an arch, and through the aperture there appeared to be an immense vault, curiously arched. We have brought this keystone up, that it may be examined by the Grand Council.

High Priest—You will present it.

Principal Sojourner presents the keystone, or trap.

High Priest (looking closely at it).—Companion King, this is a very valuable discovery indeed. It must be a keystone of a Mark Master Mason.

King—I think that is the stone wrought by our Grand Master, Hiram Abiff.

High Priest—What think you of it, Companion Scribe?

Scribe—It is undoubtedly the stone wrought by our Grand Master, Hiram Abiff.

High Priest (drawing the keystone across his forehead, and giving the sign).—The keystone of a Mark Master! Holiness to the Lord.

King and Scribe do and say the same.

High Priest (to candidates).—This is a very valuable discovery indeed. No doubt it will lead to some important treasure, of inestimable value to the craft. Are you willing to pursue your labors, and endeavor to penetrate this secret vault?

Principal Sojourner (after consulting candidates).—We are, even to the risk of our lives.

High Priest—Go; and may the God of your fathers be with you. Preserve every thing that falls in your way.

The Principal Sojourner returns with the candidates to the place where they lifted the trap, and they there consult together as to who shall descend into the vault. One of the candidates agreeing to go, they put a rope seven times around his body, leaving two long ends.[1]

---

[1] Candidates at the present day usually descend the vault by means of a ladder.

Principal Sojourner (to candidate who is about to descend).—Companion, it is necessary you should take a little precaution. Should you wish to descend still lower, pull the rope in your left hand: if you wish to ascend, pull that in your right hand.

Two companions take hold of each end of the rope, letting the candidate down eight or ten feet, to another trap-door, where he finds three small trying squares; and, giving the signal of ascending, is drawn up.[4]

Each candidate taking a square, they repair to the Grand Council. As they present themselves, the High Priest reads the following passage from the fourth chapter of Zechariah:

"This is the word of the Lord unto Zerubbabel, saying, Not by might, nor by power, but by my spirit. Who art thou, O great mountain? Before Zerubbabel thou shalt become a plain, and he shall bring forth the headstone thereof with shoutings, crying, Grace, grace unto it. Moreover, the word of the Lord came unto me, saying, The hands of Zerubbabel have laid the foundation of this house; his hands shall also finish it; and thou shalt know that the Lord of hosts hath sent me unto you. For who hath despised the day of small things? For they shall rejoice, and shall see the plummet in the hand of Zerubbabel with those seven."

High Priest (to the King).—Companions, have you any further business for the Grand Council?

King—I have nothing, Most Excellent.

High Priest (to Scribe).—Have you any thing, worthy companion?

Scribe—Nothing, Most Excellent.

High Priest—I know of nothing, unless the workmen from the ruins have something for our inspection.

Principal Sojourner—We have examined the secret vault, Most Excellent, and here is what we have found in it. (Presenting the three trying squares.)

High Priest (drawing one of the squares across his forehead).—The jewels of our ancient Grand Masters, King Solomon, Hiram, King of Tyre, and Hiram Abiff! Holiness to the Lord.

The King and the Scribe each take one and imitate the High Priest.

High Priest (to candidates).—Are you willing to continue your labors, and still further penetrate this secret vault?

---

[1] A candidate is said to be EXALTED, when he receives the Degree of Holy Royal Arch, the Seventh in York Masonry. Exalted means *elevated* or *lifted up*, and is applicable both to a peculiar ceremony of the Degree, and to the fact that this Degree, in the rite in which it is practised, constitutes the summit of ancient Masonry.—*Lexicon.*

Principal Sojourner—We are, even to the risk of our lives.

High Priest—Go; and may the God of your fathers be with you; and remember that your labors shall not go unrewarded.

The Principal Sojourner leads the candidates back as before, and winds the rope round one of them, who is let down the trap, still further down than before, where he finds the Ark, when he gives the signal and is drawn up.

The party immediately return to the Grand Council, two of them carrying the Ark, where they present themselves in the same manner as before, and the High Priest directs them to come forward and give an account of their labors.

Principal Sojourner—Most Excellent, in pursuance of your orders, we repaired to the secret vault, and let down one of our companions. The sun at this time was at its meridian height, the rays of which enabled him to discover a small box, or chest, standing on a pedestal, curiously wrought, and overlaid with gold. On discovering it, he involuntarily found his hand raised in this position (giving the sign as shown in Fig. 36), to guard his eyes from the intense light and heat reflected from it. The air becoming offensive, he gave the signal for ascending, and was immediately drawn out. We have brought this chest up for the examination of the Grand Council.

High Priest (looking with surprise at the Ark).—Companion King, this is the Ark of the Covenant of God.

King (looking at it).—It is undoubtedly the true Ark of the Covenant, Most Excellent.

Scribe (looking at the Ark).—That is also my opinion.

High Priest (taking the Ark).—Let us open it, and see what valuable treasure it may contain. (Opens the Ark, and takes out a book.)

High Priest (to King).—Companion, here is a very ancient-looking book; what can it be? Let us read in it. (Reads first three verses of first chapter of Genesis:)

"In the beginning, God created the heaven and the earth," &c.

After reading these verses, the High Priest turns over to Deuteronomy XXXI., and reads from the 24th to the 26th verses, as follows:

"And it came to pass, when Moses had made an end of writing the words of this law in a book, until they were finished, that Moses commanded the Levites, which bare the Ark of the Covenant of the Lord, saying, Take this book of the law, and put it in the side of the Ark of the Covenant of the Lord your God, that it may be there for a witness against thee."

The High Priest then turns back to Exodus XXV., and reads the 21st verse, as follows:

EMBLEMS OF THE ROYAL ARCH DEGREE

1. The Keystone. 2. The Three Jewels of the Ancient Grand Masters. 3. The Ark. 4. Book of the Law. 5. Pot of Manna. 6. Aaron's Rod. 7. The Key. 8. Grand Omnific Word.

"And thou shalt put the mercy-seat above upon the Ark; and in the Ark thou shalt put the testimony that I shall give thee."

High Priest—This is a book of the law—long lost, but now found. Holiness to the Lord. (He repeats this again, twice.)

King—A book of the law—long lost, but now found. Holiness to the Lord!

Scribe repeats the same.

High Priest (to candidates).—You now see that the world is indebted to Masonry for the preservation of this sacred volume. Had it not been for the wisdom and precaution of our ancient brethren, this, the only remaining copy of the law, would have been destroyed at the destruction of Jerusalem.[1]

[1] The foundations of the Temple were opened and cleared from the accumulation of rubbish, that a level site might be procured for the commencement of the building. While engaged in excavations for this purpose, *three fortunate sojourners* are said to have discovered our ancient stone of foundation, which had been deposited in the secret crypt by Wisdom, Strength, and Beauty, to prevent the communication of ineffable secrets to profane or unworthy persons. The discovery having been communicated to the prince, priest, and prophet of the Jews, the stone was adopted as the chief corner-stone of the re-edified building; and thus became, in a new and expressive sense, the type of a more excellent dispensation. An avenue was also accidentally discovered, supported by seven pairs of pillars, perfect and entire, which, from their situation, had escaped the fury of the flames that had consumed the Temple, and the desolation of war which had destroyed the city. This secret vault, which had been built by Solomon as a secure depository for certain valuable secrets, that would inevitably have been lost without some such expedient for their preservation, communicated by a subterranean avenue with the King's palace; but at the destruction of Jerusalem, the entrance having been closed by the rubbish of falling buildings, it had been now discovered by the appearance of a *keystone among the foundations* of the Sanctum Sanctorum. A careful inspection was then made, and the invaluable secrets were placed in safe custody.—*Historical Landmarks*, vol. II. p. 434.

In preparing the foundations, as we are told by the Jewish Rabbins, the workmen discovered a subterranean vault or cavity, supported by seven pairs of pillars supporting so many arches. This vault, at the destruction of Jerusalem, having been filled with the rubbish of the building, escaped observation, and was indicated at the present period by the discovery of *a keystone among the foundations*. The Rabbins add, that Josiah, foreseeing the destruction of the Temple, commanded the Levites to deposit the Ark of the Covenant in this vault, where it was found by some of Zerubbabel's workmen. But there is no ground for this belief; for if the secret of the vault had been known to Josiah, it must have been known also to his idolatrous predecessors, who would doubtless have plundered it of its valuable contents, and exposed them to the world, in contempt of the true God to whom they referred, and whom these degenerate monarchs had wholly renounced. It is much more probable, that in the latter years of Solomon, when he had almost forgotten God, his visits to this vault were discontinued, and the entrance being curiously concealed among the caverns underneath his palace, the secret died with him, and the communication was forever closed. It is certain, however, if the tradition of this vault be correct, that *the Ark of the Covenant was not found in it; for* it was one of the invaluable gifts of God which the second Temple did not contain, and consequently it could not have been preserved by Josiah.—*Historical Landmarks*, vol. II. p. 436.

High Priest (taking a little pot out of the Ark).—Companion King, what can this be? a pot of manna? We will read in the book of the law, and see what that says: (Reads, *Exodus* XVI. 32-34.)

"And Moses said, This is the thing which the Lord commandeth: Fill an omer of the manna to be kept for your generations, that they may see the bread wherewith I have fed you in the wilderness, when I brought you forth from the land of Egypt. And Moses said unto Aaron, Take a pot, and put an omer full of manna therein, and lay it up before the Lord, to be kept for your generations. As the Lord commanded Moses, so Aaron laid it up before the testimony, to be kept for a token."

High Priest—A Pot of Manna! Holiness to the Lord!

King—A Pot of Manna! Holiness to the Lord!

Scribe repeats the same.

High Priest—Companions, we read in the book of the law, that he that overcometh, will I give to eat of the hidden manna. Come forward, Companions, you are entitled to it. (Each one receives a small lump of sugar.) But how it came deposited here, we cannot now particularly speak. You must go higher in Masonry before you can know.

The High Priest looks again into the Ark, and finds a stick with some buds upon it, which he shows to the King and Scribe, and after a consultation, they decide that it is Aaron's Rod, and the fact is thus proclaimed in the same manner as the discovery of the manna.

High Priest then reads the following passage, Numbers XVII. 10:

"And the Lord said unto Moses, Bring Aaron's rod again before the testimony, to be kept for a token."

And also, Hebrews IX. 2-5:

"For there was a tabernacle made: the first, wherein was the candlesticks, and the table, and the shew-bread, which is called the sanctuary: and after the second veil, the tabernacle, which is called the Holiest of all; which had the golden censer, and the ark of the covenant, overlaid round about with gold; wherein was the golden pot that had manna; and Aaron's rod, that budded, and the tables of the covenant; and over it the cherubim of glory, shadowing the mercy seat; of which we cannot now speak particularly."

Looking again into the Ark, the High Priest takes out four pieces of paper, which he examines closely, consults with the

King and Scribe, and then puts together, so as to show a *key* to the ineffable characters of this Degree:

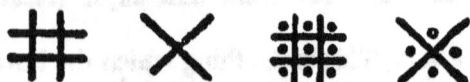

⊞ ✕ ▦ ✻

The key to the ineffable characters, or Royal Arch Cipher, alluded to above, consists of right angles, in various situations, with the addition of a dot. By transposition, it forms twenty-six distinct characters, corresponding with the twenty-six letters of the English alphabet. There are two methods of combining these characters for secret correspondence. One method is to call the first sign, , *a*; the second, , *b*; the third, , *c*; and so on, reading from left to right, thus:

a   b   c   d   e   f   g   h   i   j   k   l   m

n   o   p   q   r   s   t   u   v   w   x   y   z

The second way to read the alphabet is as follows:

a   b   c   d   e   f   g   h   i   j   k   l   m

n   o   p   q   r   s   t   u   v   w   x   y   z

The upper left angle without a dot is *a*; the same with a dot is *b*, &c.

High Priest then reads Exodus VI. 2, 3:

"And God spake unto Moses, and said unto him, I am the Lord: and I appeared unto Abraham, unto Isaac, and unto Jacob, by the name of God Almighty; but by my name Jehovah was I not known to them."

After examining the Key, he proceeds to read, by the aid of it, the characters on the four sides of the Ark.

High Priest (reading first side).—Deposited in the year three thousand. Second side—By Solomon, King of Israel. Third side —Hiram, King of Tyre, and Hiram Abiff. Fourth side—For the good of Masonry, generally, but the Jewish nation in particular.[1]

High Priest (to candidates).—Companions, here are three mysterious words, in a triangular form, upon the Ark, which, when first found, were covered with three squares, the jewels of our three ancient Grand Masters; and from this circumstance, we supposed it to be the long-lost Master Mason's word; and, on applying our Key to it, it proved our suspicions to be correct.. It is the name of Deity in three languages, viz., Chaldaic, Hebrew and Syriac, which is the long-lost Master Mason's word, or Logos, and has now become the Grand Omnific Royal Arch word.

It is the divine Logos, or Word, to which reference is had in John (i. 1-5):

"In the beginning was the word (Logos), and the word was with God, and the word was God; the same was in the beginning with God: all things were made by him, and without him was not any thing made that was made; in him was life, and the life was the light of men: and the light shineth in darkness, and the darkness comprehended it not."

This word was anciently written only in these sacred characters, and thus preserved from one generation to another.. It was lost by the death of Hiram Abiff, was found again at the building of the Temple, and will now be given to you; and you will remember the manner you receive it, and that you have sworn never to give it to others except in that particular manner.

The candidates, instructed by the Principal Sojourner, now learn the Grand Omnific Royal Arch Word, as follows:

Each one takes hold with his right hand of the right wrist of his companion on the left, and with his left hand takes hold of the left wrist of his companion on the right. Each one then

---

[1] The author of *Ahiman Rezon* has stated that he could convey his mind to an ancient Mason in the presence of a modern Mason, without the latter knowing whether either of them were Masons. He further asserted that he was able, with a few Masonic implements, i. e., two squares and a common gavel or hammer, to convey any word or sentence of his own, or the immediate dictations of a stranger, to a skilful and intelligent Freemason of the ancient order, without speaking, writing, or noise; and that to any distance, when the parties can see each other, and at the same time be able to distinguish squares from circles. This Masonic system of cipher-writing is now well understood.—*Origin of the English Royal Arch*, p. 48.

places his right foot forward with the hollow in front, so that the toe touches the heel of his companion on the right. This is called "three times three;" that is, three right feet forming a triangle, three left hands forming a triangle, and three right hands forming a triangle. They balance in the same manner, and then, with hands raised, repeat the words Jah-buh-lun, Je-ho-vah, G-o d, at low breath, as described before. (See pp. 224-25, Fig. 32.)[1]

[1] The WORD of the Royal Arch Degree, as worked in England, is *Jao-Bul-On*.

"Macrobius, in his Saturnalia (lib. I. 18), says that it was an admitted axiom among the heathen, that the triliteral JAH, or rather IAΩ, was the sacred name of the Supreme God. And the Clarian oracle, which was of unknown antiquity, being asked which of the deities was named IAΩ, answered in these memorable words:

"'The initiated are bound to conceal the mysterious secrets. Learn thou, that IAΩ, is the Great God Supreme, who ruleth over all.'

"Now it so happens, that in the gems of the early Christians we find these very letters, IAΩ, which are an abbreviation of the name of JEHOVAH, used as a monogram to express the name of the Saviour of mankind, who was thus represented as existing before time was, and shall exist when time shall be no more. It was first adopted by the Eastern Church, and signified *Ιησους, Αλφα Ομεγα*, Jesus, Alpha Omega, or in other words: Jesus, the First and the Last."—*The Insignia of the Royal Arch*, p. 32.

The Royal Arch Word to have been perfectly in keeping with the Degree, and with the general construction of Masonry, should have been a triad, not only of syllables, but also of letters. Our transatlantic brethren have seen it in its true light; but they have corrected the error unlearnedly. It ought to have been, if the principle of its construction be allowed, to be orthodox:

Syriac	*Chaldee*	*Hindoo*
___ ___	___ ___	___ ___

The Insignia of the Royal Arch, p. 34.

That is to say, instead of JAO-BUL-ON, or JAH-BUH-LUN, Dr. Oliver suggests:

Syriac	*Chaldee*	*Hindoo*
JAO	BEL	AUN
OR	OR	OR
JAH	BUL	AUM

For at page 15 of *The Insignia*, he writes thus:

"But the Royal Arch Degree is founded on the number *three*, and therefore each member of the word ought to have been triliteral. ... Among the Syrians, the Chaldeans, the Phœnicians and others, the ineffable name of the Deity was Bel, Bal, Bul, Baal, or Belin. ... Again, the Egyptians and Hindoos reverenced On or Om, i. e., Aun, or Aum, as the name of their chief Deity."

And vide *Historical Landmarks*, vol. II. p. 549:

"One says it was Jau, another thinks it was Jaoth, a third, Java; others, Juba, Jao, Jah, Jehovah, and Jova. In a word, the letters of the name are perishable, and the pronunciation of little moment; but the Being himself is ineffable, incomprehensible, and worthy of our utmost veneration. He was called by the Romans Jove, or Jah; by the Chaldeans, the Phœnicians, and the Celts, Bel or Bul; and by the Indians, Egyptians, and Greeks, Om or On."

The signs of this Degree are now given to the candidates, as follows:

First, raise the right hand to the forehead, the hand and arm horizontal, the thumb toward the forehead; draw it briskly across the forehead, and drop it perpendicularly by the side. This constitutes the duegard and sign of this Degree, and refers not only to the penalty of the obligation, but alludes also to the manner in which the brother who descended into the vault, and found the Ark, found his hands involuntarily placed, to protect his head

Fig. 86

Fig. 87

ROYAL ARCH DUEGARD AND SIGN

ROYAL ARCH GRAND HAILING SIGN[1]

from the rays of the meridian sun. (See Fig. 36.) This sign must be given to the High Priest, upon entering and retiring from a Chapter.

High Priest (placing crowns upon the heads of candidates).— Companions, you are now invested with all the important secrets

[1] The grand hailing sign is made by locking the fingers of both hands together, and carrying them to the top of the head, the palms upward. Then let them drop to the sides.

of this Degree, and crowned and received as worthy Companions Royal Arch Masons.

The High Priest then reads to them from a book the charge in this Degree, informing them that the Degree owes its origin to Zerubbabel and his associates, who rebuilt the Temple by order of Cyrus, King of Persia. He likewise informs them that the discovery of the secret vault and the inestimable treasures, with the long-lost word, actually took place in the manner represented in conferring this Degree, and that it is the circumstance upon which the Degree is principally founded.

The initiation being over, the High Priest begins the closing lecture, which is a repetition, by questions and answers, of the opening of a Chapter, and the advancement of a companion of this Degree. It begins as follows:

High Priest (to Captain of the Host).—Are you a Royal Arch Mason?

Captain—I am that I am.

High Priest—How shall I know you to be a Royal Arch Mason?

Captain of Host—By three times three.

High Priest—Where were you made a Royal Arch Mason?

Captain of the Host—In a just and legally constituted Chapter of Royal Arch Masons, consisting of Most Excellent High Priest, King and Scribe, Captain of the Host, Principal Sojourner, Royal Arch Captain, and the three Grand Masters of the Veils, assembled in a room or place representing the Tabernacle erected by our ancient brethren, near the ruins of King Solomon's Temple.

The High Priest continues his questions as to the station and duties of each officer of the Chapter, and every particular relative to the organization thereof, the initiation or advancement of candidates, &c. The Captain of the Host rehearses or describes the whole precisely as we have given it. These closing lectures are intended to perfect members in the full understanding of each Degree.

After the lecture, the Chapter is closed in the same manner as the opening, up to the raising of the Living Arch. The companions join hands by threes, in the same manner, and say in concert:

> As we three did agree
> The Sacred Word to keep—
> As we three did agree
> The Sacred Word to search;
> So we three do agree
> To close this Royal Arch.

They then break, and the High Priest reads the following prayer:

"By the wisdom of the Supreme High Priest may we be directed, by his strength may we be enabled, and by the beauty of virtue may we be incited to perform the obligations here enjoined upon us, to keep inviolable the mysteries here unfolded to us, and invariably to practise all those duties out of the Chapter which are inculcated in it."

Companions—So mote it be. Amen.

High Priest—I now declare this Chapter of Royal Arch Masons closed.[1]

It is generally conceded by Masonic writers, that ancient Masonry closes with the Royal Arch. In an edition of "The Illustrations of Masonry," by Mr. Preston, published in London, 1829, the editor, Mr. Oliver, observes:

"All Degrees beyond the Royal Arch ought to be carefully separated from genuine Masonry, as they are mostly founded on vague and uncertain traditions, which possess not the shadow of authority to recommend them to our notice."[2]

---

[1] At my first exaltation, I was taught to believe it an ancient degree; but I confess, that even at that period I entertained considerable doubts on the point. The Degree is too incongruous to be of any great antiquity. It exhibits too many evidences of modern construction to be received with implicit credence as a ceremony practised by the ancient Dionysiacs, or even the more modern colleges of Freemasons, or confraternities of the Middle Ages. The earliest mention of it in England which I can find, is in the year 1740, just one year after the trifling alteration, sanctioned by the modern Grand Lodge, already mentioned.—*Origin of the English Royal Arch*, pp. 19, 20.

[2] The fact is, the grand omnific *(all-creating) lost word*, it will be seen in the sequel, was eventually found in a vault under the ruins of Solomon's Temple; and the difficulty was, *rationally* to account for the manner in which it got there. This, therefore, is the grand object of the *Select Master's Degree;* and, at the same time, so to locate the word as symbolically to represent its archetype, the sun *lost* in the inferior hemisphere. For this purpose a history of the order was manufactured by its founders, of which the following is a sketch:

"The three Grand Masters, at the building of the Temple, entered into a solemn agreement not to confer the Master's Degree until the Temple should be completed; that all three must be present when it should be conferred, and if either should be taken away by death prior to the finishing of the Temple, the Master's Degree should be lost.

"After this *wise* arrangement, lest the knowledge of the arts and sciences, together with the patterns and valuable models which were contained in the Temple, should be lost, they agreed to build a *secret vault* under ground, leading from Solomon's most retired apartment, a *dus west course*, and ending under the *sanctum sanctorum* of the Temple, to be divided into *nine separate arches*. The ninth arch was to be the place for holding the grand council, and also for a deposit of a true copy of all those things which were *contained in the sanctum sanctorum above.*

"After the ninth arch was completed, the three Grand Masters deposited therein those things which were important to the craft, such as the Ark of the Covenant, a pot of manna, the rod of Aaron, the book of the law, etc.

The additional Degrees, including those considered legitimate, amount to upward of fifty. These are founded partly upon astronomical principles, agreeing with the ancient worship of the Egyptians, and partly upon the Hebrew and Christian doctrines.

It may be remarked in general, that many of the degrees of knights are founded on the Christian knighthoods got up in the time of the Crusades, in the twelfth century; and that the ceremonies thereof are an imitation of those superstitious establishments. A former Grand High Priest of the Chapters in the State of New York informs me, that he initiated a French gentleman into the Degree of Knight of Malta, who told him he was a member of the ancient order of that name, and that the ceremonies were very similar.

At the time those old knighthoods were founded, "superstition mingled in every public and private action of life; in the holy wars it sanctified the profession of arms; and the order of chivalry was assimilated in its rights and privileges to the sacred orders of priesthood. The bath and the white garment of the novice were an indecent copy of the regeneration of baptism; his sword, which he offered on the altar, was blessed by the ministers of religion; his solemn reception was preceded by fasts and vigils; and he was created a knight in the name of God, of St. George, and of St. Michael the archangel."—*Rees's Cycl.*

The emblem of the Royal Arch Degree is called the *Triple Tau*, and is a figure consisting of three tau crosses. It was adopted at Chicago, 1859, by the General Grand Chapter of the United States, and is worn printed on all aprons of the Royal Arch Degree.

LECTURE ON THE SEVENTH, OR ROYAL ARCH DEGREE.— SECTION FIRST

Question. Are you a Royal Arch Mason?
Answer. I am that I am.
Q. How shall I know you to be a Royal Arch Mason?
A. By three times three.
Q. Where were you exalted to the most, sublime Degree of a Royal Arch Mason?

"Prior to the completion of the Temple, Grand Master Hiram Abiff was assassinated, and by his death the Master's Word was lost. The two kings were willing to do all in their power to preserve the *Sacred Word*, and as they could not communicate it to any, by reason of the death of Hiram, they agreed to place it in the *secret vault*, that if the other treasures were ever brought to light, the *Word* might be found also."—*Fellows's Inquiry into the Origin, History, and Purport of Freemasonry*, pp. 308, 309.

A. In a regularly and duly constituted Chapter of Royal Arch Masons assembled in a place representing a Tabernacle, erected by our ancient brethren near the ruins of King Solomon's temple.

Q. How many constitute a Chapter of Royal Arch Masons?

A. Nine Regular Royal Arch Masons—consisting of Most Excellent High Priest, Excellent King, and Scribe, Captain of the Host, Principal Sojourner, Royal Arch Captain, and three Masters of the veils.

Q. Who do the three former represent?

A. Those of our ancient brethren who formed the first Most Grand Council at Jerusalem, and held their meetings in a tabernacle.

Q. Who did the three latter represent?

A. Those of our ancient brethren, who directed and brought to light the principal secrets of this Degree, after they had lain buried in darkness from the death of our Grand Master Hiram Abiff, until the erection of the second temple, and as a reward for their zeal, fortitude and attachment to Masonry, were exalted to become the three Grand Masters of the veils.

Q. How many veils were they?

A. Four.

Q. What were their colors?

A. Blue, purple, scarlet and white.

Q. What does blue denote?

A. Friendship, and is the principal color of a Master Mason.

Q. What does purple denote?

A. It being composed of blue and scarlet, it is placed before the first and third veils of the colors, to denote the intimate connection between this most sublime degree, and ancient Craft Masonry.

Q. What does scarlet denote?

A. That fervency and zeal which should actuate all Royal Arch Masons, and is the peculiar color of this Degree.

Q. What does white denote?

A. That purity of life and rectitude of conduct which should govern all those who seek to gain admission into that Sanctum Sanctorum, or Holy of Holies.

Q. To whom do the four veils allude?

A. To the four tribes of the children of Israel, who bore the banners through the wilderness, viz.: Judah, Reuben, Ephraim and Dan, emblematically represented by the strength of the Lion, the intelligence of the Man, the patience of the Ox and the swiftness of the Eagle.

Q. Where were the veils placed?

A. At the outer courts of the tabernacle.

Q. Why there?

A. To serve as a covering for the tabernacle and stations for the guards.

Q. Why were guards stationed there?

A. To take special pains that none pass or repass, except such as were duly qualified, as none were permitted to enter the presence of the Most Excellent High Priest, Excellent King, and Scribe, except the true descendants of the twelve (12) tribes of the children of Israel.

Q. How did the children of Israel make themselves known to the several guards?

A. By the same words and signs given by God to Moses. He was commanded to conduct the children of Israel out of the land of Egypt from the bands of bondage.

SECOND SECTION

Q. Where were you prepared to be exalted to the Most Sublime degree of a Royal Arch Mason?

A. In a room adjoining a regular and duly constituted Chapter of Royal Arch Masons.

Q. How were you prepared.

A. I was divested of my outward apparel, in a working posture, hoodwinked, and a cable-tow seven times around my body, accompanied by two (2) brethren possessed of like qualifications, in which condition we were conducted to the door of the Chapter, where a regular demand was made by seven (7) distinct knocks.

Q. To what do the seven (7) distinct knocks allude?

A. To the seventh Degree of Masonry, it being that upon which I was about to enter.

Q. What was said to you from within?

A. Who comes here?

Q. Your answer?

A. Three worthy brothers (or brethren) who have been duly initiated, passed to the Degree of Fellow Craft, raised to the Sublime Degree of Master Mason, advanced to the Degree of Mark Master Mason, regularly passed the Chair—have been received and acknowledged as Most Excellent Masters, and now wish further promotion in Masonry, by being exalted to the Most Sublime Degree of a Royal Arch Mason.

Q. What were you then asked?

A. If it was an act of my own free will and accord, if I was worthy and well qualified, duly and truly prepared, if I had made suitable proficiencies in the preceding Degree, and was properly vouched for—all of which being answered in the affirmative, I was asked by what further right or benefit I expected to obtain this important privilege.

Q. Your answer?

A. By the benefit of the pass.

Q. Give the pass?

A. Rabboni.

Q. What does it signify?

A. Good Master, or Most Excellent Master.

Q. What was then said to you?

A. We were directed to wait until the Captain of the Host could be informed of our request, and his answer returned.

Q. What was his answer when returned?

A. Let the candidates enter and be received in due and ancient form.

Q. How were you received in a Chapter of Royal Arch Masons?

A. Under a living arch.

Q. Why under a living arch?

A. To imprint upon my mind in the most solemn manner that the principal secrets of this Degree should be communicated only under a living arch.

Q. How were you then disposed of?

A. We were conducted once around the outer courts of the tabernacle, there caused to kneel at the altar and invoke a blessing from Deity.

Q. After invoking a blessing from Deity, how were you then disposed of?

A. We were again conducted around the outer courts of the tabernacle, where we were met by the Captain of the Host, who demanded of us who comes here, and what were our intentions.

Q. Your answer?

A. As at the door.

Q. Of what did the Captain of the Host inform you?

A. That in pursuing our intentions, we should be under the disagreeable necessity of travelling those rough and rugged paths, which all Royal Arch Masons have done before us, but before pursuing further it would be necessary for us to kneel at the altar in due form, and take upon ourselves the solemn oath or obligation of a Royal Arch Mason.

Q. What was that due form?

A. Kneeling upon both knees, both hands covering the Holy Bible, square and compasses, in which due form I took upon myself the solemn oath or obligation of a Royal Arch Mason.

Q. Have you that oath?

A. I have.

Q. Will you give it?

A. I will with your assistance.

Q. Proceed. (I, A. B., etc., etc.)

Q. After the oath how were you then disposed of?

A. We were again conducted around the outer courts of the tabernacle, where was exhibited the symbol of the burning bush.

Q. Why was the symbol of the burning bush exhibited to you at this point of your exaltation?

A. To impress upon my mind in the most solemn manner, that the words and signs following were of divine origin, and as such were regarded sacred by the children of Israel—by them transmitted to their posterity, as words and signs by which they should make themselves known and be distinguished by each other for ever after.

Q. How were you then disposed of?

A. We were again conducted around the outer courts of the tabernacle, where a representation of the destruction of the temple took place.

Q. By whom was it destroyed?

A. By Nebuchadnezzar, King of Babylon, who in the eleventh year of Zedekiah, King of Jerusalem, went up, besieged and took the city, seized on all the holy vessels, together with the two brazen pillars; and the remnant of the people who escaped the sword, he carried away captives to Babylon.

Q. What was the period of their captivity?

A. Seventy (70) years.

Q. By whom were they delivered?

A. By Cyrus, King of Persia, who in the first year of his reign issued his yearly proclamation saying: "Thus says Cyrus, King of Persia," etc., etc. (See Monitor.)

Q. Who did you then represent?

A. Those of our ancient brethren being released from their captivity. -

Q. In that case what answer did you make Cyrus, King of Persia?

A. But behold when I come unto the children of Israel, etc., etc. (Monitorial.)

Q. What answer did you receive from the Captain of the Host?

A. I am that I am, I am hath sent me unto you.

Q. Did you pursue your journey?

A. We did, the rough and rugged paths.

Q. What do the rough and rugged paths denote?

A. The sojourning of the children of Israel through the wilderness.

Q. Did you meet with any obstructions?

A. We did, several.

Q. Where did you meet with the first obstruction?

A. At the first veil, where on making the regular demand, we heard the Master of that veil exclaim, "Who dares approach this first veil of our sacred tabernacle?" and he, supposing an enemy to be approaching, hailed his companions, who on being assembled demanded, "Who comes here?"

Q. Your answer?

A. We are of your own brethren and kin—children of the captivity—descendants of those noble Giblemites, we were received and acknowledged Most Excellent Masters at the completion and dedication of the first temple—were present at the destruction of that temple by Nebuchadnezzar, by whom we were carried captives to Babylon, where we remained servants to him and his successors, until the reign of Cyrus, King of Persia, by whose order we have been liberated, and have now come up to help, aid, and assist in rebuilding the house of the Lord, without the hope of fee or reward.

Q. What were you then asked?

A. By what further reward or benefit we expected to obtain this important privilege.

Q. Your answer?

A. By the benefit of the pass.

Q. Give it? (I am that I am, I am hath sent me unto you.)

Q. Did this give you admission?

A. It did within the first veil.

Q. What was then said to you?

A. Good men and true you must have been, to have come thus far to promote so noble and good an undertaking; but further you cannot go without my word, sign, and word of explanation.

Q. What was the word of the Master of the first veil?

A. I am that I am, I am hath sent you unto us, Shem, Ham, and Japheth.

Q. What is his sign?

A. It is in imitation of that given by God to Moses when he was commanded to cast his rod upon the ground, and it became a serpent.

Q. What was his word of explanation?

A. It was explanatory of the sign as recorded by Moses, and is as follows. "And Moses answered and said, But behold they will not believe me, nor hearken unto my voice, for they will say, The

Lord hath not appeared unto thee; and the Lord said unto him, What is that in thine hand, and he said, A rod; and He said, Cast it on the ground. And he cast it on the ground and it became a serpent, and Moses fled from before it; and the Lord said, Put forth thine hand and take it by the tail; and he put forth his hand and caught it, and it become a rod in his hand, that they may believe that the God of their fathers, the God of Abraham, the God of Isaac, and the God of Jacob hath appeared unto thee.

Q. Where did you meet with the next obstruction?

A. At the second veil, where, on making the regular demand, we heard the master of that exclaim as before.

Q. Your answer?

A. As before.

Q. What were you then asked?

A. By what further right or benefit we expected to obtain that important privilege.

Q. Your answer?

A. By the word and sign given us by the master of the first veil.

Q. Did this gain you admission?

A. It did within the second veil.

Q. What was then said to you?

A. Good men and true you must have been, to have come thus far to engage in so noble and glorious an undertaking, but further you cannot go without my word and sign, and word of explanation.

Q. What was the word of the master of the second veil?

A. I am that I am, I am hath sent me unto you, Shem, Ham, and Japheth.

Q. What is his sign?

A. It is in imitation of that given by God to Moses, when he commanded him to put his hand into his bosom, and when he took it out, behold it was as leprous as snow.

Q. What is his word of explanation?

A. It is explanatory of that sign, is recorded by Moses, and is as follows: And the Lord said unto Moses, Put now thine hand into thy bosom, and he put his hand into his bosom, and when he took it out, behold, his hand was leprous as snow. And He said, Put thine hand into thy bosom again, and he put his hand into his bosom again, and plucked it out of his bosom, and behold it was turned again as his other flesh. And it shall come to pass if they will not believe thee, neither hearken to the voice of the first sign, that they will believe the voice of the latter sign.

Q. Where did you meet with the next obstruction?

A. At the third veil, where, on making the regular demand, we heard the master of that veil exclaim as before.

Q. Your answer?

A. As before.

Q. What were you then asked?

A. By what further right or benefit we expected to obtain this important privilege.

Q. Your answer?

A. By the benefit of the word and sign given us by the masters of the first and second veils.

Q. Did they gain you admission?

A. They did within the third veil.

Q. What was then said to you?

A. Good men and true you must have been, to have come thus far to promote so noble and good an undertaking, but further you cannot go without my sign and word of explanation and *signet.*

Q. What was his sign?

A. It is in imitation of that given by God to Moses, when he commanded him to take of the water of the river and pour it upon the dry land.

Q. What is his word of explanation?

A. It is explanatory of that sign, is recorded by Moses, and is as follows: And it shall come to pass if they will not believe also these two signs, neither hearken unto thy voice, that thou shalt take of the water of the river and pour it upon the dry land, and the water which thou takest out of the river shall become blood upon the dry land.

Q. Where did you meet with the next obstruction?

A. At the fourth veil or sanctuary, where on making the regular demand, we heard the Royal Arch Captain exclaim, "Who dares approach the fourth veil or sanctuary, where incense burns upon our holy altar both day and night? Who comes here?"

Q. Your answer?

A. Three worthy sojourners, who have come up to help, aid, and assist in the rebuilding of the house of the Lord, without the hope of fee or reward.

Q. What were you then asked?

A. Whence came you?

Q. Your answer?

A. From Babylon.

Q. Of what were you then informed.

A. That by a degree of the *Grand Council,* then in session,

made in consequence of difficulties having arisen by the introduction of strangers among the workmen, none are permitted to
enter the presence of the Most Excellent High Priest, Excellent
King, and Scribe, while sitting in council, excepting the true descendants of the twelve tribes of the children of Israel; it was
therefore necessary that we be more particular in tracing our
genealogy, and demanded who we were.

Q. Your answer?

A. We are of your brethren and kin—children of the captivity
—we have been received as Most Excellent Masters, and as such
have made ourselves known to the several guards, and now wait
permission to enter the presence of the Grand Council.

Q. What were you then asked?

A. By what further right or benefit we expected to obtain this
important privilege.

Q. Your answer?

A. By the benefit of the words and signs given us by the masters
of the first, second and third veils, together with the signet.

Q. What was then said to you?

A. We were directed to wait until the Captain of the Host
could be informed of our request and his answer returned.

Q. What answer did he return?

A. Let them be admitted.

Q. By whom were you received?

A. By the Captain of the Host, who conducted us into the presence of the Grand Council, who examined us as to our proficiency
in the preceding degree, and expressed satisfaction at our meeting,
after which we were asked what part of the work we were willing
to undertake.

Q. Your answer?

A. Any part, even the most servile, to promote so noble and
glorious an undertaking.

Q. Of what were you then informed?

A. That from the specimens of skill which we had exhibited,
the Grand Council had confidence and belief that we were able
to undertake any part, even the most difficult, but that it was
necessary that some more of the rubbish be removed from the
northeast part of the ruins, and they instructed us to observe and
preserve everything that we might discover of value, for they had
no doubt that there were many valuable monuments of art there
which would be essential to the craft.

Q. What followed?

A. The Captain of the Host furnished us with the necessary
working tools, and we repaired to the place as directed, where

we wrought diligently four days without discovering anything of interest, excepting passing the ruins of several columns of the order of architecture; on the fifth, still pursuing our labors, we experienced that which we at first supposed to be an impenetrable rock, but on my companion striking it with his crow, it reverberated a hollow sound, upon which we redoubled our assiduity, and removing some more of the rubbish, we found it to resemble the top of an arch, in the apex of which was a stone having on it certain characters which by length of time were nearly effaced. Night now drawing on, we repaired with it to the Grand Council.

Q. What was their opinion of the stone?

A. That it was the keystone to the principal arch of King Solomon's Temple, and from the place in which it was found, they had no doubt it would lead to important discoveries; upon which we were asked if we were willing on the morrow to descend the arch in search of them.

Q. Your answer?

A. That the task would be attended with difficulties and dangers, yet we were willing even at the risk of our lives to promote so noble and glorious an undertaking.

Q. What followed?

A. We repaired to the place as before, and removed some more of the rubbish, after which we placed a cable-tow seven times around the body of one of my companions to assist him in descending, and it was agreed, should the place become offensive, either to health or sight, he should swing it to the right as a signal to ascend; but should he wish to descend he should swing it to the left. In this manner he descended and found three squares, which they had no doubt had long been concealed; he gave the signal and ascended, and with them we repaired to the Grand Council.

Q. What was their opinion of the squares?

A. That they were masters' jewels, most probably worn by our ancient Grand Masters, Solomon, King of Israel, Hiram, King of Tyre, and Hiram Abiff, and from the place in which they were found they had no doubt they would lead to still further and more important discoveries, upon which we were asked if willing again to descend the arch in search of the treasures.

Q. Your answer? (As before.)

Q. What followed?

A. We repaired to the place as before, which I descended as before. The sun shone forth with such redoubled splendor that I was enabled to descend; in the eastern-most part thereof was a trunk of curious form, overlaid with gold, having on its top and sides certain mysterious characters; availing myself of this I gave the signal, and ascended; on arriving at the top of the arch I found my hands involuntarily placed in this position to guard my eyes from the intense light and heat that arose therefrom above; with the trunk we repaired to the Grand Council.

Q. What was their opinion of the trunk?

A. That it was the Ark of the Covenant.

Q. What were its contents?

A. A pot, a rod, and a book.

Q. What was their opinion of the pot?

A. That it was the pot of manna, which Moses by divine command, laid up in the side of the ark as a memorial of the miraculous manner in which the children of Israel were supplied with that article of food for forty years in the wilderness.

Q. What was their opinion of the rod?

A. That it was Aaron's rod, that budded and blossomed, and bore fruit in a day, which Moses also, by divine command, laid in the side of the ark as a testimony, to be kept for a token.

Q. What was their opinion of the book?

A. That it was the book of the law in which it is written, I am the Lord, I appeared unto Abraham, unto Isaac and Jacob by the name of God Almighty, but by my great and sacred name was I not known unto them.

Q. What does it contain?

A. A key to the mysterious characters upon its top and sides, by which they found those upon its sides to be the initials of our three ancient Grand Masters, S. K. of I., H. K. of T., and H. Abiff. Those upon its top, the Grand Omnific or Royal Arch word, which we as Royal Arch Masons should never give except in the presence of three Royal Arch Masons, we first agreeing by three times three, and under a living arch.

Q. How were your merits rewarded?

A. The Grand Council descended and invested us with the secrets of the Degree.

Q. How were they communicated?

A. The Grand Omnific Royal Arch word in the presence of three regular Arch Masons, we first agreeing by three times three, and under a living arch.

Q. Have you a sign in this Degree?

A. I have several.

Q. Show me a sign? (Hand to forehead. See sign.)

Q. What is that called?

A. The duegard.

Q. To what does it allude?

A. To the way and manner in which my hands were involuntarily placed on arriving at the arch, to guard my eyes from the intense light and heat that arose therefrom above.

Q. Show me another sign? (Give sign.)

Q. What is that called?

A. The sign.

Q. To what does it allude?

A. To the penalty of my obligation, that I would sooner have my skull struck off than divulge any of the secrets of this Degree unlawfully.

Q. Give me another sign? (Give sign.)

Q. What is that called?

A. The grand hailing sign, or sign of distress of a Royal Arch Mason

Q. To what does it allude?

A. To the additional portion of the penalty of my obligation, that I would sooner have my skull clove off, and have my brain exposed to the scorching rays of a noonday sun, than divulge any of the secrets of this Degree unlawfully.

Q. What are the working tools of a Royal Arch Mason?

A. The pick, spade, and crow.

Q. What does the spade teach us as Royal Arch Masons? (Monitorial.)

Q. What is the use of the crow?

A. It is used by operative masons to describe circles—every part of the circumference of which is equally near and equally distant from its centre; so is every creature whom God hath made equally near and equally dear.

Q. What is the equilateral or perfect triangle upon which the word is formed emblematical of?

A. The three certain attributes of Deity—namely, Omniscience, Omnipotence, and Omnipresence, for as the three equal legs or angles form but one triangle, so the three attributes constitute but one God.

EXTRACTS FROM "A DICTIONARY OF SYMBOLICAL MASONRY, INCLUDING THE ROYAL ARCH DEGREE," BY THE REV. G. OLIVER, D. D.

ACHILLES.—Perhaps some worthy people may stare when we point out Achilles as a Freemason. What! we hear them exclaim, is it possible that that fierce and ferocious man-slayer, nay, man-eater at heart, for he exhibited a strong propensity to cannibalism in longing to have devoured the dead body of Hector—is it possible that he could have been one of our philanthropic society? Yes, we reply, such is the actual fact, and Bonaparte was one, too, in the highest degree. But, if you will not believe Homer, or us, believe your own eyes, if, indeed, you are a Mason. *Ecce signum!* Behold Achilles giving Priam THE HAND, when the latter is supplicating for the body of his slain son:

"Thus having spoken, the old man's *right hand at the wrist*
He grasped, that he might not in any respect be alarmed in mind."

Such is the Masonic and literal translation of the text by that illustrious Grecian and brother, Christopher North; and who will say, now, that Achilles was not a Mason?—*Freemasons' Quarterly Review.*

[According to this, *Brother* Achilles gave *Brother* Priam the Master Mason's Grip, but there is no evidence to show whether they used the word MAH-HAH-BONE, and the Five Points of Fellowship.]

ESSENTIAL SECRETS.—The essential secrets of Masonry consist of nothing more than the signs, grips, pass-words, and tokens, essential to the preservation of the society from the inroads of impostors; together with certain symbolical emblems, the technical terms appertaining to which served as a sort of universal language, by which the members of the fraternity could distinguish each other, in all places and countries where Lodges were instituted. —*Stone.*

EVESIGHT.—He who has been temporarily deprived of his sight is reduced to the condition of a new-born babe, or of one of those unfortunate individuals whose natural infirmity renders the presence of a conductor indispensably necessary; but when there are no outward objects to distract his attention, it is then that with the eye of reflection he probes into the deepest and darkest recesses of his own heart, and discovers his natural imperfections and impurities much more readily than he could possibly have done had he not been deprived of his sight. This short deprivation of sight has kindled in his heart a spark of the brightest and purest flame. . . . We must further admit, that those who have been deprived of their sight, and who have hopes of being restored to it, strive most industriously and diligently to obtain it; that they have no greater desire, and that *they will most readily pledge themselves to do all that can be required of them*, in order to obtain that inestimable blessing.

A man who has been deprived of his sight may be introduced into places where he is surrounded by the strangest and the rarest objects, *without a possibility of his becoming a traitor.* At the same time, those who are in possession of their sight cannot feel the care of their guides so much as those who are hoodwinked, and who feel that without the constant attention of their conductors they would be much more helpless than they now are; but, however many proofs of attention and care they may receive, there is still something left to wish for; and to the question, What is your chief desire? the answer will ever assuredly be, "Light."
—*Gadicke.*

FIVE POINTS OF FELLOWSHIP.—The five points of fellowship were thus illustrated in the lectures used by the Athol Masons of the last century:

1. When the necessities of a brother call for my support, I will be ever ready to lend him a helping hand to save him from sinking, if I find him worthy thereof.

2. Indolence shall not cause my footsteps to halt, nor wrath to turn them aside; but, forgetting every selfish consideration, I will be ever swift of foot to save, help, and execute benevolence to a fellow-creature in distress, but more particularly to a brother Mason.

3. When I offer up my ejaculations to Almighty God, I will remember my brother's welfare, even as my own; for as the voice of babes and sucklings ascends to the throne of grace, so, most assuredly, will the breathings of a fervent heart ascend to the mansions of bliss.

4. A brother's secret, delivered to me as such, I will keep as I would my own, because, if I betray the trust which has been reposed in me, I might do him an irreparable injury; it would be like the villany of an assassin, who lurks in darkness to stab his adversary when unarmed and least prepared to meet an enemy.

5. A brother's character I will support in his absence, as I would

in his presence. I will not revile him myself, nor suffer it to be done by others, if it is in my power to prevent it.

Thus, by the five points of fellowship, we are linked together in one indivisible chain of sincere affection, brotherly love, relief, and truth.

GUTTERAL.—The gutteral sign alludes to temperance, which demands such a cautious habit of restraint, as may be necessary to preserve us from the risk of violating our obligation and *incurring its penalty.—Hemming.*

[This alludes to the "Duegard of an Entered Apprentice."]

LANDMARKS.—What are the landmarks? is a question often asked, but never determinately answered. In ancient times, boundary-stones were used as landmarks, before title-deeds were known, the removal of which was strictly forbidden by law. With respect to the landmarks of Masonry, some restrict them to the O. B. signs, tokens, and words. Others include the ceremonies of initiation, passing, and raising; and the form, dimensions, and support; the ground, situation, and covering; the ornaments, furniture, and jewels of a Lodge, or their characteristic symbols. Some think that the Order has no landmarks beyond its peculiar secrets. It is quite clear, however, that the order against removing or altering the landmarks was universally observed in all ages of the Craft.

METAL.—Many men dote on the metals silver and gold with their whole souls, and know no other standard whereby to estimate their own worth, or the worth of their fellow-beings, but by the quantity of these metals they possess, thereby debasing and degrading those qualities of the mind or spirit by which alone mankind ought to be estimated. He who wishes to be initiated into Free Masonry must be willing to relinquish all descriptions of metal, and all the adventitious circumstances of rank and fortune, for it is the MAN that is received into Free Masonry, and not his rank or riches.—*Gadicke.*

ORIGINAL POINTS.—Ancient Masonry admitted twelve original points, which constitute the basis of the entire system, and without which no person ever did or can be legally received into the Order. Every candidate is obliged to pass through all these essential forms and ceremonies, otherwise his initiation would not be legal. They are—opening, preparing, reporting, entering, prayer, circumambulation, advancing, obligation, intrusted, invested, placed, closing.

PENAL.—The penal sign marks our obligation, and reminds us also of the fall of Adam, and the dreadful penalty entailed thereby on his sinful posterity, being no less than death. It intimates that the stiff neck of the disobedient shall be cut off from the land of the living by the judgment of God, even as the head is severed from the body by the sword of human justice.

[This applies as well to the Entered Apprentice's as to the Royal Arch Mason's "Duegard."]

PHRASES OF ADMISSION.—When a candidate receives the first Degree he is said to be *initiated*, at the second step he is *passed*, at the third, *raised*; when he takes the Mark Degree, he is *congratulated* (advanced); having passed the chair, he is said to have *presided*; when he becomes a Most Excellent Master, he is *acknowledged* and *received*; and when a Royal Arch Mason, he is *exalted*.

SIGN OF DISTRESS.—In a society whose members ought fraternally to love and assist each other, it is to be expected that they should have a sign whereby they could make themselves known immediately to their brethren, in however distressed circumstances they might be placed, and thereby at the same time claim their assistance and protection. This is the sign of distress, in conjunction with a few words. He who falls into the greatest difficulty and danger, and supposes that there is a brother within sight or hearing, let him use this sign, and a true and faithful brother must spring to his assistance.—*Gadicke*.

UNIFORMITY.—It is almost unnecessary to argue the question in relation to Uniformity of Work, because such can never be; we say never, as long as we live up to the teachings of the Fathers and communicate, *orally*, the mysteries to candidates. To obtain uniformity, the work must be written, and that will never be done, so long as Freemasons regard their obligations. A Gen. G. Lodge should be, if the fraternity, at any time foolish enough to sanction such an organization, which they never will, might, in imitation of such bodies among modern associations, attempt for the sake of having uniformity, by its dicta authorize the work to be written, but under no other circumstances could or would such a thing be attempted; and even in that case there would be a general uprising of the craft to prevent such a violation of obligation. Uniformity in all things is not absolutely necessary, nor was it ever so considered. It cannot be expected that different persons will communicate the same ideas in precisely the same language; besides language changes in its import and ideas change with the progress of science and advance of philosophy. It was well enough for the ancients to advance that the sun rises in the East, that this earth is stationary as a tree or a house is stationary, and that the sun moves around this little globe of ours; but the day of these ideas is past. Now, by a change of verbiage, the ideas are expressed consistent with sound philosophical principles, as the sun in the east opens and adorns the day, etc., and thus it must necessarily be in relation to Masonic language and Masonic ideas. The language used to express an idea several thousand years ago, or even a few hundred years ago, would be unintelligible, and not understood. To expect uniformity of language for all time, is a vain expectation, and can never be attained.—*Key Stone.*[1]

VAULT.—Vaults are found in every country of the world as well as in Judea, and were used for secret purposes. Thus Stephens, speaking of some ruins in Yucatan, says: "The only way of descending was to tie a rope around the body, and be lowered by the Indians. In this way I was let down, and almost before my head had passed through the hole, my feet touched the top of a heap of rubbish, high directly under the hole, and falling off at the sides. Clambering down it, I found myself in a round chamber, so filled with rubbish that I could not stand upright. With a candle in my hand, I crawled all round on my hands and knees. The chamber was in the shape of a dome, and had been coated with plaster, most of which had fallen, and now encumbered the ground. The depth could not be ascertained without clearing out the interior."

WAGES.—The tradition respecting the payment of the workmen's wages at the building of Solomon's Temple, may or may not be accurate, as I am ignorant of the authority on which the calculations are founded. Indeed the probability is, that the tradition has been fabricated in a subsequent age, without the existence of any documents to attest its authenticity.

[1] This is not taken from Dr. Oliver's Dictionary, but is quoted from a popular Masonic journal, and embodies the sentiments of a great majority of the fraternity.

THE TRIPLE TAU

APPENDIX

NOTE A, page 12.—In some Lodges the Tyler *takes* the sword from the altar.

NOTE B, page 18.—Some Masters repeat the words, "O Lord my God," three times.

NOTE C, page 19.—Masters differ about the proper manner of placing the three lights around the altar. In most Lodges they are placed as represented in the engraving, page 19; but many Masters have them placed thus:

The square represents the altar; the figures 1, 2, and 3, the lights; the letter A, the kneeling candidate, and the letter B, the Master.

NOTE D, page 21.—Some Masters say: "I now declare this Lodge opened in the Third Degree of Masonry *for the dispatch of business.*

NOTE E, page 39.—In spelling this word, "Boaz," always begin with the letter "A," and follow the alphabet down as the letters occur in the word.

NOTE F, page 42.—In some Lodges the reply is: "Try me, and disapprove of me if you can;" in others, "I am willing to be tried."

NOTE G, page 43.—Some say, "In an anteroom adjacent to a Lodge of Entered Apprentice Masons."

NOTE H, page 44.—Some say, "Three times around the Lodge."

NOTE I, page 51.—Some say, "On the highest hills and lowest valleys."

NOTE J, page 89.—In some Lodges, the Deacon omits the single rap (●), and opens the door when the three raps (●●●) are given.

NOTE K, page 205.—In most Lodges the candidate does not halt at the Junior Warden's station, but passes on to the Senior Warden.

NOTE L, page 125.—Master says: "I shall now proceed to give and explain to you the several signs and tokens belonging to the Degree." Here the Master places his hands as the candidate's were when he took the oath of a Master (see Fig. 5, page 17), and explains. Makes sign of a Master Mason, and explains. (See Fig. 6, page 18.) Makes the grand hailing sign, and explains. (See Fig. 7, page 18.) Gives grip of a Master Mason, and explains. (See Fig. 16, page 97.) Gives strong grip, and explains. (See Fig. 17, page 120.)

NOTE M, page 235.—The Principal Sojourner should say: "We are of your own brethren and kin—children of the captivity—descendants of those noble Giblemites, we were received and acknowledged Most Excellent Masters at the completion and dedication of the first temple—were present at the destruction of that temple by Nebuchadnezzar, by whom we were carried captives to Babylon, where we remained servants to him and his successors until the reign of Cyrus, King of Persia, by whose order we have been liberated, and have now come up to help, aid, and assist in rebuilding the house of the Lord, without the hope of fee or reward." (See lecture.)

NOTE N, page 236.—Instead of saying: "You surely could not have come thus far unless you were three Most Excellent Masters," etc., the Master of the First Veil should say: "Good men and true you must have been, to have come thus far to promote so noble and good an undertaking, but further you cannot go without my word, sign, and word of explanation." (See lecture.)

NOTE O, page 235.—In some Chapters they only stamp seven times.

NOTE P, page 140.—In some parts of the country the second section of the lecture is continued as follows:

Q. What followed?

A. They travelled as before; and as those, who had pursued a due westerly course from the temple, were returning, one (1) of them, being more weary than the rest, sat down on the brow of a hill to rest and refresh himself, and on rising up caught hold of a sprig of acacia, which easily giving way excited his curiosity; and while they were meditating over this singular circumstance they heard three frightful exclamations from the cleft of an adjacent rock. The first was the voice of Jubelo, exclaiming, "Oh! that my throat had been cut from ear to ear, my tongue torn out by its roots and buried in the sands of the sea at low water mark, where the tide ebbs and flows twice in twenty-four hours, ere I had been accessory to the death of so great and good a man as our Grand Master Hiram Abiff." The second was the voice of Jubela, exclaiming: "Oh! that my left breast had been torn open, my heart plucked from thence and given to the beasts of the field and the birds of the air as a prey, ere I had been accessory to the death of so great and good a man as our Grand Master Hiram Abiff." The third was the voice of Jubelum, exclaiming more horridly than the rest, "It was I that gave him the fatal blow! it was I that slew him! oh! that my body had been severed in twain, my bowels taken from thence and burnt to ashes, the ashes scattered before the four (4) winds of heavens, that no more resemblance might be had, among men or masons, of so vile a wretch as I am, ere I had been accessory to the death of so great and good a man as our Grand Master Hiram Abiff." Upon which, they rushed in, seized, bound, and brought them before King Solomon, who ordered them to be taken without the gates of the city and executed according to their imprecations. They were accordingly put to death.

Q. What followed?

A. King Solomon ordered the twelve fellow crafts to go in search of the body, and if found, to observe whether the master's word, or a key to it, was on or about it.

Q. Where was the body of our Grand Master Hiram Abiff found?

A. A due westerly course from the temple, on the brow of the hill, where our weary brother sat down to rest and refresh himself.

Q. Was the master's word, or a key to it, on or about it?

A. It was not.

Q. What followed?

A. King Solomon then ordered them to go with him to endeavor to raise the body, and ordered that as the master's word was then lost, that the first sign given at the grave, and the first word spoken after the body should be raised, should be adopted for the regulation of all Master Masons' Lodges until future ages should find out the right.

Q. What followed?

A. They returned to the grave, when King Solomon ordered them to take the body by the entered-apprentice grip and see if it could be raised; but on taking the body so it was putrid, it having been dead fifteen days, the skin slipped from the flesh, and it could not be raised.

Q. What followed?

A. King Solomon then ordered them to take it by the fellow-craft grip and see if it could be so raised; but on taking the body by that grip the flesh cleft from the bone, and it could not be so raised.

Q. What followed?

A. King Solomon then took it by the strong grip of a Master Mason, or lion's paw, and raised it on the five (5) points of fellowship, which are foot to foot, knee to knee, breast to breast, hand to back, cheek to cheek, or mouth to ear. Foot to foot, that we will never hesitate to go on foot, and out of our way, to assist a suffering and needy brother; knee to knee, that we will ever remember a brother's welfare in all our adorations to Deity; breast to breast, that we will ever keep in our own breasts a brother's secrets, when communicated to us as such, murder and treason excepted; hand to back, that we will ever be ready to stretch forth our hand to aid and support a fallen brother; cheek to cheek, or mouth to ear, that we will ever whisper good counsel in the ear of a brother, and in the most tender manner remind him of his faults, and endeavor to aid his reformation, and will give him due and timely notice that he may ward off all approaching danger.

Q. What did they do with the body?

A. They carried it to the temple and buried it in due form. And masonic tradition informs us that there was a marble column erected to his memory, upon which was delineated a beautiful virgin weeping; before her lay a book open, in her right hand a sprig of acacia, in her left an urn, and behind her stood Time with his fingers unfolding the ringlets of her hair.

Q. What do these hieroglyphical figures denote?

A. The broken column denotes the untimely death of our Grand Master Hiram Abiff; the beautiful virgin weeping, the temple unfinished; the book open before her, that his virtues lie on perpetual record; the sprig of acacia in her right hand, the timely discovery of his body; the urn in her left, that his ashes were then safely deposited to perpetuate the remembrance of so distinguished a character; Time unfolding the ringlets of her hair, that time, patience, and perseverance accomplish all things.

Q. Have you a sign belonging to this Degree?

A. I have several.

Q. Give me a sign? (Penalty.)

Q. What is that called?

A. The duegard of a Master Mason.

Q. Has that an allusion?

A. It has, to the penalty of my obligation, and when our ancient brethren returned to the grave of our Grand Master Hiram Abiff, they found their hands placed in this position to guard their nostrils from the disagreeable effluvia that arose there from the grave.

Q. Give me a token. (Pass grip.)

Q. What is that called?

A. The pass grip from a fellow craft to a Master Mason.

Q. What is its name?

A. Tubal Cain.

Q. Who was Tubal Cain?

A. The first known artificer or cunning worker in metals.

Q. Pass that? (Strong grip.)

Q. What is that?

A. The strong grip of a Master Mason, or lion's paw.

Q. Has it a name?

A. It has.

Q. Give it me?

A. I cannot, nor can it be given except on the five (5) points of fellowship, and heard then in a low breath.

Q. Advance and give it.

A. The word is right.

Q. How many grand masonic pillars are there?

A. Three.

Q. What are they called?

A. Wisdom, Strength and Beauty.

Q. Why are they so called?

A. Because it is necessary there should be wisdom to contrive, strength to support, and beauty to adorn, all great and important undertakings.

Q. By whom are they represented?

A. By Solomon, King of Israel, Hiram, King of Tyre, and Hiram Abiff, who were our first three Most Excellent Grand Masters.

Q. Why are they said to represent them?

A. Solomon, King of Israel, represents the pillars of wisdom, because by his wisdom he contrived the superb model of excellence that immortalized his name; Hiram, King of Tyre, represents the pillar of strength, because he supported King Solomon in this great and important undertaking; Hiram Abiff represents the pillar of beauty, because by his cunning workmanship, the temple was beautified and adorned.

Q. What supported the temple?

A. It was supported by 1453 columns and 2906 pilasters, all hewn from the finest Parian marble.

Q. How many were employed in building the temple?

A. Three Grand Masters, three thousand three hundred masters, or overseers of the work, eighty thousand fellow crafts in the mountains and in the quarries, and seventy (70) thousand entered apprentices, or bearers of burdens. All these were classed and arranged in such a manner by the wisdom of King Solomon, that neither envy, discord, nor confusion was suffered to interrupt that universal peace and tranquillity which pervaded the world at this important period.

Q. What is meant by the three steps usually delineated on the Master's carpet?

A. They are emblematical of the three principal stages of human life, viz.: youth, manhood, and age, etc., etc. (Monitorial.)

Q. How many classes of Master's emblems are there?

A. Nine.

Q. What is the ninth (9th)?

A. The setting maul, spade, coffin, and sprig of acacia. The setting maul was that by which our Grand Master Hiram Abiff was slain; the spade was that which dug his grave; the coffin was that which received his remains, and the sprig of acacia was that which bloomed at the head of his grave. These are all striking emblems of morality, and afford serious reflections to a thinking mind; but they would be still more repining were it not for the sprig of acacia that bloomed at the head of the grave, which serves to remind us of that imperishable part of man which survives the grave and bears the nearest affinity to the Supreme Intelligence which pervades all nature, and which can never, never, never die. Then, finally, my brethren, let us imitate our Grand Master Hiram Abiff in his virtuous conduct, his unfeigned piety to his God, and his inflexible fidelity to his trust, that like him we may welcome the grim tyrant Death, and receive him as a kind messenger, sent by our Supreme Grand Master to translate us from this imperfect to that all perfect, glorious, and celestial lodge above, where the Supreme Architect of the universe presides.

NOTE Q., page 148.—(*Extract from the Annual Address of M. W. P. M. Tucker, G. M. of Vermont.*)

In my address of last year I endeavored to condense what little information I had about the Masonic lectures, and that attempt has been, in general, quite favorably noticed by the Craft. In one distinguished Masonic quarter, however, some parts of my address on this subject seem to have met with marked disfavor. One particular thing found fault with is, that I thought myself justified in saying that the lectures in use, received through Webb and Gleason, were the *true* lectures of Preston. I certainly did not mean to say that they were identical in *length* with those of Preston. I had already said that Webb changed the arrangement of Preston's sections, but that he had left the body of the lectures as Preston had established them. Perhaps I should have said, the *substance* instead of the "*body*" of those lectures. I now state, what I supposed was well understood before by every tolerably well-informed Mason in the United States, that Webb *abridged* as well as *changed the ar-*

rangement of the lectures of Preston. I believed that I knew *then*, and I believe I know *now*, that Webb learned and taught the Preston lectures *in full*, as well as that he prepared and taught his own abridgment of them. I have a copy in key, both of Webb's abridgment and of Preston in full, which I have reasons, wholly satisfactory to myself, for believing are true manuscripts of both those sets of lectures, as Gleason taught them. But my reviewer has got the "very rare" book of a certain J. Browne, published in London in 1802, called the "Master Key," containing the *whole* course of lectures in an "abstruse cypher," and *presumes* them to be the Prestonian lectures. Reviewers, it seems, tolerate "presumption" in themselves, while nothing short of demonstration is allowable with them as to others, who are required to speak from "their own knowledge." I am ready to compare my copy of the Preston lectures in *full* with J Browne's "*Master Key*," if my reviewer understands Browne's "abstruse cypher,"—a fact about which he has not yet informed us. Again, I am criticized for saying that Gleason visited England and exemplified the Preston lectures, as he had received them from Webb, before the Grand Lodge of England, whose authorities pronounced them correct, and I am charged with taking this from "hearsay," and my critic places "no faith in it." I received that statement from the *highest* authority—from one who *knew*—and I wrote it down at the time. There are existing reasons why I do not choose to gratify my critic by naming that authority at this time, and I leave the Craft to judge whether my *statement* of that fact, upon undoubted authority, is not worthy of as much credit as *any* reviewer's *doubt* about it. I do not possess anything in writing or published of Gleason's, as to his lecturing before the *Grand Lodge* of England, but that Masonry abroad did not ignore the lectures, as Gleason taught them, we have his own published letter to prove. In the 2d edition of the Masonic Trestleboard, under the date of Nov. 26th, 1843, in a letter from him to Brother Charles W. Moore, I find the following language:

"It was my privilege, while at Brown University, Providence, R. I., (1801/2), to acquire a complete knowledge of the lectures, in the *three* first degrees of Masonry, *directly* from our much esteemed Brother T. S. Webb, author of the Free Mason's Monitor; and, in consequence, was appointed and commissioned by the Grand Lodge of Massachusetts and Maine, Grand Lecturer, devoting the whole time to the instruction of the Lodges under the jurisdiction,—and, for many years subsequently (as Professor of Astronomy and Geography), visiting all the different States in the Union, and (1829/30) many parts of Europe—successfully communicating, to numerous Lodges and Associations of Brethren, the same 'valuable lectures of the Craft,' according to the ancient landmarks."

Here, then, we have the assertion of Gleason himself, that the lectures he received from Webb were, "in many parts of Europe," as well as in the States at home, communicated by him to "numerous Lodges and Associations of Brethren, according to the ancient landmarks," without the slightest hint or intimation of any objection being made to them abroad, as not being the true lectures of the Order. This is, at least, *prima facie* evidence of their having been substantially what I claimed them to be. But if I am still told that it carries no conclusive evidence that Brother Gleason knew anything of the *true* Preston lectures, I call that brother upon the stand again. On the 24th day of June, 1812, "Brother Benjamin Gleason, A. M.," delivered an "*Oration*" at "Montreal, Lower Canada," before St. Paul's Lodge No. 12, and Union Lodge No. 8, by "special request" of the former Lodge. It was published at Montreal, and a second edition of it was soon after published at Boston. I copy from this second edition the following remarks of Brother Gleason:

"On the subject of our Lectures, we notice with pleasure, this day, the venerable Preston of England, whose 'Illustrations of Masonry' redound to the honor of the Craft, and whose *estimable system of improvements*, while with precision and certainty they define, with purity and eloquence, aggrandize, the immovable *landmarks* of our ancient Society."

Brother Gleason then, *did*, upon his own statement, understand Preston's "estimable system of improvements," their "precision and certainty," their "purity and elegance," and their relation to our "immovable landmarks." And with these and Webb's teachings fully in his mind, was probably as good a judge as any modern critic, of the relations they bore to each other. Can any reasonable man, in this state of things, believe that if they had *conflicted* with each other he did not know it, or that, if conflicting, he would have taught *both;* or that he could have taught either "in Europe" without objection, had they not been substantially the *same* teachings, differing only in their *length?*

But my critic says:—"It is wrong to talk in this careless strain of the Prestonian lectures as existing in the United States, while in all probability they never did, and most certainly never will. It is time to quit writing Masonic history in this loose and random style."

It is no part of my purpose to *convince* my reviewer that the "Prestonian lectures" exist in the United States, or to *persuade* him, that (though confessedly a strong Masonic writer), he does not quite embody in his learning *all* the Masonry of this Western continent. His liberality might perhaps concede that, *among* all who have made Masonry a study, or with their *united* investigations, enough of Masonic learning *might* have been preserved to

make itself respected at least as against simple negation. But I
do not write to *convince* or satisfy *him*. I do so that the Craft
may have an opportunity to understand something of their own
affairs, as they exist; to examine and investigate them as matters
of fact and principle; and that they may have no apology for
"pinning their faith" upon the mere negations of any writer,
whatever may be the strength of his masonic reputation. In an
account of the Installation of Mount Lebanon Lodge at Boston, on
the 29th of December, 1858, Brother Charles W. Moore, Editor of
the *Freemasons' Monthly Magazine*, has the following remarks:
"Among the Past Masters of this Lodge we notice the name of
the late Benjamin Gleason, Esq., who was the associate and co-
laborer of the late Thomas Smith Webb, in introducing into the
Lodges of New England, and subsequently into other sections of
the country, what is known as the Prestonian system of work and
lectures. The labor of promulgating the work mainly devolved on
Brother Gleason, and it is not too much to say, that as an accurate,
consistent, and intelligent teacher, he had no superior, if an equal,
in this country. He was a thoroughly educated man, and he understood the literary as well as the mental requirements necessary to
a faithful and creditable discharge of the important duty he had
assumed. In 1804, the Grand Lodge of Massachusetts adopted the
Preston ritual as its standard of work, and employed Brother
Gleason to communicate it to the Lodges under its jurisdiction,
then including what is now the State of Maine. In the performance of this duty, he was exclusively employed during the whole
of the year named, on account of the Grand Lodge; and we think
a large part of the following two or three years, on his own private
account. Indeed he never ceased his labors, as a lecturer, until
his death in 1847, and there are many brethren now living—among
them myself—who will ever take pride in remembering and
acknowledging him as their master and teacher, in the purest and
most perfect Masonic ritual of ancient Craft Masonry ever practised
in this country. It was the work' of Masonry, as revived by
Preston, and approved and sanctioned by the Grand Lodge of
England, near the close of the last century, and practised by
authority of that body, until the 'union' in 1813, when, for the
purpose of reconciliation, it was subjugated to a revision, which,
in some respects, proved to be an unfortunate one, inasmuch as
the revised system, though exceedingly beautiful, has so many
incongruities and departures from the original, and is so elaborate
withal, that it has never met with that cordial approval, even
among our English brethren, which is necessary to its recognition
and acceptance as a universal system. The verbal ritual, as re-

vised by Preston, was brought to this country about the year 1803—not by Webb, as we have seen it stated, for he never went abroad—but by two English brethren, one of whom, we think, had been a pupil of Preston, and both of whom had been members of one of the principal Lodges of Instruction in London. It was first communicated to Webb, and by him imparted to Gleason, who was at the time a student in Brown University, at Providence, and being an intelligent and zealous brother, became a favorite of Webb, who was his senior both in years and in Masonry. On being submitted to the Grand Lodge of this Commonwealth it was approved and adopted, and Brother Gleason was employed to impart it to the Lodges, as before stated. From that time to the present it has been the only recognized Masonic work of Massachusetts, and though we are not unmindful that many unwarrantable liberties have been taken with it, and that innovations have crept in, which would have been better out—yet, as a whole, we are happy to know that it has been preserved in the Lodges of this city—and in view of the recent instructions, by authority of the Grand Lodge, we may add, the Lodges of this Commonwealth —in a remarkable degree of purity; and that it is still taught in the Lodge of which, in 1809, Brother Gleason was Master, with so close a resemblance to the original, that if it were possible for him to be present at the conferring of the degrees to-day, he would find very little to object to in the work of his successors. The system underwent some modifications (which were doubtless improvements) in its general arrangement and adaptation—its mechanism—soon after its introduction into this country; but in all other respects it was received, and has been preserved, especially in the Lodges of the older jurisdictions, essentially, as it came from the original source of all our Craft Masonry. In many parts of the country it has hitherto had to contend against the corrupting influences of ignorant itinerant lecturers and spurious publications; but it is believed that an effectual check has been put to this class of dangerous evils, and that they will hereafter be treated as they deserve. If so, we may reasonably hope to be able to preserve the ritual, and transmit it to our successors, in something like its original purity, but not otherwise." We have, then, added to Gleason's own assertion as to his knowledge of Preston's "estimable system of improvements," the statement of one of the most intelligent and reliable Masons in this country, that Webb had "the Prestonian system of work and lectures," and that the labor of promulgating them "mainly devolved on Brother Gleason." And I wholly content to let that evidence stand as my authority and justification against the remarks of a reviewer who accuses me of "talking in a careless strain" when I maintain that these lectures exist in the United States.

Our Grand Lecturer has compared, with critical care, my copy of the Preston with that of the Gleason Lectures. I have not had sufficient leisure since the former has been in my possession, to compare them, as fully as I design to do hereafter. The Preston Lectures are very lengthy, and if written out in full the Grand Lecturer thinks they would cover nearly one hundred pages of foolscap paper. He thinks them wholly too long for ordinary use, and that if all Masons were required to commit them *in extenso*, it would be a task which very few would successfully accomplish; and so far as my own examination has gone, I entertain the same opinion. The Grand Lecturer also entertains the opinion that Webb has preserved, in the abridgment and new arrangement of them, all that was substantially of practical value, and that the language used by him is preferable to much that was used by Preston.

I regret to say that in the criticism of which I have spoken, there appears a most palpable intention to undervalue *all* the lectures of Masonry. The believers in the importance of preserving the lectures intact are sneered at; called "parrot Masons," who, taken off the "beaten path," know "nothing at all of Masonry, of its history, its philosophy, or its symbolism." And we are dismissed with the cool remark—"Let us talk more, therefore, of the philosophy of Masonry, and something less of the Lectures of Webb," and as opposed to the idea of the importance of the Lectures, we are called on, "in Heaven's name, to inaugurate a new era."

This is, at least, sufficiently cool for a teacher of Freemasonry.

"Inaugurate a *new* era." That is the idea precisely. Some of us ignorant Masons had supposed that, at least, some portion of our Masonic "history, philosophy, and symbolism," was *suggested* in our Lectures. Our "history"—written and unwritten—the "philosophy" of our system, and something of our "symbolism," were imagined to be secure in the past. But a "new era." About what? Can our "*history*" be changed; can our "*philosophy*" be changed? Not a million of critics, however distinguished, can brush the first particle of consecrated dust from either. "There they stand, and there they will stand forever—unshaken by the tests of human scrutiny, of talents and of time."

THE END

OTHER MASONIC TITLES

A Dictionary of Freemasonry
Freemasonry and its Etiquette
Freemasonry at a Glance (Answers to 555 Questions)
Freemasonry Character Claims
Morals and Dogma of Freemasonry
Order of the Eastern Star
Revised Duncan's Ritual Vol. 1
Revised Duncan's Ritual Vol. 2
Revised Knight Templarism Illustrated
Scottish Rites Masonry Vol. 1
Scottish Rites Masonry Vol. 2
Secret Societies Illustrated
The History of Freemasonry
The Illustrated History of Freemasonry

MASONIC RELATED TITLES:

Freemasonry and Judaism
Freemasonry Interpreted
Freemasonry and the Vatican

WWW.LUSHENABKS.COM

NOTES

NOTES

NOTES

NOTES

NOTES

NOTES

110319-200-3-60W